R .

To Paddy
     Ashdown,
Constitutional
     Reforms
With best Wishes
     From
     Vernon
     Bogdanor

POLITICS AND THE CONSTITUTION

For Judy, Paul and Adam, who all helped – with thanks

POLITICS AND THE CONSTITUTION

Essays on British Government

VERNON BOGDANOR

Reader in Government, Oxford University and Fellow of Brasenose College

Dartmouth

Aldershot ● Brookfield USA ● Singapore ● Sydney

Published by
Dartmouth Publishing Company Limited
Gower House
Croft Road
Aldershot
Hants GU11 3HR
England

Dartmouth Publishing Company
Old Post Road
Brookfield
Vermont 05036
USA

British Library Cataloguing in Publication Data
Politics and the Constitution:Essays on British Government
 I. Bogdanor, Vernon
 320.941

Library of Congress Cataloging-in-Publication Data
Bogdanor, Vernon, 1943–
 Politics and the constitution : essays on British government /
Vernon Bogdanor.
 p.   cm.
 Includes bibliographical references.
 ISBN 1-85521-760-0
 1. Great Britain—Politics and government.   2. Great Britain—
Constitutional history.   3. Elections—Great Britain—History.
4. Decentralization in government—Great Britain. I. Title.
JN231.B59   1996
324'.0941'09045—dc20   95-44460
                                                        CIP

ISBN 1 85521 760 0

Typeset in Times by Raven Typesetter, Chester and printed
in Great Britain by Athenaeum Press Ltd, Gateshead, Tyne & Wear.

Contents

List of Tables

List of Figures

Introduction: Exorcising Dicey's Ghost

I

A constitution forms the basis of the legal order of the state. But a constitution is also a 'power-map' tracing the normative relationships between government and citizen.[1] Thus constitutions, insofar as they are concerned with power, are as much the concern of the political scientist as of the constitutional lawyer. The essays collected together in this book offer a political scientist's view of the British Constitution. They seek to show why it is that the Constitution, having departed from the political agenda in the 1920s, reappeared in the 1970s, and has remained part of that agenda despite all the efforts of politicians to exorcise it. If any excuse is needed for trespassing in a field seemingly reserved for constitutional lawyers, it is that the debate on the constitution is also a debate about the future shape of democratic government. It is for this reason that, in Britain, 'the constitutional lawyer and the political scientist are for ever undivided'.[2]

The constitutional structure of a mature and civilized society will normally display a certain inner logic or coherence and it is this inherent conceptual structure which it is the task both of the constitutional lawyer and the political scientist to expose. This task, difficult enough in itself, is made vastly more complicated when there is no codified constitution which can provide a starting-place, a point of departure for analysis. In Britain, where there is no officially sanctioned collection of constitutional rules, constitutional lawyers have generally fallen back on the work of A. V. Dicey (1835–1922) who has become Britain's substitute for a codified constitution. Indeed, it has been claimed that 'Dicey's word has in some respects become the only written constitution we have', and his ghost still dominates all accounts of the British Constitution.[3] For it was Dicey who elucidated the conceptual structure which still dominates thinking about the Constitution. These essays seek to examine the implications of Dicey's thinking, although some of them reach conclusions which he would have strongly repudiated.

Dicey, although himself a lawyer, was insistent that the political scientist has an equally important role in elucidating a constitution which is not only unentrenched, but also both indistinct and indeterminate.[4] For these characteristics mean that in Britain what is constitutional and what is politically feasible often coincide. In Britain, even more than in countries with codified constitutions, constitutional law and politics tend to merge into each other.

In his classic work, *Introduction to the Study of the Law of the Constitution* (1885), Dicey suggested that 'a lawyer cannot master even the legal side of the English [*sic*] constitution without paying some attention to the nature of those constitutional understandings which necessarily engross the attention of historians or of statesmen'. Thus he devoted the third and final part of his classic, *Law of the Constitution*, to those 'understandings' whose purpose it was to secure 'though in a roundabout way, what is called abroad the "sovereignty of the people" '.[5]

It was Dicey's singular achievement to have understood that any introduction – perhaps prolegomenon would be a better word – to the study of the law of the constitution must emphasize its *historical* nature. In his unpublished lectures on comparative constitutions, Dicey characterized the British Constitution as an 'historic' constitution, and this is a far more accurate and illuminating description than the misleading platitude that it is 'unwritten'.[6] For Dicey understood that the 'principles' of the British Constitution, since it is uncodified, could be nothing more than a summation of historical experience, inductive generalizations based upon the past behaviour of politicians as well as judges. It is this that makes the British Constitution so difficult to elucidate and understand. In 1904, one of the most perceptive students of British government, Sidney Low, declared that

> There is one reason why the English method of government is so hard to describe. Any account of it must be like the picture of a living person. If you want to see exactly how the original appears, you do not refer to a photograph taken twenty or thirty years ago. The features may be the same, but their expression, their proportion, and their whole character have changed. In the interval between one examination of our public polity and another, the formal part may not have greatly altered, but the conventional, the organic working portion has been modified in all sorts of ways. The structural elements, it is true, exhibit a wonderful superficial permanence. The Crown, the two Houses of Parliament, the Council of Ministers, the Electorate, the Judicature, and the mutual relations of their various powers and authorities, are the material of all the historians and jurists. There is the same machine, or at least a machine which is painted to look the same.[7]

The British Constitution, then, is not something logically anterior to government, comprising a consciously enacted set of principles of the kind generally to be found embodied in 'non-historic' or enacted constitutions. Nor is British constitutional law a normative fountain from which specific statutes flow; rather it is a resumé of her historical experience, something logically consequent upon a pre-existing governmental structure. Indeed, the very absence of a codified constitution is a consequence (and not a cause) of a background of stability and consensus.[8]

From this, important consequences flow. The evolutionary conception of the British Constitution leaves no place for a theory of the state nor for principles which can limit public power. Where then are the limits upon government to be found? For the essence of constitutionalism lies in the notion of a *limit* upon the power of government.[9] Yet Dicey's central principle – that of the sovereignty of parliament – effectively denies the possibility of any *legal* limit to the power of government. This is not, of course, to suggest that Dicey favoured unlimited or omnicompetent government. But for him the limits to government were to be found not in the law but in public opinion. It was the force of opinion in society which served effectively to limit the power of government. There is indeed a very close connection between the juridical doctrines of the *Law of the Constitution* and the historical analysis embodied in his *Lectures on the Relation Between Law and Public Opinion in England During the Nineteenth Century* (1905).

The idea of a limitation of power is as basic to the British Constitution as it is with any effective constitution, but, until recently at least, it has been understood in a unique way. Both Bentham, in Chapter IV of his *Fragment on Government* and in his postscript to the *Introduction to the Principles of Morals and Legislation*, and Dicey in the *Law of the Constitution*, are as attached to the idea of a limit on government as any Continental jurist, but they understand it differently. For they are disinclined to the notion of a statutory limit on government, preferring to base the limitation of power in political habits, and in opinion. There is, in the British Constitution, then a form of *garantisme*, but it is extra-statutory. Indeed this hostility to statutory forms of *garantisme* has long been a fundamental feature of British thought about the constitution.[10] Thus any understanding of the British Constitution requires a grasp of those procedures and understandings which give life to the idea of a limitation of power and that is as much a matter for the political scientist as for the constitutional lawyer.

II

An important part of Dicey's aim was to show how it is that constitutional conventions help to achieve the aim of securing the sovereignty of the people. One crucial convention helping to secure that sovereignty was that of ministerial responsibility. For this was designed, in Dicey's view, to ensure 'that the Crown, or the Ministry, must ultimately carry out, or at any rate, not contravene the wishes of the House of Commons'. And since

> the process of representation is nothing else than a mode by which the will of the representative body of the House of Commons is made to coincide with the will of the nation, it follows that a rule which gives the appointment and control of the government mainly to the House of Commons is at bottom a rule which gives the election and ultimate control of the executive to the nation.[11]

'The one principle', Dicey believed, 'which under the present state of England lies at the bottom of all constitutional habits or conventions is that Parliament ought to conform to the clearly expressed will of the nation'.[12]

In his insistence that Britain's constitutional arrangements ought to secure the sovereignty of the people, Dicey rejects the Whig view of the constitution, 'a view of Parliamentary sovereignty which made Parliament in the strictest sense the sovereign power'.[13] He would have been the first to repudiate the erroneous misinterpretation, standard among defenders of executive power, according to which parliamentary sovereignty has come to be equated with the power of an omnicompetent government to do what it likes, regardless of public opinion, a standpoint attacked by Lord Hailsham – when in opposition in the 1970s though not when in power in the 1980s – as one of 'elective dictatorship'.[14]

Dicey is in fact much less orthodox than he seems. He is far from being an uncritical eulogist of the British Constitution. Nor was he 'one of the many Fellows of All Souls who were to devote their talents to draping the attorney's mantle about the shoulders of arbitrary power'.[15] He was in fact a constitutional reformer who sought persistently for a method by which fundamental laws could be preserved and indeed entrenched in a political system with a sovereign parliament. He came to believe, indeed, that only the people themselves, through the referendum, could provide an authoritative check upon a democratic and omnicompetent government. Dicey was the first person in Britain to advocate, in an article entitled 'Ought the Referendum to be Introduced into England?', published in the *Contemporary Review* in April 1890, the referendum as an instrument to correct the defects of parliamentary government, and in particular of the working of the party system.

Dicey, then, is in no way a Whig defender of the status quo. His place in the history of ideas lies rather with those great liberal individualists, J. S. Mill and Ostrogorski, both radical critics of the growing rigidity of the party system.[16] As early as 1889, Dicey had composed a Memorandum on English Party Government in which he asserted that 'Under all forms of popular government there must be political parties. Englishmen assume that the existence of political parties involves the existence of our system of party government. This argument is both historically and logically unsound.'[17] Dicey, like Ostrogorski, believed that use of the referendum could mitigate the excesses of the party system.

The weakness of the argument is that the referendum cannot of itself bear the great weight which Dicey puts upon it. For Dicey, like most of those who advocated the referendum, believed that it could be employed only for a small number of constitutional issues. He did not see it as something that would be used regularly, but as an instrument to be used only on infrequent occasions. Dicey was correct in predicting that the referendum would come to be used in the vast majority of democratic states, but in almost all democracies – with Switzerland being the major exception – it is used as an occasional device rather than as a regular part of the machinery of government. Thus Dicey's one remedy for the deep-seated ills of the party system – the referendum – seems too feeble to cure the malady which he diagnosed.

Ostrogorski and Mill believed that the single transferable vote method of proportional representation was an even more important reform which, through the mechanism of preferential voting, would weaken the party machine. For the single transferable vote conceptually linked a primary election to a general election. The elector would be voting for a candidate of his or her choice as well as the party of his or her choice. Thus it would be impossible for a party to impose its favoured candidates in safe seats. Indeed the whole concept of the safe seat would disappear since candidates would have to compete for preferential votes with other candidates from their own party as well as with candidates from the opposition parties. Voters would thus be able to choose between candidates of their favoured party; the political system would become candidate-based rather than party-based and for this reason more responsive to popular choice.

Dicey gave but perfunctory attention to proportional representation in his introduction to the 8th edition of the *Law of the Constitution* (1915), the last to be published in his lifetime, and declared himself an opponent. One sympathetic commentator, however, ended his review of the 8th edition with

an expression of wonder how it is that Mr. Dicey is to be reckoned an opponent. His Introduction is largely, if not entirely, critical of modern developments in politics. He is specially severe on the 'machine'. He is distrustful of pure democracy, yet of suggested constitutional changes he favours the referendum only . . . .[18]

The tradition of thought which Dicey represented was resuscitated in 1980 by S. E. Finer who also advocated the referendum in his book, *The Changing British Party System, 1945–1979*.[19] My own book, *The People and the Party System: The Referendum and Electoral Reform in British Politics*, published in 1981,[20] advocated both the referendum and the single transferable vote method of proportional representation as democratic checks upon the party system, as ways indeed of undermining the dominance of party in the constitution.

III

The first edition of *Law of the Constitution* was published in 1885, a peculiarly difficult year in which to delineate constitutional conventions. For the general election of that year was the first to be held under the new electoral regime created by the 1884 Reform Act and the 1885 Redistribution Act providing for male household suffrage in predominantly single-member constituencies. It was far from clear what constitutional form the nascent democracy would assume. Hitherto, the aim of constitutional reformers had been to extend the franchise so that it embraced the whole nation rather than a mere section. They had been concerned with how the people could *obtain* power. By 1885, it had become clear that this aim was near fulfilment. Constitutionalists, therefore, turned their attention to the question of how democratic power could be restrained, how power, exercised by the people's representatives in the Commons, could be *controlled*.

The eighth edition of *Law of the Constitution*, published in 1915, contained an introduction dealing with proposals for reform such as the referendum and proportional representation. It was published three years before the 1918 Reform Act provided for universal suffrage for men and for women over 30 – the age for women was lowered to over 21 in 1928. These reforms seemed to bring the movement for constitutional reform to an end, since its main aim – universal suffrage – had been achieved. For this reason, the coming of universal suffrage led to a freezing of political institutions parallel and analogous to the freezing of major party alternatives that was first noticed by Lipset and Rokkan.[21] For the newly mobilized electorate was interested less in constitutional questions than in the improvement of social and economic conditions.

So it was that constitutional questions came to be eclipsed by socioeconomic questions which replaced them at the centre of the political agenda. In Britain, politics became the politics of the democratic class struggle and the movement for constitutional reform seemed to have been played out. Moreover, measures of constitutional reform, measures designed to increase participation and the popular control of government, would have threatened the interests of the major parties which were coming to dominate the political system. Democracy came to be identified with rule by tightly organized mass political parties which, it was thought, offered the best means for the stability of democratic government. Constitutional reform would inevitably undermine the prerogatives of these tightly organized mass parties, which, therefore, called a halt to the liberal democratic movement. It was only with the decline in the authority which mass political parties were able to exert over their electorates in the 1970s that constitutional issues came back once more into British politics. Their return to politics was a response to the gap left by the weakening of party loyalties, a response to dealignment. Since fewer electors seemed to 'belong' to a political party by virtue of their social class or religion, so they would be less willing to accept the unquestioning authority of party leaders. In addition, wider social changes in economic life – the spread of ownership of property, shares and other assets – have helped to undermine attitudes of deference and diffuse attitudes of political effectiveness. There has been an increasing emphasis on consumerism and choice in both public and private services. It would be unrealistic to expect that these changes would not have their consequences in the political sphere. The demand for greater accountability and participation has grown, and it is this that has helped fuel the movement for constitutional reform.

Thus the certainties of the Diceyan analysis came to be undermined as political divisions widened, with the decline of consensus in the 1970s and 1980s. It came to be asked whether informal limits on power were still sufficient to deter a determined government, or whether something more was needed. The informal limits were based upon convention, but the last two decades have seen the death of convention as an influence capable of limiting government. In particular, Margaret Thatcher's style of government showed that the Diceyan principle of parliamentary sovereignty was no longer compatible with limited government through the operation of commonly understood and shared constitutional conventions. It was Margaret Thatcher's period in office which saw the death of convention since she showed how a determined prime minister could override what had hitherto been regarded as unassailable conventions of the constitution.

The question now is whether the conventions of the constitution can be resuscitated. This question is as much a political one as it is one of constitutional law. For, in the absence of abstract constitutional principles, the British Constitution is unusually dependent upon procedures and understandings whose interpretation will depend upon the distribution of authority in society. So it is that many constitutional rules – for example those concerning central/local relations – will be a product of the distribution of authority rather than of any process of ratiocination or intellectual debate; they are the outcome of political battles and not of legal rulings. In such situations it appears that 'the constitutional and political limits to the use of power tend to coincide'.[22] So it is that, in Britain, the notion of constitutionalism is crucially linked with the distribution of political power, rather than with pre-existing constitutional norms. Constitutional *forms*, as Ostrogorski understood so well, depend upon political *forces*, which in turn are the product of culture and ideas.

IV

The essays in this volume share an underlying *leitmotif*. It is that, to preserve the notion of constitutionalism as a limitation of power, we need to depart from the Diceyan insistence upon power and sovereignty being located at one point, at Westminster. Instead, it is high time that we learnt how to share power. These essays argue for the sharing of power with the European Union, with the nations and regions of the United Kingdom through devolution, with local government, and with the people themselves through use of the referendum.

The essays on party politics pursue the theme of the sharing of power in a different way. 'The Ghost of Peel and the Legacy of Disraeli' shows that, contrary to received wisdom, the Conservative Party's procedure for electing its leaders has been much more democratic than is usually imagined. It is precisely because the Conservatives have been willing to share power in their internal relations that the leaders of the Party have been so well attuned to the needs of the electorate. The electoral procedures of the Conservative Party have been pre-eminently those of a political party which, despite Margaret Thatcher, has generally operated without ideology. The Conservatives have also been much more willing than parties of the Left to countenance coalitions and electoral pacts with their political opponents and this too has helped to keep them in power for much of the twentieth century. The politics of the 1980s teaches the same lesson for the parties of the Left as the politics of the period before the First World War – that the two parties of the Left need to co-operate if they are to wrest electoral hegemony from the Conservatives.

At the time of writing, it appears that Britain may once again be on the brink of major constitutional change. For the first time since the First World War, the main opposition party – Labour – finds itself committed to a whole raft of constitutional reforms. Among other reforms, Labour proposes devolution to Scotland and Wales and the abolition of the voting rights of hereditary peers in the House of Lords. Most important of all, John Smith in 1993 proposed a referendum on electoral reform, and this commitment has been echoed, albeit with some hesitancy, by the present leader of the Labour Party, Tony Blair.

Electoral reform would be the most fundamental constitutional change of all. For it would permanently alter the style of British politics, making coalition politics the norm rather than the exception. Such a reform would make British politics appreciably more like that of the Continent. It would play its part in helping Britain to accommodate herself to European Union. Most important of all, it would herald a new configuration of power in British politics and a new political settlement, one no less fundamental than that ushered in by the great Reform Act of 1832.

Yet the debate on electoral reform, like the constitutional issues discussed in this book, while seemingly part of an abstract constitutional argument, is in reality a debate about the distribution of political power. The resolution of the debate, therefore, will depend not only upon the abstract merits of the arguments deployed, but also upon the outcome of a political struggle. That struggle will involve the people as well as the politicians. For Dicey was at least right in this, that on great constitutional issues, the opinion of the nation counts for more than the opinion of Parliament. That was the case in 1832, at the time of the Great Reform Bill, and in 1910, over the Parliament Bill. So it may be again if new constitutional measures reach the statute book. The outcome of the constitutional debate, therefore, is one that will be determined by the people. Only in this way will it be possible finally to exorcise Dicey's ghost, which has become all the constitution that we have left.

The essays in this book are drawn from the following sources.

The introduction above is based upon the papers 'Constitutional Law and Politics', *Oxford Journal of Legal Studies*, 1987, pp. 454–64 and 'Dicey and the Reform of the Constitution', *Public Law*, 1985, pp. 652–72.

Chapter 1 is taken from *Constitutions in Democratic Politics*, edited by me and published by Gower in 1988. Chapter 2 is from *The Thatcher Effect*, edited by Dennis Kavanagh and Anthony Seldon and published by Oxford University Press in 1989. Chapter 3 was first delivered as a lecture to the Institute for Advanced Legal Studes in London University in 1993 and partially reprinted in *Government and Opposition*, 1994, pp. 676–95. Chapter 4 is from *The Conservative Century*, edited by Stuart Ball and Anthony Seldon and published by Oxford University Press in 1994. Chapter 5 is from the journal *Government and Opposition*, 1992, pp. 283–98 and Chapter 6 from *Electoral Studies*, 1993, pp. 203–24. Chapter 7 is from *Electoral Politics*, edited by Dennis Kavanagh, and published by Oxford University Press in 1992.

Chapter 8 is taken from *The Changing Constitution*, 3rd edition, edited by

Jeffrey Jowell and Dawn Oliver, and published by Oxford University Press in 1994. Chapter 9 is from a pamphlet produced for the Society of Local Authority Chief Executives (SOLACE) in 1994 entitled 'Local Government and the Constitution'. Chapter 10 is from the *Political Quarterly*, 1979, pp. 36–49 and Chapter 11 from *Options for Britain*, edited by David Halpern and Stuart White and published by Dartmouth in 1996.

Chapter 12 is taken from *Referendums Around the World*, edited by David Butler and Austin Ranney and published by the American Enterprise Institute in 1994, and *Référendums*, edited by Francis Delperée, published by CRISP, Brussels in 1985. Chapter 13 is from *Parliamentary Affairs*, 1980, pp. 249–63 and Chapter 14 from *Bicameralisme*, edited by H. W. Blom, W. P. Blockmans and H. de Schepper, published by Sdu, s'Gravenhage in 1992.

Grateful acknowledgments are due for permission to reprint. I am grateful also to William Field for collaborating with me on Chapter 6.

Notes and references

1   Ivo Duchacek (1973), *Power-Maps: Comparative Politics of Constitutions*, Santa Barbara: ABC-Clio.
2   S. A. de Smith (1960), 'The Lawyers and the Constitution', Inaugural Lecture delivered at the London School of Economics, 10 May, 6.
3   Jeffrey Jowell and Dawn Oliver (1985) (eds), *The Changing Constitution*, 1st edn, Clarendon Press, v.
4   S. E. Finer, Vernon Bogdanor and Bernard Rudden (1995), *Comparing Constitutions*, Clarendon Press, 40 ff.
5   A. V. Dicey (1885), *Law of the Constitution*, 10th edn (1959), 417–18.
6   These lectures are to be found in the Codrington Library, All Souls College, Oxford, MS 323 LR 6 b 13.
7   Sidney Low (1904), *The Governance of England*, T. Fisher Unwin, 5.
8   See Benjamin Akzin (1956), 'On the Stability and Reality of Constitutions' in *Scripta Hierosolymitana*: Vol. III: *Studies in Economics and the Social Sciences*; Jerusalem: Magnes Press, esp. 337.
9   Giovanni Sartori (1962), 'Constitutionalism: A Preliminary Discussion', *American Political Science Review*.
10   W. H. Morris-Jones (1965), 'On Constitutionalism', *American Political Science Review*, 439–40.
11   *Law of the Constitution*, 431.
12   Dicey to St Loe Strachey, 2 July 1909, Strachey Papers, S/5/5/12: House of Lords Record Office.
13   *Law of the Constitution*, 435.
14   Lord Hailsham (1978), *The Dilemma of Democracy*, Collins.
15   As Professor Heuston appeared to believe. See R. F. V. Heuston (1964), *Essays in Constitutional Law*, 2nd edn, Stevens, 1.
16   J. S. Mill (1861), *Representative Government*. Moisei Ostrogorski (1902), *Democracy and the Organisation of Political Parties*.

17 This memorandum is to be found, with Dicey's lectures, in the Codrington Library, All Souls College, Oxford, MS 323 LR 6 b 13.
18 J. Fischer Williams (1915), 'Mr. Dicey and Proportional Representation,' *Represent-ation*, **32**, June.
19 American Enterprise Institute, 1980.
20 Cambridge University Press, 1981.
21 S. M. Lipset and Stein Rokkan (eds) (1967), Introduction to *Party Systems and Voter Alignments: Cross-National Perspectives*, New York: Free Press.
22 Graeme C. Moodie (1957), 'The Monarch and the Selection of the Prime Minister: A Re-Examination of the Crisis of 1931', in *Political Studies*, 19.

PART I
THE CONSTITUTION AS
POLITICS

1 The Political Constitution

I

En Angleterre, on reconnaît au parlement le droit de modifier la constitution. En Angleterre, la constitution peut donc changer sans cesse, ou plutôt elle n'existe point. Le parlement, en même temps qu'il est corps législatif, est corps constituant. (Tocqueville: *De la Démocratie en Amérique*, Pt I, Ch. 6)

If by 'constitution' we mean simply the rules, whether statutory or not, regulating the powers of government and the rights and duties of the citizen, then Britain, like other civilized states, has always possessed a constitution; but clearly this was not what Tocqueville had in mind when he made his famous declaration that Britain had no constitution. What, then, did he mean?

There are two senses in which it is correct to say that Britain has no constitution. First, Britain lacks a single specifically enacted document containing the main rules which regulate the powers of government and the rights and duties of the citizen. Second, since Parliament in Britain is sovereign, except perhaps in relation to European legislation, no distinction can be drawn between 'ordinary' laws and 'constitutional' laws, laws of fundamental importance which can be changed only through some special legislative procedure. Of these two senses of the term 'constitution', it is the second which is of greater significance. That Britain knows nothing of fundamental law is far more important than the fact that it has no enacted constitution. Nevertheless it is the absence of an enacted constitution that is the first feature to strike the student of British government.

Why is it that Britain lacks an enacted constitution? It is, with Israel and New Zealand, one of only three democracies without such a document. The reason is not difficult to find. Constitutions are generally drawn up to symbolize the birth of a nation, a new beginning in the aftermath of war or revolution. A constitution marks the start of a new political order, a new epoch in a nation's development. A document, so it is generally held, is an essential pre-requisite to the legitimation of a new regime, since it lays out the goals

3

which the political community is expected to pursue and the means by which they may be attained. A constitution, therefore, marks a sharp discontinuity in the history of a state, a radical break with previous practice.

England, however, has been spared such discontinuities since the seventeenth century. Its progress has been evolutionary, unpunctuated by revolutionary upheaval or foreign occupation. The English people have hardly ever felt the need to ask themselves whether they ought to summarize their historical experience in a fundamental document. England's whole constitutional experience seems to show that there is neither any need for, nor any virtue in, an enacted constitution. England, so it might appear, has been constructed in a different way from most other democracies, and in a more durable way. English exceptionalism has been providential, a matter for congratulation and not for regret.

What was true of England was not, of course, necessarily true of Britain or 'the United Kingdom', to give the state its official title. For the United Kingdom came into existence as a result of specific and datable acts – the Articles of Union of 1706 abolishing the Scottish and English Parliaments, and establishing one Parliament of Great Britain; the Union with Ireland Act of 1800 abolishing the Irish Parliament but providing for Irish representation in the new Parliament of the United Kingdom; and the Anglo-Irish Treaty of 1921, removing the 26 counties of the Irish Free State from the jurisdiction of the Parliament of the United Kingdom. All these measures, it might be argued, were of the nature of constituent instruments creating the state as it has existed since 1922, the date when the present borders of the United Kingdom were delimited. Yet the courts, not only in England, but also in Scotland, have never accepted that the Acts of Union with Scotland or Ireland legally restrict Parliament's legislative powers. The courts have held that questions of obligation deriving from the Acts of Union are not legally justiciable. (*Ex p. Canon Selwyn* (1872) 36 J.P.54; *MacCormick v. Lord Advocate* (1953) S.C.396; *Gibson v. Lord Advocate* (1975) S.L.T. 134.) If these Acts create obligations, then they are obligations which rest upon convention, rather than law; they are to be understood as obligations of honour, rather than legal limits upon the power of Parliament. For practical purposes, nevertheless, the legal effect of the Acts of Union has been assimilative. England as the largest of the units comprising the United Kingdom has been able to impose its own particular conception of constitutional development upon Scotland and Northern Ireland.

What is the significance of the fact that Britain lacks an enacted constitution? In his unpublished lectures on the Comparative Study of Constitutions, the constitutional lawyer A.V. Dicey distinguished between historic and non-historic constitutions. An historic constitution such as the English (as Dicey persisted in misnaming the British Constitution), was distinctive not only by its antiquity, but also through its originality and spontaneity. It was the product, not of deliberate design, but of historical development.

The characterization of the British Constitution as an 'historic' constitution is, so it is suggested, more accurate than the common description of it as unwritten. The expression 'unwritten Constitution' was, in Dicey's view, nothing more than a lay and popular one. It is, of course, true that the articles of the British Constitution are not to be found, as are the articles of, for example, the American, French or Belgian Constitutions, in any definite documents or enactments; yet this, for Dicey, was 'a mere matter of form'.[1] For considerable parts of the British Constitution are in fact to be found in written documents or statutes. Magna Carta, the Bill of Rights, the Act of Settlement and the Parliament Acts, all contain a good deal of the British Constitution, in the sense of providing norms for the regulation of government activity and the rights of citizens. There seems no *a priori* reason why the vast jumble of statutes, judicial decisions, precedents, usages and conventions, which comprise the British Constitution, should not be reduced to a single parliamentary enactment. The essential substance of the constitution need not be changed through its translation into written form.

One important provision of a written British constitution, however, would have to be that it could always be amended or repealed in exactly the same way as any other Act of Parliament. Such a provision would be needed to give effect to the principle of the sovereignty of Parliament which was, for Dicey, 'from a legal point of view the dominant characteristic of our political institutions'.[2] Indeed, there is a sense in which the British Constitution can be summed up in eight words: What the Queen in Parliament enacts is law. The essence of the British Constitution is thus better expressed in the statement that it is an historic constitution whose dominating characteristic is the sovereignty of Parliament, than in the statement that Britain has an unwritten constitution. But precisely because the sovereignty of Parliament is the central principle of the British Constitution, it has seemed pointless to rationalize it in an enacted constitution which could forbid nothing, nor could it provide a list of basic freedoms which governments would be unable to infringe.

That the British Constitution is not to be found in a single document is a fact of more interest to the constitutional lawyer than to the political scientist; that Parliament is sovereign is a fact of central importance to both. For it follows from the sovereignty of Parliament that Britain knows no distinction between ordinary laws and constitutional laws, laws with a status higher than mere ordinary laws, the amendment of which requires some special legislative procedure. There is, in Britain, a single process for all legislation which requires but a simple majority in the House of Commons (the Lords can in theory delay a non-money bill, but this is a power which has been used only once since the time of the 1949 Parliament Act). When Tocqueville stated that, Parliament having the right to change the Constitution, there was no Constitution, he meant that Britain knew nothing of fundamental law. Statutes concerning the organization of government or the rights of the citizen can be passed or repealed by the same simple majority procedure as is required for all other legislation. Thus the term 'unconstitutional' cannot in Britain mean contrary to law; instead it means contrary to convention, contrary to some understanding of what it is appropriate to do. But unfortunately, there is by no means universal agreement on what the standards of appropriateness are or ought to be. As Sidney Low put it in 1904, 'British government is based upon a system of tacit understandings. But the understandings are not always understood'.[3] It is perhaps easier to secure consensus and stability in such a system than in one based upon constitutional principles where interpretations of what the constitution requires will often vary with the political beliefs of the interpreter. But in Britain, doctrinal disagreement can be masked by attachment to a common stock of historical precedents; the standard of appropriateness is *internal* to the system, not external to it. For there is no objective reference point, no *pouvoir neutre* beyond Parliament, which is able to erect a standard for what is constitutional.

Yet, although legally supreme, Parliament is in reality largely controlled by the government of the day. In the contemporary world of disciplined parties, the House of Commons is an electoral college rather than a genuine legislative body; and in practice, the supremacy of Parliament serves to legitimize the omnicompetence of government. Britain, *pace* Maitland, has substituted the authority of the Crown for a theory of the state.[4]

II

The ability of a government unilaterally to alter the rules of the political game could, in theory, allow for a very considerable abuse of power. Yet the abuse of power has been the exception and not the rule in British twentieth-century politics. The basic reason for this is that, for most of the twentieth century, the British Constitution has remained above politics. Whatever other differences there have been between the political parties, they did not seek to dispute the fundamental rules through which political activity was regulated. Even in the 1930s when political conflict was at its sharpest, there was surprisingly little questioning of Britain's constitutional arrangements. The Constitution has only been genuinely under strain during the years 1910–14 when the dispute over Irish Home Rule and the Ulster question threatened the very foundations of the political system and might easily have led to civil war. Indeed, some historians believe that the impasse over Ulster would have had this consequence, had it not been for the coming of the First World War in August 1914.

No other issue has so menaced the civic order of Britain this century. Nevertheless, there have been two other periods when constitutional questions formed a central part of the agenda of politics – the thirty years before the First World War, and the period since 1969. These were years of constitutional *ferment* in British politics, years in which the contours of the constitution were blurred and its future seemed uncertain.

Britain adopted universal male suffrage for men over 21, and universal female suffrage for women over 30, in 1918. (Women aged between 21 and 30 were enfranchised in 1928.) Yet, the real battle over the suffrage had been won much earlier – in 1884, 1867 or perhaps even in 1832; and from the 1880s, constitutional reformers began to turn to other issues, and in particular to a consideration of the relationship between the new democratic electorate and the institutions of government.

A. V. Dicey's classic *Introduction to the Study of the Law of the Constitution* was first published in 1885 at the beginning of this period of constitutional ferment. For the eighth edition published in 1915 – the last edition for which he was personally responsible – Dicey contributed a long introduction surveying the constitutional debates of the previous thirty years: women's suffrage, Home Rule, proportional representation and the referendum. These constitutional issues formed a central part of the political agenda in the three decades before the First World War. For there was a deep-seated disagreement both within and between the parties on the future shape of British democracy. Until 1911, it was uncertain whether Britain would retain a bicameral legislature, or whether Parliament would become effectively unicameral; and uncertain whether the referendum would become a part of the British Constitution, a proposal endorsed by the Conservative leader, A.J. Balfour, shortly before the December 1910 General Election. Moreover, until the secession of the 26 counties of the Irish Free State in 1921, it was possible to believe that Irish Home Rule might be the prelude to 'Home Rule All Round', transforming Britain into a quasi-federal state. Most important of all, it was by no means implausible to suppose that Britain would adopt the alternative-vote electoral system or some system of proportional representation; and the issue remained genuinely in doubt until 1918 when, in the Fourth Reform Act, Parliament decided, almost by default, to retain the plurality electoral system in single-member constituences.

These three measures – the 1911 Parliament Act, the 1918 Representation of the People Act, and the Anglo-Irish Treaty of 1921 – served to remove constitutional issues from British politics for almost 50 years. The Parliament Act not only put paid to the possibility of referring legislation to the electorate; it also ensured that there was no body other than the government of the day which could make a judgment on the constitutional propriety of legislation. The Parliament Act established an effectively unicameral system of government in Britain. It was, Dicey claimed, 'the last and greatest triumph of party government', and underlined the fact that party government was 'not the accident or corruption, but, so to speak, the very foundation of our constitutional system.'[5] What made Britain unusual was that party government was henceforth to operate within a political system which, unlike most democracies, contained nothing to check the untrammelled power of the majority party.

Retention of the plurality system of election in the 1918 Representation of the People Act made possible Conservative hegemony in the interwar period, enabling the party to gain an overall majority in the Commons in 1922 on only 38 per cent of the vote. The vast extension of the franchise in 1918, together with the growth of class feeling, contributed to the restoration of a two-party system, but one in which Labour, not the Liberals, was the chief opponent of the Conservatives. Labour took the view that the central issues of politics were socioeconomic, not constitutional; while the Conservatives, in power for most of the time, were happy to accept the status quo.

The removal of the vast majority of Irish MPs from the House of Commons as a result of the Anglo-Irish Treaty made single-party majority government more likely. Before 1918, any British Government needed around 100 more seats than the main opposition party if it was to be assured of a working majority for a full Parliament and avoid reliance on the 80-odd Irish Nationalists regularly returned to the Commons after 1885. Four out of the eight elections held between 1885 and December 1910 had led to hung parliaments in which the government was dependent upon the Irish members. Further, the Anglo-Irish Treaty also removed the constitutional issue of Irish Home Rule from British politics, taking with it – so at least it seemed for 50 years – both devolution and the Ulster question.

In the 1920s, the British party system was taking on the shape which it was to assume for over 50 years – a two-party system within which both parties emphasized the priority of socioeconomic concerns. The Liberals, a party for whom constitutional questions formed the very stuff of political life, were replaced by Labour, a party whose political focus was directed at problems of economic management and social welfare. This new party system was buttressed by the growth of social solidarity and political consciousness among the working class. For the process leading to universal adult suffrage, slow as it was, preceded the 'embourgeoisement' of the working class. The existence of a wide suffrage combined with a politically conscious working class created the preconditions for a fairly rigid two-party system within which the Conservative and Labour Parties battled for control over terrain whose contours were primarily socioeconomic, while constitutional issues were pushed off the map as a tiresome irrelevance. In opposition for much of the 1920s,

1930s, 1950s and 1980s, Labour's aim was nevertheless to capture the state, not to transform it; while the Conservatives dug themselves in around a defensive stockade, enjoying the supreme power bestowed on them by the Constitution, while assuming that the forces of radical change could be kept at bay for ever and ever. It was a high-risk strategy, but it worked.

Moreover, as Michael Steed has pointed out,[6] the very development of tightly organized mass parties had the consequence of fossilizing the movement for constitutional change. For the parties succeeded in identifying all that was beneficent about democracy with their own dominance. One of the central concerns of constitutional reformers had been the extension of participation. Yet defenders of the party system could argue that the parties themselves were perfectly adequate channels of participation, and that reforms such as devolution, the referendum or primary elections were unnecessary. Sociology and ideology thus went hand in hand in underwriting the party system evolving in Britain in the 1920s; the party system was seen as being congruent both with social reality and with ideological attitudes.

III

It is hardly a coincidence, then, that the processes of social change which have produced embourgeoisement, have also stimulated the decline of ideological and class loyalties, greater threats to the two-party system, and the return of constitutional issues to British politics. Indeed, since the late 1960s constitutional issues have formed a central part of the political agenda. In 1968, the civil rights movement in Northern Ireland erupted into violence and threatened the rule of the Ulster Unionists. As the Northern Ireland problem forced itself upon the attention of successive British governments, so they found themselves proposing constitutional innovations for that troubled province which they would not have dreamt of contemplating for the mainland. The year 1973 saw three constitutional reforms, consequent upon the abolition of the Northern Ireland Parliament. A border poll was held to display the allegiance of the province to the United Kingdom; a new legislature was proposed in the Northern Ireland Constitution Act which, departing significantly from the Westminster model of single-party majority government, was to be based upon the principle of power-sharing between the Unionist majority and the Nationalist minority. Further, the Assembly would be elected by the single transferable vote method of proportional representation, and the new district councils in Northern Ireland would also be elected by this method. It is hardly surprising that the Electoral Reform Society, which had been campaigning for the single transferable vote for nearly 90 years, called 1973 a 'Red Letter Year' and declared that:[7]

The reform this Society seeks is no longer an academic matter, capable of being dismissed as the concern of a few enthusiasts; it is now something actually operating within the United Kingdom . . . The whole subject is topical as it has not been for half a century.

Changes in Northern Ireland, however, had comparatively little effect upon opinion in the rest of the United Kingdom for whom that province had, for many years, been seen as a rather peculiar entity subject to laws of its own and with no wider relevance. Yet the 1970s saw the introduction of another momentous issue into British politics, Britain's entry into the European Community, which not only had major constitutional implications, but also very considerable consequences for the political parties, since it was one of the issues which led to the split in the Labour Party and the secession of many on the Right wing to form the Social Democratic Party in 1981. Britain's entry into the Community was bound to pose problems for the theory of parliamentary sovereignty. Admittedly, the strains have not been as immediate or as obvious as might have been predicted; nevertheless, the central consequence of entry has been that decisions previously taken by the British Government are now taken by a body – the Council of Ministers – which is not and cannot be responsible to Parliament at Westminster. This transference of power from Britain to the institutions of the Community is underlined by the Single European Act of 1986 and the Maastricht Treaty of 1991, which render a wider area of Community decision-making subject to qualified majority voting. This will tend to shift decision-making power still further away from Britain, and also shift the balance of parliamentary responsibility from Westminster to the European Parliament. Britain's entry into the Community may not have caused any immediate constitutional revolution; but it was a change of major constitutional importance which led to a further constitutional innovation – the first nation-wide referendum, held in 1975, on the question of whether Britain should leave the Community or remain on the basis of the terms renegotiated by the Labour Government which had come to office in 1974.

Entry to the Community had yet another effect upon constitutional thinking in Britain. It exposed British politicians and lawyers to Continental political and legal systems, and showed them that the simple stereotypes which they had often used to disparage them were distortions of reality. In particular, direct elections to the European Parliament, first held in 1979, helped to keep the issue of proportional representation in the forefront of political debate. For supporters of proportional representation could claim that if, as turned out to be the case, Britain retained the single-member plurality system, it would prove to be the only member of the Community not employing one or other of the various systems of proportional representation for these elections. Not only would Britain be the odd man out, but the misrepresentation of British opinion would have a highly distorting effect upon the strength of the party groupings in the European Parliament. They also argued that MPs could support proportional representation for elections to the European Parliament without necessarily committing themselves to proportional representation for elections to the House of Commons, since the European Parliament, unlike the Commons, was not required to sustain a government. The counter-argument employed by opponents – that proportional representation would lead to weak and/or unstable government – was therefore irrelevant.

Yet a third constitutional issue in addition to Northern Ireland and the European Community haunted Parliament in the 1970s – devolution. This too raised important constitutional questions relating to parliamentary sovereignty and federalism, issues which the 1974–9 Labour Governments sought, not wholly successfully, to avoid. Ministers faced the same question as had confronted Gladstone's Liberals in the 1880s and 1890s. Was it possible to provide for legislative devolution in only one part of a unitary state without causing intolerable anomalies in parliamentary representation and in the distribution of financial resources? Was there a genuine halfway house between the unitary state and 'Home Rule All Round' or federalism? The problem was in some respects even more complex than it had been 90 years earlier, since the existence of a developed Welfare State and the requirements of a managed economy seemed to impose crucial limitations upon the extent to which power could be transferred from Westminster and Whitehall.

Like the Northern Ireland question and the European Community, devolution also involved a choice of electoral system. In October 1973, the Report of the Royal Commission on the Constitution (Kilbrandon Commission) was published, and among its few unanimous recommendations was a proposal that any assemblies established in Scotland, Wales or the English regions, should be elected by the single transferable vote method of proportional representation. This recommendation was rejected, however, by the Labour government of the 1970s which was prepared to accept the risk that, in a four-party political system in Scotland, the Scottish Nationalists might gain control of the Scottish Assembly, and claim a mandate for independence on a vote of 40 per cent or less. Fear of such an outcome was one of the factors inhibiting the Scottish electorate from giving whole-hearted endorsement to the devolution proposals in the referendum of March 1979.

The government found that devolution, like Britain's membership of the Community, was not an issue which could be satisfactorily resolved through normal parliamentary procedures, but needed popular endorsement by the electorate to gain legitimacy. Indeed, the devolution legislation would probably not have secured parliamentary approval at all had the government not been willing to commit itself to a referendum. So it was that the referendum on Britain's membership of the Community, justified by ministers in terms of the unique nature of the issue, was followed by referendums in Scotland and Wales four years later. A further innovation was the 40 per cent rule, a provision inserted in the Scotland and Wales Acts against the wishes of the government, which required that 40 per cent of the electorate, as well as a majority of those voting, cast a 'Yes' vote for the legislation to come into effect.[8]

IV

In the 1970s, then, three major problems – Northern Ireland, the European Community, and devolution – brought constitutional concerns back to the centre of politics. For a time, it seemed that British politics was actually dominated by constitutional issues. However, the period of constitutional ferment ended with the defeat of the devolution proposals in the referendums held in March 1979, and the return of the Conservatives to office in May. For the Conservative Party, under Mrs Thatcher, took the view that constitutional issues were a distraction from the real tasks facing government. Previous administrations, so it was argued, had spent too much time tinkering with the Constitution and reorganizing the institutions of government. Mrs Thatcher's administration, by contrast, would focus its attention ruthlessly upon the socioeconomic and cultural causes of Britain's long economic decline.

Yet, although her Government stuck obstinately to its conviction of leaving constitutional issues alone, Mrs Thatcher was not able entirely to exorcise the constitution. Evicted from one door, it soon returned by another. The problems of Northern Ireland, of course, remain to torment British governments, whether Labour or Conservative; while the gradual and seemingly inexorable transfer of powers to Europe continued to pose difficult questions for those wedded to Britain's traditional constitutional arrangements.

In other areas also, new constitutional issues arose as a result of the policies of the Thatcher Government. In two areas in particular – trade union reform and the reform of local government – constitutional issues arose which the government would have preferred to have kept submerged. Coming to power in 1979, shortly after the so-called 'Winter of Discontent' in which a series of strikes had led to the closure of schools, the disruption and blocking of hospitals and even a refusal to bury the dead, it was inevitable that the Conservatives would seek to do away with the legal immunities which the trade unions had enjoyed since 1906, and to impose a new legal framework for the regulation of union affairs. The 1984 Trade Union Act was a part of this approach, and it provided, among other things, that unions should be required to test the opinion of their members every decade on whether they still wished to maintain a political fund from which, *inter alia*, affiliation payments were made to the Labour Party. This raised the whole question of the role of institutions – whether trades unions or companies – in the financing of political parties. On grounds of fairness, it seemed wrong to regulate trade union financing of the Labour Party, while leaving unregulated company financing of the Conservatives. It could be claimed that a system in which the two major parties were financed by industry and the trade unions polarized politics and encouraged confrontational attitudes, as well as handicapping parties, such as the Liberal Democrats, which did not enjoy close links with unions or companies. Some put forward the view that state aid to political parties was the only way to avoid undue reliance upon institutional interests. So what seemed at first sight an issue merely of trade union reform began to pose questions about the relationship between organized interests and political parties, and indeed raised fundamental issues about the very nature of the British party system. These issues are, in essence, constitutional – although, like other constitutional issues, their resolution depends largely upon the future configuration of party politics.

The relationship between central and local government was another area in which, unexpectedly, constitutional issues arose. Relations between central government and local authorities, although regulated to a certain extent by statute, had always been based more upon shared understandings as to the proper role of the centre and of localities than upon precise legal regulations. These shared understandings were undermined when the Conservatives took office in 1979 – for two interconnected reasons. The first was that the government was committed to a large reduction in public expenditure as part of its programme of containing inflation. This would inevitably fall heavily upon local authorities, which are responsible for around a quarter of total public expenditure. Secondly, the Conservatives found that, in many urban authorities, power had passed from an older generation of Labour councillors to a new generation determined to implement genuinely socialist policies at local level, to make local government into a laboratory for the testing of socialism. This made them even more unwilling to heed government requests for restraint in public expenditure. It seemed that the consensual framework needed to sustain a partnership between the two levels of government no longer existed.

The Conservative Government decided to adopt drastic measures to deal with the problem. First, it intervened directly to curb the financial independence of local authorities. A series of legislative measures provided for the rigorous control of local government expenditure – whether financed from the block grant provided by central government, the Rate Support Grant, or from local government's own resources, primarily the rates. These measures culminated in the 1984 Rates Act, empowering the Secretary of State for the

Environment to impose maximum rate levels upon local authorities.

But the Conservatives took an even more direct step to deal with their political opponents in the Local Government Act 1985, abolishing the Greater London Council and the six metropolitan county councils, authorities for Britain's major conurbations established by a previous Conservative Government in the 1972 Local Government Act. These authorities had all been captured electorally by the Labour Party, and had formed a powerful focus of opposition to many of the government's social and economic policies.

The Conservatives' opponents accused them not only of undermining local autonomy, but also of breaking important conventions of the constitution. The Rates Act breached the principle that local authorities should be free to decide for themselves how much money they wished to raise locally. For, until 1984, it had been generally accepted that local authorities should be free to decide what level of rate to set, and to provide for services to meet the level of rates which they could raise. Governments, if they wished to limit local authority expenditure, did so through varying the level of central grant paid to local authorities, not by directly controlling the level of rates. The Rates Act, however, for the first time restricted the power of local authorities to set their own rates. This was a very different matter from central government restricting its *own* contribution to local authorities. That local authorities should be free to raise what money they required from those who elected them had hitherto been thought to be a cornerstone of local democracy in Britain. The abolition of the Greater London Council and the metropolitan authorities was also held to be a breach of constitutional convention because it undermined the right of local electors to have local services provided by directly elected local authorities. The 1985 Act did *not* replace the GLC and the Metropolitan Counties with a unitary system of local authorities, for comparatively few functions were devolved from the GLC and the Metropolitan Counties to the London Boroughs and Metropolitan Districts respectively. Most of their functions were transferred to London or county-wide bodies which were not directly elected; others were transferred directly to Whitehall. Thus, the upper tier of local government would remain but, instead of being directly elected, it would be administered through joint boards, committees, government 'quangos' (quasi-autonomous non-government organizations) and by the Minister. The unilateral abolition of elections to a tier of government was held by some to raise constitutional issues of great magnitude, and to set a dangerous precedent for any future administration seeking to abolish an elected body of which it disapproved.

The measures taken by the Conservatives had the consequence of calling into question traditional relationships between central government and local authorities, and made many ask whether there were any constitutional principles which ought to govern these relationships, and whether there was a need of constitutional protection for the values of local self-government. The various Royal Commissions and departmental committees established in the 1960s and 1970s to examine local government as a prelude to its reorganization were required by their terms of reference rigorously to exclude constitutional questions. The consequence has been that central–local relations were governed by no discernible principles, but operated on a pragmatic and *ad hoc* basis. It is doubtful whether this can any longer be sustained. The major Opposition parties – Labour and the Liberal Democrats – have committed themselves to policies involving a restoration of local autonomy, and to Scottish and Welsh devolution; they are also sympathetic to the establishment of a layer of regional authorities in England. And many believe that even a Conservative government would have to reconsider the basis of central–local relations, since the arrangements proposed in the Local Government Act of 1985 for the administration of London and the metropolitan authorities are, in the view of their critics, so ramshackle and unstable that they cannot possibly survive. But this re-examination of local government will, inevitably, involve the introduction of those very constitutional issues so rigorously excluded in the past.

The policies pursued by the Conservative Government have not only stimulated constitutional discussion on the financing of political parties and the role of local government. They have also given rise to a more general concern at the consequences of omnicompetent government. Lacking the checks and balances which exist in most democracies, Britain can easily approach the condition identified by Lord Hailsham as 'elective dictatorship'.[9] How, then, can the balance, at present so heavily tilted in the executive's favour, be redressed? Among the proposed remedies have been reform of the House of Lords so that, with a more rational composition, it can gain the authority to check the government of the day; a Bill of Rights – which in practice would mean incorporating the European Convention of Human Rights into British law; and a Freedom of Information Act providing for more open government. These reforms, however, do not enjoy the popular salience of the major constitutional issues discussed earlier.

V

Northern Ireland, the European Community, devolution and central–local relations all involve questions of territorial politics in which local allegiances cut across party political loyalties. The history of the measures taken to deal with these issues shows how remarkably ill-attuned British party and parliamentary procedures are to issues of territorial politics. Britain remains a unitary state, but it contains a territorially heterogeneous population. The question is whether this unitary structure can be preserved when challenged by the development of a distinctive political consciousness in some of its component parts, such as Northern Ireland, Scotland and also possibly some of the English regions. British politicians find it difficult to think in territorial terms; and the party structure, with the exception of the Scottish and Welsh nationalist parties and the Northern Ireland parties, is based mainly upon socioeconomic rather than territorial cleavages. It is for this reason that territorial issues have placed such severe strain upon the cohesiveness of Britain's political parties. The European Community and devolution, in particular, were issues which split both parties, dividing allies while uniting those who were normally political opponents.

Part of the reason why British governments have found it difficult to cope with territorial issues lies with the ideological heritage of Dicey, who was inclined to confuse the purely formal legal doctrine of the sovereignty of Parliament with the more controversial statement that Britain's political stability depended upon the existence of an omnicompetent Parliament. This entailed the absence of any competing legislative authorities, even if subordinate, which might challenge this omnicompetence. As a consequence, governments have been ideologically ill-equipped to deal with territorial problems whose resolution requires less an assertion of sovereignty than acceptance of the principle of power-sharing.

The return of territorial issues into British politics challenged the legislative dominance of Westminster, and required, so it seemed, something over and above the normal legislative procedures if they were to be resolved. Locke in his *Second Treatise of Government* declared (para. 141) that the power of Parliament was but a delegated power from the People, and that Parliament could not transfer its power of making laws without the approval of the People. So it is that Parliament has provided that Northern Ireland shall not cease to be a part of the United Kingdom without a border poll, and that the questions of Britain's membership of the European Community and of devolution could only be settled through a referendum. Legitimacy seemed to require, not just a positive vote by Parliament, but the endorsement of the People as well. Thus, to the question of where a constitutional reference point can be found in a political system with a sovereign Parliament, the British system can now answer – in the referendum. The electorate itself can be a democratic check upon the processes of representative government.

In Britain, the referendum has proved to be, as Dicey predicted, a method of securing *de facto* entrenchment in a country without a rigid constitution. It offers a means of drawing a distinction between ordinary laws and constitutional laws, such as is commonly drawn in countries with constitutions which can only be amended by a special procedure. Thus, if a government ever wished to deprive Northern Ireland of its membership of the United Kingdom or to provide for legislative devolution, it would be difficult to do so without a referendum. The degree of entrenchment secured is, of course, greater if a hurdle in the form of a qualifying majority is imposed, such as the 40 per cent rule in the Scottish and Welsh referendums.

VI

The fundamental reason why constitutional issues have again become a part of the British political agenda is that the party system has found itself unable to accommodate them. It has become frozen.

British politics, more than that of most other democracies, is marked by the dominance of party, and more particularly by the dominance of the two major parties. Although political parties in Britain are not recognized in law, the law nevertheless helps them retain their dominance. It does so in two ways. First, it provides for an electoral system – the plurality method of voting in single-member constituencies – which discriminates against third parties lacking concentrated class or geographical support. Thus, it re-inforces the existence of a class-based party system, in which the central political cleavage is socioeconomic. Secondly, Britain is quite unique among developed Western democracies in the extent to which the two major parties are financed from institutional sources – companies and trade unions. The bulk of the contributions made to the central organizations of the two major parties are the result of corporate rather than individual decisions, private donations, but not necessarily voluntary ones. It is difficult for a new party, not enjoying a privileged relationship with the trade union movement as the Labour Party does, and unable to attract large company contributions as the Conservatives do, to overcome this disadvantage. So the methods by which the parties are financed in Britain, like the electoral system, seem to reward those parties able to exploit one type of political cleavage – class conflict – at the expense of others.

The British political system, then, depends primarily upon the operation of party. In Britain, the parties not only control the game of politics; they also control the rules under which the game is played. This is perfectly acceptable when there is widespread agreement on what these rules should be, and when cohesive parties provide a rational framework for political debate based upon the real issues of the day. These preconditions have been met for much of the twentieth century, but it is questionable whether they are still met in the Britain of the 1990s. Until the Second World War, the British party system was given fluidity by a periodic process of realignment. Modern party politics began in Britain after the Second Reform Act in 1867. Yet, by the

1880s, realignment was beginning to occur. The right wing of the Liberal Party – the Whigs – were already finding that Gladstonian Radicalism was incompatible with a Whig interpretation of Liberalism, and they were beginning to move towards the Conservative Party, even before Gladstone's espousal of Irish Home Rule in 1885–6 hastened the process. The defection of Joseph Chamberlain in 1886 added a powerful element of populism to the Conservative Party, and the Unionist coalition ruled Britain almost continuously in the twenty years after 1886. In 1903, however, a new issue cut across the old politics – Tariff Reform, introduced suddenly and without warning by Chamberlain, the only politician in modern British history to split both major political parties. This caused defections from the Conservatives – an 1886 in reverse, although the numbers involved were much smaller. They did, however, include the young Winston Churchill, destined to be one of the radical social reformers in the 1905–15 Liberal Governments.

Meanwhile, the birth and development of the Labour Party which, over a period of 25 years, came to replace the Liberals as the main Opposition party on the left, introduced a further element of flexibility into the political system; while the splits within the Liberal Party which followed the formation of the Lloyd George coalition government in 1916 helped to ensure that Liberal values would be promoted in the Conservative and Labour Parties. In 1931, the formation of the National Government split the Labour and Liberal Parties, giving a new accretion of strength to the Conservatives, and enabling old battles on issues such as Free Trade and Empire to be settled peacefully.

Thus between 1880 and 1931, party alignments changed constantly in response to a changing political agenda. The realignment of 1931, however, was to prove the last for 50 years. The prime reason for this was ideological. Labour regarded the defection of MacDonald and his followers in 1931 as a unique betrayal, while the Conservatives benefited electorally from the disunity of their opponents, and were not disposed to throw away the advantage of party unity.

The end of realignment would not have mattered if there had been a real unity of feeling and purpose in the Conservative and Labour Parties. But instead the party system became frozen, emphasizing the ritualistic issues of the past, while ensuring that others – the European Community in the 1950s, the role of sterling in the 1960s, the decentralization of power in the 1970s, and above all the economic modernization of Britain – were submerged in a directionless consensus. At the same time, many of the crucial lines of division in British politics were found to lie within the parties, not between them, and the real conflict often seemed to be found between warring intra-party factions, rather than in the more manufactured disagreement of the House of Commons and the hustings.

In the 1970s, however, it seemed that the parties were coming to take their rhetoric more seriously, and the 'adversary politics' thesis was put forward to show how the two-party system could be dysfunctional to the maintenance of Britain's position as an advanced industrial society.[10] In the immediate post-war period, the consensual aspects of British politics had seemed to discourage open debate on the real policy choices facing the country. In the 1970s, the party battle, which had hitherto appeared a sham fight, came alive. But, at the same time, support for the two major parties was seen to be waning. In the first eight elections after the Second World War, between 1945 and 1970, the average percentage of the vote gained by the winning party was 47.4; in the next six elections between February 1974 and 1992, the average percentage was only 41.1, a little over two-fifths of the vote. In the two general elections of 1974, no party succeeded in gaining as much as 40 per cent of the vote, while the Conservative landslides in 1983 and 1987 were gained on just over 42 per cent of the vote, a lower percentage than was gained by any government with a comfortable majority since 1922, during another period of realignment. Indeed, the percentages of the vote gained by the Conservatives in 1983, 1987 and 1992 were lower than that gained by the main Opposition party in *every* election between 1945 and 1974, except those of 1945 and 1966.

Pressures for party realignment were associated, as they had been in previous political crises in the twentieth century, with a programme of economic modernization. It is striking that so many of those who have put the modernization of the British economy at the forefront of their political programme – Joseph Chamberlain, Lloyd George, the Keynesian radicals of the interwar years, and David Owen – have found themselves unable to work within the orthodox two-party system, and have been driven to seek new political combinations. They saw the party system as an alienated superstructure, distorting and suppressing the real political choices which needed to be made.

Thus, the final outcome of the constitutional debate in British politics depends crucially upon the vicissitudes of party politics. Dicey argued that one central weakness of Britain's party constitution was that constitutional change came to be muddled up with party considerations. The question of the best constitutional arrangement came to be mixed with other political questions, and above all, with the question of which party ought to be in government.[11] For the British Constitution is essentially a *political* constitution, one whose operation depends upon the strength of political factors and whose interpretation depends upon the will of its political leaders. If the two-party system reasserts itself, then constitutional change is unlikely. If, however, the party system remains in a state of flux, the constitutional conventions which are the product of the two-party system will no longer be sustainable. Coalition or minority government could come to replace single-party majority government as the norm, and British politics could again become what it was before 1867 – multi-party politics. A necessary condition of such an outcome is probably the introduction of proportional representation, something which would reinforce new political alignments. Proportional representation is, as it were, the key in the lock, the precondition for unfreezing the party system and so making possible other constitutional reforms.

But the strength of the various political forces in Britain cannot be divorced from the processes of social change. For political parties reflect these processes, and are to some extent their product. The party system is in flux because British society is also in a state of flux. There has come to be a lack of congruence between the rules regulating the framework of party politics, and the social and economic patterns which in the past sustained it. It is impossible to foresee how Britain's institutions, its 'living Constitution' in Karl Llewellyn's phrase,[12] something amended not by the courts or Parliament, but in the last resort by the people themselves, will adapt itself to changing social conditions. In the words of Disraeli's Sidonia:[13]

A political institution is a machine; the motive power is the national character [what political scientists today call political culture]. With that it rests whether the machine will benefit society, or destroy it. Society in this country is perplexed, almost paralysed; in time it will move and it will devise. How are the elements of the nation to be again blended together? In what spirit is that reorganisation to take place?

'To know that', replied Coningsby, 'would be to know everything.'

Notes and references

1   A. V. Dicey, Lectures on the Comparative Study of Constitutions, MS 323 LR 6 b 13.
2   A. V. Dicey (1959), *Introduction to the Study of the Law of the Constitution*, 10th edn, Macmillan, 39.
3   Sidney Low (1904), *The Governance of England*, T. Fisher Unwin, 12.
4   F. W. Maitland (1936), 'The Crown as Corporation', in H. D. Hazeldine, G. Lapsley and P. H. Winfield (eds), *Selected Essays*, Cambridge University Press.
5   Dicey (1915), Introduction to 8th edition of *Law of the Constitution*, Macmillan, ci.
6   Michael Steed (1972), 'Participation through Western Democratic Institutions', in Geraint Parry (ed.), *Participation in Politics*, Manchester University Press.
7   *Representation* (Journal of the Electoral Reform Society), **13** (53), October 1973, 54.
8   See Vernon Bogdanor (1979), *Devolution*, Oxford University Press.
9   Lord Hailsham (1978), *The Dilemma of Democracy*, Collins.
10   S. E. Finer (ed.) (1975), *Adversary Politics and Electoral Reform*, Anthony Wigram.
11   Dicey, Lectures on the Comparative Study of Constitutions, *loc. cit.*
12   See, for example, Karl Llewellyn (1934), 'The Constitution as an Institution', *Columbia Law Review*, **34**, January.
13   Benjamin Disraeli (1844), *Coningsby*, Book IV, Chapter XIII.

2 Mrs Thatcher and the Constitution

Each period of history has its own characteristic motif. The 1970s were marked by a crisis of authority in British politics as the jurisdiction of the state seemed to be threatened by trade unionists, Ulster loyalists, and Scottish nationalists. The most memorable emblems of that decade were Saltley pickets, the masked gunmen of Northern Ireland, and cancer patients turned away from hospitals. For political scientists, the central themes were ungovernability and overload. The state was under threat because it was trying to do too much; and, precisely for this reason, it was unable to fulfil its basic responsibilities effectively. The fundamental task of government, so it seemed, was not only to alter the direction of economic management, but to restore the authority of the state.

The 1980s, by contrast, are best understood through a quite different concept – elective dictatorship – coined by Lord Hailsham to characterize the weak Labour governments of the 1970s, but more applicable to the regime of Mrs Thatcher in which he was himself to serve. The juxtaposition – ungovernability, elective dictatorship – neatly sums up both the strengths and weaknesses of Mrs Thatcher's decade. For, having restored the authority of the state, she also weakened the democratic underpinning which makes that authority tolerable. It would be a mistake, however, to ascribe this duality solely to the personality of Mrs Thatcher, or to that ill-defined jumble of qualities labelled 'Thatcherism'. It stems, rather, from a deep-seated instinct in conservatism itself. Hayek, often cited as one of Mrs Thatcher's ideological mentors, has noticed

the characteristic complacency of the conservative toward the action of established authority, and his prime concern that this authority be not weakened rather than that its power be kept within bounds – he believes that if government is in the hands of decent men, it ought not to be too restricted by rigid rules.[1]

In her commitment to a strong state and her aversion to any reform of the constitution which might limit its sway, Mrs Thatcher was doing no more than following a well-worn Conservative tradition.

Restoration of the authority of the state required, first and foremost, a positive answer to the constitutional question: could government govern against the wishes of the trade unions? From 1969, when Harold Wilson capitulated to the union barons over *In Place of Strife*, to 1985, when Mrs Thatcher inflicted a final defeat on Arthur Scargill, this was the dilemma which haunted British politics. In four general elections – 1970, October 1974, 1979 and 1983 – the problem lay in the background as an implicit constraint on government; in the fifth, that of February 1974, it moved into the foreground, becoming an explicitly constitutional issue and bringing about the fall of Edward Heath. As a result, governments found themselves paralysed over wide areas of policy-making – not only in industrial relations, but also in areas such as education and health, where the trade union veto operated to prevent new policy departures. It was the removal of that veto which made possible the reforms of Mrs Thatcher's third term – the Education Reform Act of 1988 and the NHS reforms. Whether the teachers' unions or the health service unions favoured these reforms was now irrelevant, for they had lost the power to destroy legislation with which they disagreed. The era which Bernard Donoughue christened as one of producer socialism was now quite dead.

Mrs Thatcher thus took one major constitutional issue – the government versus the unions – entirely out of politics, probably for good. The removal of this issue from the political agenda was an essential precondition not only for the promotion of a market economy favoured by the Conservatives, but even perhaps for the policies favoured by the opposition parties. They too may have cause to be grateful to her for removing the union veto, which was a veto on the policies of Labour governments as well as Tory.

Restoration of the authority of government is in essence a Tory idea. Yet it was sought as a means to ends which were far from Tory. For Mrs Thatcher's aim was to create not a hierarchical society, one governed through rank and degree, but its opposite, a society marked by freedom and individual responsibility. How was this aim to be achieved – by the method of constitutionalism, as in the German Federal Republic, or by the exercise of sovereign power as in Britain.

In Germany, the social market economy is buttressed by constitutional provisions designed to limit state action. Government is constrained by very general constitutional rules, and especially by a federal division of power which ensures that the implementation of much federal legislation is left to the *Länder*. Fundamental to the German constitution is a conception of the dispersal of public authority as an essential concomitant of economic liberalism. For neo-liberal thinkers such as Hayek and Nozick, the constitutional dispersal of power is vital to the achievement of the free economy. For them, the methods by which the state acts, the forms which such action takes, are as important as the content of state action. For this reason, Hayek explicitly rejects the notion of parliamentary sovereignty, which he sees as but the legal counterpart of omnicompetent government; it means in effect 'the abandonment of constitutionalism which consists in a limitation of all power by permanent principles of government'.[2] Yet in Britain, by contrast, Mrs Thatcher, far from seeking to limit the power of government, made use of it to a far greater extent than her predecessors. The scope of government may be limited, but its ambit became infinite.

The reason for this should be clear. In a Germany ruined by Hitler, there seemed little alternative to the disciplines of the market. In Britain, on the other hand, attitudes conducive to the maintenance of a free economy could not be assumed, but had to be conjured into existence. Thus, Mrs Thatcher's aim was not only to reconstruct the state, but also to transform society. The impact of over 30 years of social democracy and the Welfare State had been to weaken the primacy of competitive relationships, making individuals over-reliant on 'society', rather than on their own efforts. Thus, the project to re-establish the free economy had also to be one that reshaped social relations. In Andrew Gamble's words, 'The citizens have to be forced to be free and enterprising, otherwise there is no guarantee they will be so.'[3]

Human nature, in the Conservative view, is not naturally inclined towards freedom and individual responsibility. For this reason, Mrs Thatcher's policy for society, as opposed to her policy for the economy, could not be one of *laissez-faire*. The success of a competitive economy, as Japan shows so clearly, rests not upon a sense of rampant individualism, but upon quite different values. The primary need, therefore, was to restore a sense of discipline and morality without which individuals would be ill equipped to take their places in the competitive market. Thus the transformation which Mrs Thatcher sought was as much cultural as economic. This certainly marked a definite break with the past. Previous Conservative administrations – those of Baldwin, Macmillan, even perhaps of Heath – had sought to conserve a society whose values they saw as supportive of Conservatism. Mrs Thatcher, by contrast, saw herself living in a society undermined by the permissive 'adversary culture' of the 1960s and saturated with values which were far from Conservative. If the measures taken to correct this situation happened to invade what liberals of the left chose to think of as civil liberties, that had to be accepted in the interests of the broader goal.

Since 1979, therefore, civil liberties issues – freedom of information, rights to freedom of speech and expression, the rights of unpopular minorities such as suspected terrorists and homosexuals – have played a much more prominent part in constitutional debate than in any other period since the end of the war. Indeed, one proposition on which the opposition parties were broadly agreed was that Mrs Thatcher constituted a threat to civil liberties. This agreement was the basis of the Charter 1988 movement, a critique of what its authors saw as creeping authoritarianism, but also a possible agenda for party realignment. Yet, here again, while Mrs Thatcher may have gone much further than previous administrations, it is difficult to see her basic concerns as being essentially different in kind from those of, say, Lord Salisbury, Sir William Joynson Hicks, or Henry Brooke, all of whom seem to have believed that human beings needed to be fenced around with stern prohibitions if they were to be made fit for the rigours of competitive life.

But Mrs Thatcher's programme had to involve, in addition, policies designed to topple the bastions of social democracy – not only the trade unions, but also local government, the education system, the National Health Service, and even the professions themselves, carriers of a quite different ethos from that of the competitive market. It was in seeking to transform those institutions whose function is to offer collective provision that Mrs Thatcher unwittingly brought the constitution back into the centre of British politics.

As head of a government dedicated to turning back the tide of collectivism, Mrs Thatcher found herself confronted by institutions whose very purpose was that of providing for collective needs. The most important of these institutions is local government, and it is no coincidence that Mrs Thatcher's administrations raised, in a very acute form, the constitutional question of the proper relationship between central government and local authorities. It is, in particular, in Scotland and the great conurbations of the North of England that this relationship has been put under strain to such an extent that there is now, in some parts of Britain, a real question mark over the moral legitimacy of the actions of central government.

To criticisms that the government's actions strained the limits of the constitution, ministers replied that Britain is a unitary state in which Parliament enjoys the power to alter political relationships as and when it pleases. This conception of the constitution, however, puts too much weight on one of Dicey's principles – the sovereignty of Parliament – while ignoring another – the conventions of the constitution. For the territorial constitution of the United Kingdom is governed less by statute than by convention; it depends upon a spirit of mutual accommodation, and it rests upon a sense of identification by the governed with those who have authority over them. An assertion of the unbridled right of an omnicompetent government is apt to conflict with the practicalities of political management in a country already sharply polarized by an electoral system which effectively excludes much of the North of England and Scotland from a share in the exercise of political power. The traditional defence of territories so excluded has been the power of constitutional convention. But the years of Mrs Thatcher's rule saw the death of convention.

It is a paradox that a programme designed to widen individual choice had as one of its consequences a massive increase in the power of central government, and a decline in the influence of local communities and intermediate institutions. The explanation for this paradox was foreseen as long ago as 1946 in a brilliant if little-noticed reply to Hayek by Herman Finer, entitled *The Road to Reaction*. Finer argued perceptively that the free-market programme, like its seeming opposite, socialism, was a global philosophy of politics, and that it could not coexist with other centres of power. As *The Economist* noticed in December 1979, 'The trouble with being a non-interventionist government is that in order to go from intervention to non-intervention you have to intervene to challenge the way things are done.'

In a democracy, any government, whatever its political colour, will find itself faced with a society in which competing conceptions of the good life jostle for attention. Faced with the reality of social pluralism, two responses are possible: to share power or to curb its competitors. An ideological government, whether free market or socialist, finds itself compelled to adopt the latter alternative. For it is of the essence of its philosophy that any competing viewpoint is somehow illegitimate and its continued expression a threat to good government. It was Thomas Hobbes who called institutions which lie between government and the individual, worms in the entrails of the body politic; for they serve to eat away at the sovereignty of Leviathan. It is this conception of sovereignty which Mrs Thatcher carried to its limits.

At first sight, this view of the role of the state seems peculiarly associated with the brand of Conservatism espoused by Mrs Thatcher. Previous Conservative governments, whether led by Churchill, Macmillan, or Heath, felt little impulse to reconstruct society, seeking instead to coexist with other centres of power, rather than to transform them. And yet Mrs Thatcher's approach was perhaps an inevitable response to the perceived unworkability of a Conservatism which sought to remain within the constraints of the post-war consensus. The Heath government sought desperately, in its final 18 months, to accommodate itself to a society whose values were deeply un-Conservative. The only way to escape from such appeasement was to break the constraints of social democracy, and seek to confront society with a radically different philosophy of government. The probability is, therefore, that any Tory leader, having lived through the crisis of Conservatism between 1972 and 1974, would have reacted as Mrs Thatcher did, and abandoned the philosophy which led her predecessor to grief. All the same, the very determination with which Mrs Thatcher pursued her goals brought into sharp focus the limitations of traditional conceptions of the British constitution. For, when confronted with a determined government, insistent upon its will, the constitution seemed unable to restrain or limit the powers of government. 'The hollowness of Diceyan liberal constitution, now exposed, is that when confronted with this drive for centralised, uncheckable power, it has no answer.'[4]

It is a paradox that a government so determined to resist constitutional change made the constitution itself a political issue. The existence of a constitution implies a set of rules determining political behaviour; but the peculiarity of the British constitution is that it lacks an umpire. It is the players themselves, the government of the day, who interpret the way in which the rules are to be applied. There is no reference point, no *pouvoir neutre*, over and above government which can offer a criterion for what is allowable and what is not. It is this deficiency which proponents of constitutional reform seek to remedy, either by establishing such a reference point in the form of a Bill of Rights or, alternatively, by ensuring, through electoral reform or reform of the House of Lords, that a single party cannot enjoy unlimited power on a minority of the popular vote. It is a striking consequence of Mrs Thatcher's decade that all of the opposition parties, without exception, now favour constitutional change of one sort or another, so that the constitution, as it now exists, depends for its survival upon the continuation of Conservative government.

But conceptions of the constitution themselves rely on alternative conceptions of human nature and of political liberty. For Mrs Thatcher, as for most modern Conservatives, freedom is in essence the freedom to compete in the marketplace. By reducing the role of the state in the economy, through abolishing controls over prices, incomes, and foreign exchange, she increased the sum total of freedom in society. By policies which encouraged the ownership of property, shares and other forms of wealth, she contributed towards a genuine decentralization of power. Freedom is devolution of power to the individual citizen; it is not something which can be guaranteed by institutions. To regard participation in government as the essence of freedom is to misunderstand the basic needs of human nature. For, as Oscar Wilde once wrote, what was wrong with socialism was that it took up too many evenings. Mrs Thatcher, by reducing the influence of intermediate institutions such as local authorities, succeeded in diminishing the scope of the political over people's lives. For the only real participation that is worth the name is participation in the marketplace; and political freedom is nothing but the withdrawal of the state from all but its most essential tasks.

The trouble with this view of freedom, however, is that it assumes away any notion of the public good. It transforms questions about, for example, the best system of education and health care for society as a whole into questions about the best system of education and health care for myself and my family. In assuming that the community is nothing more than the mere sum of individual wants, it commits the fallacy of composition. It offends against Burke's notion of a society as being a contract between generations as well as between individuals. There is, however, an alternative conception of freedom capable of taking full account of those communitarian instincts which are, in some sense, natural to mankind; and it is this alternative conception which lies at the root of the constitutionalist critique of Mrs Thatcher.

Liberty, it has been said, is power cut into pieces; and the purpose of dividing power is to make it properly accountable. Thus intermediate institutions, far from being barriers to freedom, are actually essential to it since they provide opportunities by which citizens are enabled to make decisions as to the relative priorities for society. For, whether services are to be provided publicly or privately, the determination of priorities must, in the last resort, be made politically. The market itself cannot decide how much should be spent on schools, and how much on housing. The decision must be made by a political body, either by central government or by decentralized institutions. The great advantage of the sharing of power is the much greater opportunity for popular participation which it provides. For, whereas there are only 651 MPs, and being an MP is today a full-time professional career, there are around 25 000 local government councillors, as well as a large number of people involved in local pressure groups and similar bodies. Thus the existence of a wide range of intermediate bodies allows for the diffusion of political understanding, and is part of the very essence of democracy. For it is these institutions which help to produce the 'active citizen' which ministers such as Douglas Hurd sought to call into existence to supplement gaps in welfare provision. The active citizen, however, is unlikely to be the product of a system based upon the authority of parliamentary sovereignty; he or she is far more likely to arise out of a society which diffuses and shares power. For it is, as John Stuart Mill understood, 'the discussion and management of collective interests' which 'is the great school of public spirit'.[5]

It is, in the last resort, impossible to bifurcate human beings, impossible for someone who is expected to be independent and self-reliant in his or her economic dealings not also to demand wider social and political rights. Moreover, one fundamental consequence of the information society is the dispersal of decision-making which it makes possible. Individuals, freed from the tyranny of mass production and large public sector unions, will no longer be content to see themselves as subjects, but will, increasingly, seek to become citizens.

Mrs Thatcher's constitution was at bottom an heroic attempt to restore the authority of the state in a period when the social preconditions for the restoration of authority were absent. What is distinctive about the changes she has wrought is less their originality than the colossal effort of individual will needed to bring them about. Indeed, she so strained the conventional limits of the British constitution that the constitution itself became a part of party politics, rather than a set of rules lying above politics. Yet constitutions depend not only upon political leaders, but also upon the social and economic patterns which underpin their operation, upon a country's political culture. Who is there yet able to tell whether this culture has been permanently transformed by so remarkable a prime minister?

Notes and references

1   F. A. Hayek (1960), *The Constitution of Liberty*, Routledge & Kegan Paul, 401.
2   F. A. Hayek (1979), *The Political Order of a Free People*, Routledge & Kegan Paul, 3.
3   Andrew Gamble (1988), *The Free Economy and the Strong State: The Politics of Thatcherism*, Macmillan, 35.
4   Patrick McAuslan and John F. McEldowney (1985), 'Legitimacy and the Constitution: The Dissonance between Theory and Practice', in McAuslan and McEldowney (eds.), *Law, Legitimacy and the Constitution*, Sweet & Maxwell, 38.
5   Cited in David Marquand (1988), 'Preceptoral Politics, Yeoman Democracy and the Enabling State', *Government and Opposition*, **23** (3), Summer, 273. This essay is a splendid example of an approach to constitutional thinking which lies at the opposite pole to that favoured by Mrs Thatcher.

3 Ministers, Civil Servants and the Constitution

The government's public service reforms have been described as a revolution in Whitehall. They comprise the most radical changes in our public services since, in 1870, Gladstone laid the foundations of the modern civil service by implementing the recommendations of the Northcote–Trevelyan Report. The reforms involve the devolution of functions via the 'Next Steps' programme to agencies outside Whitehall, the contracting-out of public services, market testing, privatization, and a more decentralized system of civil service pay.

These reforms are generally regarded as essentially managerial in nature. They aim to secure the more efficient delivery of services and better value for money in the public sector. It is, of course, far too early to determine whether this aim will be achieved. What is perhaps more important at the present time is to consider whether the reforms rest upon a sound substratum of constitutional principle; or whether, on the contrary, the managerial revolution needs to be complemented by a constitutional revolution if the reforms are to be effective.

The leitmotif of the reforms is that the public services will be delivered more effectively if government operates along business lines. But the analogy between government and business misleads as much as it enlightens. In particular, it prevents us from grasping how our constitutional principles are threatened by the reforms now in train. First. there is the obvious point that many of the services which are being delivered by government are a public responsibility precisely because it is not in the interests of any private business to deliver them. Many of the services provided by government are ones which no sane entrepreneur would undertake. But, more important perhaps from the constitutional point of view, it is doubtful whether there is any counterpart in the business world to those constitutional principles designed to ensure the accountability of ministers and the integrity and impartiality of civil servants, in particular the principle of ministerial responsibility, which is under threat from the ill-considered way in which the public service reforms have been carried out.

II

Ministerial responsibility is a widely misunderstood concept. It ought not to mean, and indeed it has hardly ever been interpreted to mean, that a minister is to *blame* for any mistake that occurs in his or her department, only that he or she *takes the blame* for such mistakes. The principle means, not that the minister is necessarily at fault, but that it is he or she who is responsible for taking corrective action, for putting things right, and for ensuring that the department is run effectively.

One may ask – who is responsible for failing to lock the door of the Vice-Chancellor's office at night – meaning who is to *blame* for failing to lock the door; but one may also ask – who is responsible for running the university – meaning who is the authority with the duty to take corrective action when things go wrong, and to ensure that the university is being effectively managed.

Suppose a lecturer at the university takes his clothes off in the middle of his lecture. Clearly, the lecturer is responsible in the first sense of the term, in that he is to blame. But it is the Vice-Chancellor of the university who is responsible in the second sense. The Vice-Chancellor is of course not personally at fault, but he or she must take notice of what has happened, since, in virtue of his or her position, he or she is under a duty to take corrective action, and to ensure that appropriate machinery is in place so that there is no repetition.

But there is a connection between the two senses of responsibility. For responsibility in the second sense – taking the blame – makes sense only if the Vice-Chancellor actually has some means of checking how lecturers in the university are conducting themselves, and the power to put things right. The Vice-Chancellor must be able to scrutinize what is happening in the university, and he or she must have mechanisms of feedback and control if he or she is to be able to exercise responsibility.

So also in government, the responsibility of the minister is predicated on the fact that he or she is able to scrutinize what is happening in the department, and can check on how civil servants in the department are conducting themselves. Otherwise, ministerial responsibility would become an empty husk. It is the task of the minister, therefore, to ensure that his or her department so operates that he or she is informed of important matters which arise, and that the department is in general run in an efficient way.

Now, ministerial responsibility in this sense is not intended to protect officials from the consequences of their actions. A civil servant is only entitled to such protection as of right when he or she has been carrying out an explicit order by the minister, or acting in accordance with the policy laid down by the minister. That was the doctrine laid down by Sir David Maxwell Fyfe in the debate on Crichel Down in July 1954, over 40 years ago.[1] In other circumstances, it is for the minister to take such action as is necessary when officials have made errors or failed in some way. For the purpose of the doctrine of ministerial responsibility is not to protect officials, but to locate accountability for the actions of government where, in a democracy it ought to be located, in the hands of elected politicians.

It follows that it is not, and never has been, appropriate for a minister to resign because of an error occurring in his or her department for which he or she is in no way to blame. Indeed, if ministers resigned whenever a mistake was made in a department, there would probably be very few ministers left! The circumstances under which ministers are required to resign are quite different. They have been well stated by the constitutional theorist, Geoffrey Marshall. 'Nobody doubts that Ministers should resign if they sell secrets to the enemy or have mistresses who write rude letters about them in *The Times* . . ., or if they tell lies to the House of Commons (except on matters of major policy)'.[2] Resignation for an administrative mistake which was not the minister's fault would be a punishment – a misdirected punishment – but not a remedy. What the public are entitled to expect in a democracy is the application of a remedy by the responsible minister.

It is this conception of ministerial responsibility which is under serious threat from the growth of executive agencies under the 'Next Steps' programme. The purpose of this programme is to devolve power away from Whitehall to the chief executives of agencies, who are given a substantial amount of autonomy through framework agreements, drawn up after consultation, between the minister, Whitehall officials and the chief executives themselves. The post of chief executive is normally to be filled by open competition; chief executives will be appointed for a fixed term, and their salaries will generally be linked to the achievement of targets. It is, moreover, the chief executive rather than the permanent secretary of the department, who is to be the accounting officer for operational matters within the agency, and, as such, directly accountable to Parliament.

What is novel about this arrangement is the development of new machinery outside Whitehall, agencies which are expected and encouraged to exercise leadership in the performance of their functions. Those working in the agencies will be taking decisions far removed from ministerial scrutiny and oversight. That, indeed, is one of the main purposes of establishing them.

This has two important and interrelated consequences. The first is that ministers will lose that means of securing overall control and feedback, which, as we have seen, is the essential corollary of the doctrine of ministerial responsibility. What can responsibility mean if the minister no longer enjoys the ability to check what his or her officials are doing?

Secondly, it will no longer make much sense to regard civil servants, when taking operational decisions in the agencies, as acting solely on behalf of their minister. The earlier Financial Management Initiative, which proposed a much more limited measure of devolution, seemed to the former Joint Head of the Civil Service, Sir Douglas Wass, 'hardly possible to reconcile . . . with the concept of the responsibility for departmental acts being located uniquely in the minister's office'.[3] Even more must this be the case with the agencies. If the agencies are to enjoy genuine autonomy, it is hardly plausible to regard someone working in an agency in the traditional terms of constitutional theory as being merely the mouthpiece of his or her minister. Why, then, should it not be the chief executive who is held constitutionally responsible – in the second sense of the term 'responsible' – for operational matters, so that if anything goes wrong in the agency, the chief executive takes the blame; just as it is the board of a nationalized industry which is responsible for ensuring its efficiency. If such a doctrine were to be accepted, the ultimate sanction would then be, not the resignation of the minister, which would, in any case be constitutionally inappropriate, but a vote in Parliament to reduce the salary of the chief executive, in effect a call for his or her dismissal.

Yet, the introduction of the 'Next Steps' agencies has not been accompanied by any rethinking of the doctrine of ministerial responsibility. Speaking to the House of Commons on 18 February 1988, Mrs Thatcher declared, 'There will be no change in the arrangements for accountability. Ministers will continue to account to Parliament for all the work of their departments, including the work of the agencies.'

The theory behind the 'Next Steps' proposals, however, is that the two functions, of service delivery and policy-making, can be separated. Yet, where such a separation of powers has been instituted in the past – in the nationalized industries, for example, or in the arrangements under which the universities are administered – ministerial responsibility was retained only for matters of policy; the minister was not to be constitutionally responsible for operational matters. Thus, if the train taking me from Oxford to London were late, responsibility lay not with the minister, but with the board of British Rail which had the duty to put things right. A complex undertaking such as the railways could hardly operate with any degree of success if the minister were held to be responsible for the everyday details of the railway timetable. It was the practice, therefore, for the statutes establishing the nationalized industries to distinguish control over general policy in the public interest, for which a minister was responsible to Parliament, from the ordinary business management of the industry, where the corporation was intended to be free from political interference.

No similar logic has been applied to the 'Next Steps' agencies. Yet, how can ministers be held responsible, in the second sense of that term – 'responsible' in the sense of taking the blame, not of being to blame – for what happens in the agencies? For, if agencies are to have any degree of autonomy at all, ministers will hardly be in a position to scrutinize their workings, as they can do with the work which remains in Whitehall. The position will be roughly similar to the relationship with the nationalized industries. Just as the minister could have said, 'It is not my responsibility that your train was late. Contact British Rail', so also he or she may want to say, 'It is not my responsibility that you did not receive the benefits to which you were entitled. Contact the Benefits Agency.'

Perhaps ministers will try to exercise their responsibility in which case they will come to be involved in the detailed work of the agencies, and the purpose of setting them up – freeing civil servants from ministerial interference – will be defeated. Ministers will be tempted to intervene, since what may seem a mere matter of detail in, say, the Benefits or the Employment Agency, can have enormous political repercussions. For, it is ministers whom the public will blame if they do not receive the benefits to which they are entitled, or if they are not properly informed of employment opportunities. If the political standing of the government is involved, ministers will be pressed to intervene. The agencies will be leant upon to implement the will of the minister. Boards, as Jeremy Bentham noticed, are screens. There is thus some danger that the 'Next Steps' programme will lead, not to clarification, but to a confusion of responsibility. That was the situation found in the Prison Service (which is an agency) by Sir John Woodcock in his report on 'The Escape from Whitemoor Prison on Friday 9th September 1994' (Cm. 2741, HMSO, 1994). Sir John found that 'There exists at all levels within the Service some confusion as to the respective roles of Ministers, the Agency Headquarters and individual Prison Governors. In particular, the Enquiry has identified the difficulty of determining what is an operational matter, and what is policy, leading to confusion as to where responsibility lies' (Para. 9.28). The same may become true of agencies.

If, however, ministers are genuinely prepared to exercise self-restraint, then ministerial responsibility for the operational work of the agencies will come to have little meaning.

The danger is that the incoherent arrangements for constitutional responsibility for operational failures in the agencies will work in practice to prevent responsibility being pinned on anyone. It may become easier for ministers to pass the buck. It may also become easier for ministers to treat as an operational failure what is really a failure of government policy. If a chief executive fails to achieve a particular target, he or she may not be reappointed and may become the subject of public opprobrium. Yet the chief executive concerned may have unsuccessfully pressed the minister to adopt an alternative strategy, or to provide more resources, arguing that experience had shown that the agency's target could not in fact be achieved under the existing strategy using existing resources. As a civil servant, the chief executive will be in no position to reveal this publicly, so that he or she will take the blame for the misjudgment of the minister. The principle of ministerial responsibility requires the minister to take the blame for misjudgment by officials. We are inverting this principle by requiring officials to take the blame for misjudgments by ministers.

Will anything in practice be left of ministerial responsibility for operational failure, or will the minister be able, simply, to disclaim responsibility, to refuse to take the blame? Will ministerial responsibility for the operational activities of agencies become so minimal that, like the Cheshire cat, it disappears, leaving only the grin behind? If that happens, then there will have been a significant reduction in the power of Parliament to scrutinize the activities of government and to obtain redress for citizens with grievances. And, if the minister disclaims responsibility, will the agencies be subject to any effective channels of accountability at all; do we not need to strengthen our grievance procedures, such as the Ombudsman, to provide more effective means of redress for the ordinary citizen?

Perhaps we are beginning to create a new kind of accountability, the direct accountability of the civil servant. This would be a considerable constitutional innovation. Already, however, the 'Next Steps' programme has led to one constitutional reform. The written answers of chief executives to questions from MPs are now published in *Hansard* along with written answers from ministers. Chief executives are the only civil servants whose written answers are treated in this way, and perhaps we can see in this new practice the germ of a new form of direct accountability by civil servants to Parliament. What is clear is that the respective responsibilities of ministers and civil servants need to be reformulated. If there is to be genuine devolution, there must be a specific definition of the respective responsibilities of the minister and the chief executive. This would involve three further changes.

First, the relationship between ministers and officials would need to be made explicitly contractual so that specific responsibilities were delegated to officials and put into statutory form in, for example, a statutory instrument. Ministers would then remain responsible only for the terms of the delegation. Thus the framework agreement would be converted into a legal document that would, in the last resort, be subject to judicial interpretation and might put the chief executive in a stronger position to resist ministerial interference.

Second, the direct accountability of the chief executive to the relevant select committee of the House of Commons would need to be formalized in some way, perhaps by means of a statement that the Osmotherly Rules should not apply to the evidence given by chief executives. This would mean that chief executives would not be appearing, as permanent secretaries and other civil servants do, merely in the role of spokesmen for their ministers. On the other hand, chief executives remain, of course, civil servants, and so, unlike, for example, chairmen of nationalized industries, they could not be allowed to comment on the merits of *policy*, as opposed to explaining the background to it. But they would be able to answer for their own actions in their own way on operational matters.

Third, provision needs to be made for strengthening the ability of the ordinary citizen to secure redress for operational failures on the part of the agency. This might be achieved by allowing the citizen direct access to the Ombudsman where he or she feels that there has been unfair treatment by an agency. Such direct access already exists in the case of the Health Service Ombudsman. In addition, principles of administrative law might be developed so that agencies are given a firmer structure of rules to guide them in their dealings with the ordinary citizen.

These reforms, it must be recognized, would not necessarily be sufficient to prevent ministers from intervening in the operational work of agencies. The statutes regulating the nationalized industries did not, as we know, succeed in preventing ministerial intervention, and it is indeed difficult to discover any institutional means which might prevent the kind of arm-twisting that sometimes occurred when the minister sought to persuade the board of a nationalized industry, by informal means, to conform to some governmental objective, such as the control of pay or prices.

Yet these reforms might perhaps bring out the underlying logic behind the 'Next Steps' programme. For, if carried to its logical conclusion, the 'Next Steps' principle would seem to imply nothing less than an attenuation of our traditional notion of a minister being in charge of, and responsible for, a Whitehall department. Ministers, according to this logic, should be concerned primarily with policy matters, not with management. It is indeed because ministers are required to be in charge of Whitehall departments that cabinet government is not what it ought to be, a genuinely collective forum for the making of policy. For ministers, instead of being collective policy-makers, have become too much spokesmen for a departmental point of view, and the Cabinet has degenerated into what Richard Crossman found it to be when he wrote his famous diaries, a loosely organized confederation of departments.

Of course, so radical an alteration in our conception of the role of the minister raises very fundamental questions which have, as yet, hardly been confronted, let alone answered. One obvious question is what responsibility for policy-making would actually mean if it came to be divorced from the realities of the daily administrative casework which ought to inform it. Would ministers not become even more remote from what is actually happening on the ground? Would not the Cabinet, as a result, be in danger of becoming merely a collection of disembodied wraiths brooding in glorious and isolated impotence in a void, and quite remote from the political realities? The whole direction in which the 'Next Steps' reform is leading ought surely to be given far more reflective consideration than it has yet received, if it is not to lead to unintended and irreversible changes in our structure of government.

What ought by now to be clear is that we cannot make a managerial change of the magnitude of 'Next Steps' and expect the rules relating to ministerial responsibility to remain unaffected. If 'Next Steps' succeeds in its aim of devolving the power of decision to autonomous agencies, ministerial responsibility to Parliament for the operational work of the agencies is bound to be weakened; while, if a serious attempt is made to reassert the traditional doctrine of ministerial responsibility, the agencies will find that their autonomy becomes circumscribed by ministerial interference as occurred with the nationalized industries.

III

The ethical principles which ought to guide civil servants have been laid out in the Armstrong code of 1985, entitled 'The Duties and Responsibilities of Civil Servants in Relation to Ministers'.[4] This code is itself a restatement of evidence given to the Tomlin Commission on the Civil Service by the very first Head of the Civil Service, Sir Warren Fiser, in 1931. It is, surely, remarkable that, despite the numerous changes in the Civil Service that have occurred during the intervening period of over 60 years, the principles regulating the behaviour of civil servants were not thought to be in any need of modification.

The Armstrong code restated the convention of ministerial responsibility, declaring that civil servants have no constitutional personality or responsibility separate from that of the government of the day. The code did not, however, explain what a civil servant ought to do when a minister so acts as to seek to evade the application of ministerial responsibility, either by withholding information from Parliament, or by deceiving Parliament. Is it sufficient in such circumstances simply to repeat the nostrum that the civil servant must serve the minister to the best of his or her ability? The only redress available to the official was to consult his or her superior, and then the

Permanent Secretary of the Department, and finally, as a last resort, to have the matter referred to the Head of the Home Civil Service through the Permanent Secretary. In practice, however, the vast majority of complaints were made to the Civil Service unions rather than to the very senior civil servants upon whom the promotion prospects of the complainant may depend.

The issue of civil service ethics has come to the fore in a number of recent governmental crises. Ponting, Westland and Matrix Churchill are only the most prominent examples. These crises have raised complex and difficult ethical questions which the existing machinery of government seems incapable of resolving. Was it at all realistic to expect ambitious civil servants, faced with requests which they believe might compromise their political neutrality, to take a step which they may feel would be detrimental to their career by complaining to their permanent secretary, much less to the Head of the Civil Service, who is also, as Cabinet Secretary, in effect an adviser to the Prime Minister. It is much more natural for a civil servant in such a situation to consult his or her trade union for a resolution of the dilemma.

The line between politics and administration is likely to become seriously blurred as a result of bringing into the public service more people from outside, who may be insufficiently sensitive to what the conventions of political neutrality require. An extreme example of an official who crossed the line of what was acceptable was the case of the NHS Chief Executive, a grade 1A civil servant in the Department of Health, who gave an interview to the *Daily Mail* in October 1991, which was published under the heading 'Exclusive: Kinnock's NHS privatisation myth exploded: Health Boss Slams Labour'. The interview consisted of a defence of hospital trusts, and, more generally, of the Government's health reforms against Labour's claims that these reforms would lead to the privatization of the Health Service. When asked what he thought about Labour's policies for the NHS, the civil servant replied 'It's hard to know what they are.' The civil servant in question would have been unlikely to have been able to retain the confidence of a Health Secretary in a Labour government, had Labour been returned in the General Election of 1992.

This political intervention by a civil servant during a pre-election period is but an extreme example of how the dividing lines between politicians and officials can become blurred, a result perhaps of the longest period of single-party government since the Napoleonic wars. The danger is increased with the establishment of executive agencies under the 'Next Steps' programme, since this will bring many more people into the Civil Service from outside.

The Armstrong Code, however, was imprecise about where the boundaries between proper and improper behaviour actually lie. It did not confront the question – what is it legitimate for a civil servant to do on behalf of a minister, and what steps should the civil servant take if asked to go further. The code dealt with the duties of civil servants towards ministers, but not with the duties of ministers towards civil servants.

The government issues to all ministers upon obtaining office an official document 'Questions of Procedure for Ministers' designed to guide their conduct. But it is of little help in this regard. For it contents itself with declaring that ministers have a 'duty to refrain from asking or instructing civil servants to do things which they should not do' (para. 55). That is a tautology dressed up as guidance. There ought, surely, to be a code requiring ministers to support civil servants who carry out their responsibilities in the proper manner, to ensure that officials are enabled to speak their mind, that their advice is properly considered before decisions are made, and that they are at all times treated with due personal consideration.

Above all, the Armstrong Code failed to take sufficient account of the fact that the role of the civil servant would change with the establishment of executive agencies and other developments which would require officials to be far more involved in policy initiatives than traditional doctrines allowed. Civil servants are increasingly becoming accountable for specific blocks of work, and taking decisions which cannot be understood simply as decisions taken in the name of the minister. The media have come to identify individual civil servants as being involved in policy initiatives, a development that has been emphasized by the regular appearance of civil servants before select committees. The select committees indeed have made senior civil servants public figures, known, not perhaps to the public at large, but to specialists involved in particular policy networks. The select committees have drawn back the veil of anonymity which had hitherto hidden officials from the public gaze. The consequence is that civil servants have to be much more prepared to defend in public the policies of their ministers. If civil servants were to be made constitutionally responsible to Parliament, then they would no longer enjoy the shield of ministerial responsibility as a protection from the consequences of their operational acts.

The Armstrong Code, then, could be criticized on two main grounds. First, it restated the standard conventions of the constitution, but failed to outline any effective remedy in cases when the conventions were no longer observed; and, secondly, the code failed to reformulate the traditional conventions so as to take account of changes in the Civil Service which were coming to undermine them. The Code, therefore, appeared increasingly unrealistic and anachronistic in the light of the reforms that are occurring in our public services.

For this reason, the Conservative government, in its White Paper on the Civil Service, 'Taking Forward Continuity and Change' (Cm 2748), published in 1995, proposed two reforms designed to maintain standards in the

Civil Service. The first was a new Civil Service Code. The second was a new independent line of appeal to the Civil Service Commissioners where civil servants believe that this new code has been breached.

The trouble is, however, that the proposed new code is, like the Armstrong Code, to be couched in general terms. The danger is that it will be insufficiently specific. Moreover, as with the Armstrong Code, the government appears to be envisaging a new definition of the duties of civil servants rather than of ministers. Yet, where civil servants have failed in their duties, as in the case of Ponting, this was because they believed, rightly or wrongly, that ministers were seeking to evade the application of ministerial responsibility by misleading Parliament. In the 1930s, Wing Commander Torr Anderson gave Winston Churchill private information concerning Britain's defence weaknesses which were being concealed by the government. Churchill told him that 'loyalty to the State must come before loyalty to the Service'.[5] How is this loyalty to the State to be defined?

Second, the proposed new code, if it is to be useful, must draw a precise line between what is a matter for government and what is party political. Is it appropriate, for example, to ask a civil servant to draft a party conference speech? Is it appropriate to ask him or her to assist with back-bench amendments to bills? The code gives no answer.

Third, the new code must clarify the convention of ministerial responsibility, which has come under pressure through the devolution of power within the civil service to agencies. This has enabled ministers to pass the buck by blaming publicly known officials for what are called 'operational' failures. But, what is an 'operational' failure? One official has cynically suggested that if a problem is difficult, then it is operational! Two ministers, William Waldegrave, when Chancellor of the Duchy of Lancaster, and Peter Lloyd, a junior Home Office Minister, have declared that previous arrangements for ministerial responsibility were a 'fiction'.[6] Yet the government persists in maintaining that the constitutional arrangements have not changed. What is needed, then, is a statement in modern form of the principles needed to enable the constitutional relationship between ministers and civil servants to work effectively.

In addition, however, there needs to be an independent adjudicator of disputes, a point of appeal beyond the Civil Service. The government proposes an appeal to the Civil Service Commissioners who will have the right to report to Parliament. A more powerful mechanism, however, would be the creation of a Civil Service Ombudsman, with the right to report to the Treasury and Civil Service Select Committee where the government ignores his or her recommendations. The experience of the Parliamentary Commissioner for Administration, working together with the Select Committee on the Parliamentary Commissioner, shows what a powerful weapon this mechanism can be.

Nearly a decade ago, Sir Douglas Wass, a former Permanent Secretary at the Treasury, proposed that there should be an 'Inspector General' for the Civil Service, who

> would not be removable by Ministers and he would operate in some sense in a judicial capacity. His function would be to hear complaints by a civil servant who felt that the Minister was acting in an improper way. . . . If he thought there was substance in it he would take the matter to the Minister . . . and he would invite the Minister . . . to correct the improper behaviour in some way. Thereafter if the Minister declined it might be necessary, as a final safety valve of course, for the Inspector General to have the right to report, perhaps in camera, to the relevant Select Committee.[7]

The introduction of an Inspector General, as proposed by Sir Douglas Wass, would make it easier for civil servants to continue to display their impartiality without fearing that they might be jeopardizing their careers by so doing. Like the concept of the Parliamentary Commissioner, the Ombudsman, the proposal for an Inspector General for the Civil Service would thus serve to strengthen rather than weaken ministerial responsibility. The Ombudsman strengthens ministerial responsibility by pointing out where maladministration has occurred, so making it possible for the minister to take corrective action. An Inspector General for the Civil Service would strengthen ministerial responsibility by ensuring that ministers would not be able to shuffle responsibility on to civil servants. And since, like the Ombudsman, the Inspector General would have the assistance of a select committee of the House of Commons, he or she would be able to assist Parliament in pinning responsibility on to the relevant minister.

There is a deep need within the British system of government for some moral reference point that can help determine when the conventions of government have been broken. At present, it is the government itself, advised by the Cabinet Secretary, which decides upon the rules regulating ministers and civil servants. Ministers remain judges and jury in their own case. A moral reference point, however, could help to provide a constitutional framework which would assist in the preservation of standards in public life.

There is today widespread confusion and anxiety concerning the future of the Civil Service and relationships between civil servants and ministers. It arises fundamentally because the public service reforms seek to bring the commercial ethic into the public service and minimize the deep-seated conflict between the public-service ethic and the commercial ethic. To conflate the two is like trying to connect two incompatible computers, each seeking to transfer data to the other which does not know how to receive it.

It is difficult, however, to introduce commercial accountability into the performance of many government services. The customers of, for example, the Benefits Agency, which serves in total around 20 million people, cannot remove their custom, as they can with Marks & Spencer; they cannot use market mechanisms to demand different services, nor can they ensure increased expenditure on benefits in any way other than through the ballot box. Public services are provided for an employer who cannot go out of business so that, although it may be possible to create a surrogate for market forces for some of them, the final sanction of the market – that the employer will have to close his doors – cannot apply.

But, if many public services cannot be made commercially accountable, and if, as argued above, traditional forms of accountability are being eroded by the public service reforms, then new forms of accountability are needed, the old no longer being adequate. These new forms of accountability can be provided in three different ways – through the development of a constitutional code, through strengthening Parliament, and through policies of devolution and decentralization.

A proper code of ethics for the Civil Service, which would, of course, apply to civil servants working in the agencies as much as in Whitehall, would emphasize that civil servants have duties over and above those to ministers. They would be required, as well as serving their ministers, to serve the state in the spirit of the words of Sir Thomas More, 'I am the government's good servant, but I am the state's servant first'. The constitution ought not to be defined by the government, which means, in effect, the party in power. Instead there must be some reference point, some *pouvoir neutre* over and above that of the government of the day. The introduction of the Inspector General would help to provide such a reference point.

A code of ethics should lay down the duties of civil servants to ministers, but also duties to Parliament and to the public. It would thus, for the first time, provide the Civil Service with a constitutional status, a constitutional personality of its own separate from that of the government of the day.

The problem of how to secure the accountability of the agencies for operational matters should be resolved by making the chief executives of the agencies directly accountable to Parliament for these matters. This would seem merely to draw out the logical implications of the fact that chief executives are already the accounting officers for the agencies, and that their written answers to MPs' questions are published in *Hansard*. Chief executives would then be required to give evidence on their own behalf to select committees concerning matters for which they were responsible. Such a reform would, it seems, be merely a recognition of the reality that the role of the chief executive could no longer be understood by describing him or her as simply the instrument of a minister. It would also enable Parliament more effectively to review and control the work of the agencies. As long ago as 1918, the Haldane Report proposed that any increases in efficiency which flowed from executive action must always be matched by an increase in the power of Parliament to scrutinize what the executive was doing. A strengthening of Parliament would be a natural concomitant to the devolution of power provided for in the 'Next Steps' programme.

Finally, and perhaps most fundamentally, there must be much greater accountability through locally elected bodies. For, whatever reforms are made in the machinery of central government and in parliamentary scrutiny of governmental activity, there will remain much in our public services that is unaccountable to the ordinary user. Inevitably, civil servants, whether in Whitehall or in the agencies, will be protected from the user by distance and by time. And yet, without pressure from the user, how are we ever to secure genuine improvements in our public services?

Those who favour market mechanisms for the delivery of public services do so largely because they regard the market as natural, as part of a spontaneous order which does not require the intervention of politicians. Yet, in no democracy has a market for public services arisen spontaneously in the way that it has, for example, in the case of cars or compact discs. Therefore, the market for public services must be, at best, a regulated market.

But, the question then arises – who is to do the regulating? If the answer is that it is to be central government, then, inevitably, we create a 'new magistracy' of managers.

Much has been heard in recent years of a 'democratic deficit' in the European Community. Perhaps, however, there is also a democratic deficit in British domestic politics, consisting in the replacement of elected representatives by appointed managers, largely insulated from the democratic machinery of Parliament and local government, and so inaccessible to the user of public services. Moreover, accusations are made that managers are appointed for party-political reasons rather than for the contributions that they can make to administrative efficiency.

Perhaps the public services can be made more accountable if responsibility for them is devolved as far as possible to the local level. For, in public services such as education, the market element, the possibility of 'exit' is bound to be limited. Therefore, an alternative mechanism of accountability – 'voice' – needs to be strengthened.

One key clause of the Maastricht Treaty is Article 3b on subsidiarity, which provides that no function should be carried out at Community level if it can be carried out more effectively at a lower level of government. Perhaps there is a need in the uncodified British Constitution for a subsidiarity clause providing that no public functions be carried out at the level of central government if they can, with advantage, be undertaken at a lower level.

Unless we provide ourselves with such a clause, we will be unable to re-establish the relationship between ministers and civil servants on a regularized footing. For the truth is that we have not been able to discover any method of making centralized public services properly accountable either to Parliament or to the public whom they are meant to serve. That is the fault neither of the Civil Service, nor of politicians, but rather an inevitable outcome of the doctrine of centralized government espoused by every administration since the war.

IV

The argument in this chapter has been that we are faced, in government, by a revolution which is not merely managerial, but has important constitutional implications. If it is to be successful, the managerial revolution in the public services needs to be complemented by a constitutional revolution, whose fundamental aim must be to make power accountable. Reforms at the level of central government, while necessary, are by no means sufficient to achieve this aim. They must be complemented by reforms intended to reduce the scale of government and to decentralize power. Such reforms could actually serve to strengthen the state and make it more effective by allowing the central institutions of government to pare down their activities and devote their energies to major policy-making rather than detailed administration. But, even more important, the decentralization of power would strengthen liberty which Hobbes once defined as power cut into pieces.

If power in Britain is to be made more accountable, it must be cut into pieces. Without a much more self-conscious constitutional awareness, the managerial revolution will not yield the beneficial outcomes for which its advocates have been hoping – or, to put the point another way, the managerial revolution will surely fail if it is not also accompanied by a constitutional revolution.

Notes and references

1   House of Commons, Vol. 530, Cols 1285–6, 20 July 1954.
2   Geoffrey Marshall (1989), Introduction to G. Marshall (ed.), *Ministerial Responsibility*, Oxford University Press, 7. His precepts were laid down shortly after the resignation of Cecil Parkinson in 1983.
3   Sir Douglas Wass (1985), 'The Civil Service at the Crossroads', *Political Quarterly*, **56**, 3, 230.
4   This code can most conveniently be found in Marshall (1989), *Ministerial Responsibility*, 140–4.
5   Martin Gilbert (1994), *In Search of Churchill*, HarperCollins, 126.

6   Q 1909, Q44, Minutes of Evidence taken before the Home Affairs Committee on Monday, 19 April 1993, *The Prison Service*, HC 1922–3, 612–i.
7   Evidence given to the Treasury and Civil Committee inquiry into 'Civil Servants and Ministers', HC 92, 1985–6, para. 4.13

PART II
CONSERVATIVE
HEGEMONY AND A
DIVIDED OPPOSITION

4 The Ghost of Peel and the Legacy of Disraeli: The Selection of the Conservative Party Leader

I

The leadership of the Conservative Party is a subject which gives rise to a considerable popular and even academic mythology.[1] This mythology has been embodied at different times in phrases such as 'customary processes of consultation', 'the magic circle', 'the men in grey suits'. The implication is that the Conservative Party chooses its leaders by some arcane process that has little in common with normal democratic procedures. That implication, as can be seen from an examination of past leadership changes, is almost entirely false.

Until 1922 the Conservative Party had a formal leader only when there was a Conservative prime minister in office, or when an ex-prime minister remained as leader in the House of Lords or House of Commons. Otherwise, as in the years 1881–5 and 1911–22, when the party was in opposition or in a coalition with a non-Conservative prime minister, there was a party leader in the House of Commons and a leader in the Lords. It was for the sovereign to choose which of them should be invited to form the government, although, in practice, the choice was often obvious, as with Derby in 1852, Disraeli in 1868, and Salisbury in 1885. During the twentieth century, every Conservative Prime Minister, apart from Bonar Law, became party leader *after* not before becoming Premier, until Edward Heath in 1965 became the first Conservative leader to be elected under a new electoral procedure.

In 1902, 1921, 1922, 1937, 1940 and 1955 there was no need for any procedure to be devised, since there was an obvious heir apparent. Superficially,

Table 4.1   The selection of Conservative leaders, 1902–63

Year	Leader chosen	Possible alternative candidates
1902	A. J. Balfour	Joseph Chamberlain
1911	A. Bonar Law[a]	Austen Chamberlain
		W. Long
1921	Austen Chamberlain[a]	—
1922	A. Bonar Law	[Austen Chamberlain][b]
1923	S. Baldwin	Lord Curzon
1937	Neville Chamberlain	—
1940[c]	W. S. Churchill	[Lord Halifax]
1955	Sir A. Eden	—
1957	H. Macmillan	R. A. Butler
1963	Lord Home	R. A. Butler
		Lord Hailsham
		R. Maudling

[a] Leader in the House of Commons only.
[b] Austen Chamberlain was deposed as leader by the Carlton Club meeting, after which Bonar Law was elected leader without opposition.
[c] Churchill became Prime Minister in May 1940 in preference to Halifax; by October 1940, when the party leadership became vacant because of Chamberlain's ill-health, there was no alternative candidate to Churchill.

it might seem that, in 1902, Joseph Chamberlain was a competitor, with A. J. Balfour, for the succession; but in reality that was not the case. For Chamberlain was not a Conservative, but a Liberal Unionist. As such and as a nonconformist, he was unacceptable to Conservatives, the predominant element in the Unionist coalition. Chamberlain himself recognized this, and some time before Salisbury's resignation he had assured Balfour of his support.

In 1922, following the downfall of the Lloyd George Coalition, Bonar Law was the only possible Conservative leader. But he did not accept the king's commission until he had formally been elected leader by Conservative MPs. On 19 October 1922, shortly after the Carlton Club meeting, Bonar Law was telephoned by Lord Stamfordham, the King's Private Secretary. Bonar Law told him

> that he was not the leader of the Conservative Party, that the party was for the moment broken up and, until he knew that he could count on its undivided support he would not accept office. Therefore it was indispensable that he should be

present at a meeting of the representatives of the whole Conservative Party, where he could make the above condition . . .

Stamfordham

> ventured to suggest to him that the King sent for him independently of these party considerations into which His Majesty did not enter; that, having accepted Mr Lloyd George's resignation, it was the King's duty to form a new Government as soon as possible and to send for whoever he considered was the proper person to carry out this great responsibility.[2]

But Bonar Law was not to be moved; and it was not until after a meeting of Conservative MPs and parliamentary candidates had been held on 23 October, four days after the Carlton Club meeting, that he was willing to kiss hands as Prime Minister.

In 1921 (when Austen Chamberlain succeeded Bonar Law, who had retired on account of ill health), 1937 and 1955, Conservative leaders were succeeded by heirs apparent, elected by acclamation, who had long been accepted as having a right of reversion. There would have been no point in anyone else competing for the leadership. Interestingly enough, all three were failures. Election by acclamation was not, however, something peculiar to the Conservative Party.[3] There was, after all, no election for the Liberal leadership in 1896 when Rosebery resigned, nor in 1898 when Harcourt resigned the leadership of the Liberal Party in the House of Commons, nor in 1908 when Campbell-Bannerman retired, nor in 1926 when Asquith retired, nor in 1931 when Lloyd George declined to continue as Liberal leader. It was in each case clear who the obvious successor should be. Therefore, the method by which the Conservative leader was chosen in the cases where there was no dispute as to who should be leader cannot of itself be used to sustain any generalizations about the nature of the party.

II

There has been genuine competition for the Conservative leadership on eight of the fourteen occasions this century upon which there has been a vacancy – in 1911, 1923, 1957, 1963, 1965, 1975, 1990 and 1995. The most interesting, in many ways, of all the leadership contests is that of 1911, following the resignation of Balfour, since it brings out, with stark clarity, the qualities which Conservatives seek in their leaders.[4] This was the first occasion in which there had been a vacancy in the leadership in the House of Commons with the Conservatives in opposition since Disraeli had assumed the leadership in 1849. By what procedure was the succession to be decided?

Walter Long, one of the candidates for the leadership, declared for some reason that 'the proper precedent is a meeting of our Privy Counsellors'.[5] He held that there was 'nothing so undignified as a ballot for the leadership of the great Unionist Party. I will never be a party to putting the leadership of the Unionist cause up to Dutch auction.'[6] But this was very much a minority belief. The general view was that a meeting of all Unionist MPs should be summoned to elect a leader, and that this should be done as soon as possible, to avoid the leadership being decided by constituency representatives at the party conference, due to convene shortly. But, how was the new leader to be elected? Lord Balcarres, the Conservative Chief Whip, declared on 9 November, the day after Balfour announced his resignation, 'My colleagues agree to idea of ballot – object strongly to transferable vote [he presumably means the alternative-vote system] – say we should reduce candidates to two, and then settle offhand without speeches.'[7]

This method, however, would work only if the contest could be restricted to two candidates. But a third candidate, Bonar Law, insisted on standing, and so the alternative-vote method seemed inevitable. According to Austen Chamberlain, however, Balcarres, the Chief Whip, proposed to make soundings to see if there were a clear majority for one candidate; and, if so, whether the others could be persuaded to withdraw so that the party meeting might be offered just one name.[8] As it happens, however, neither Chamberlain nor Long could command such support. In the words of Jack Sandars, Balfour's political secretary,

> It may be said against Austen Chamberlain that he comes from Birmingham, that he is a Liberal Unionist, that he is not allied by family tradition or landed estates with the traditional Conservative Party. On the other hand, Walter Long has none of these disqualifications, but he possesses every other conceivable one, and in fact his only claims are squiredom and seniority.[9]

It was, moreover, becoming clear that neither of the two candidates would be able to command the allegiance of his opponent's supporters. The Chamberlainites were 'whole-hoggers' on tariff reform, and prepared to accept food taxes, while Long's supporters were moderate Protectionists, who looked to him to continue Balfour's work of disengaging the party from food taxes.[10] Moreover, Chamberlain, as a Liberal Unionist, represented the minority wing of the Unionist coalition, while Long was generally regarded as choleric and incompetent.

Both Chamberlain and Long, therefore, were induced to withdraw in favour of the third candidate, Bonar Law. Unlike Long, Bonar Law was a man of competence representing a broader interest than that of the squirearchy, while, unlike Chamberlain, he was a Conservative and, although a tariff-reformer, less ideologically committed than the Chamberlainites. He had, for example, supported Balfour's call for a referendum on tariff reform, made immediately before the general election of December 1910; moreover, unlike Chamberlain, he had supported Balfour's policy of allowing the Parliament Bill to pass through the Lords in 1911, and so he could not be accused of disloyalty.

In any contested election, Bonar Law, it was agreed, would have won fewer votes than either Chamberlain or Long. Therefore, under the alternative-vote system, he would have been eliminated and his preferences redistributed. Bonar Law could have won election neither on the first-past-the-post nor the alternative-vote methods, yet there are good grounds for claiming that he was the right leader for the Conservatives at that time. 'The fools have stumbled on the right man by accident' was Lloyd George's comment.[11] Chamberlain's unwavering commitment to food taxes, an issue upon which Bonar Law was to show flexibility in 1913, would probably have split the party, while Long would have been unable to command the confidence of his closest colleagues. 'The decision to make Bonar Law leader of the Conservative Party', comments Robert Blake, Bonar Law's biographer, 'was reached in a strange and tortuous manner, but it probably saved the unity of the party in a way in which no other choice could have done.'[12]

Analysis of the leadership struggle of 1911 shows that, for the Conservatives, the best leader is not necessarily the person with majority support in the party, but rather the one who can best hold the party together. That was the course taken by the party, not only in 1911, but also in 1963, and perhaps in 1990 as well. Thus, the right Conservative leader is not necessarily the person who would be chosen either in a first-past-the-post ballot nor even in the majoritarian alternative-vote variant.

III

In office, before the adoption in 1965 of an electoral procedure, different methods were used to choose a Conservative prime minister when a vacancy occurred. In 1923, following Bonar Law's resignation, the king decided, after receiving a memorandum embodying what he was told were Bonar Law's views, and after consulting both Lord Balfour, the only other living Conservative ex-Premier, and a Conservative elder statesman, Lord Salisbury (son of the prime minister), to appoint Stanley Baldwin, in preference to his more experienced rival, Lord Curzon. The main reason for this choice was the inadvisability of appointing a prime minister from the Lords when Labour, now the main opposition party, was virtually unrepresented there. There was also a feeling that Curzon might prove a stalking-horse for the return to government of Austen Chamberlain and of those who had supported the Lloyd George coalition. This, in the opinion of some at least of those who had voted with the majority at the Carlton Club meeting the previous year, would be premature. It would have seemed, in the view of J. C. C. Davidson, a close friend of Bonar Law and Baldwin, 'treachery by those who had stood by Bonar and Baldwin at the Carlton Club meeting, and who represented the overwhelming majority of the rank and file of the party in the country'.[13] So the state of back-bench opinion may also have been a significant factor in the choice of Baldwin. But the decision was made by the king, using his prerogative, and there was no attempt at a systematic canvass either of the Cabinet or of Conservative MPs.[14]

In 1957, by contrast, the sovereign's decision was influenced largely by the view of the Cabinet, and perhaps also by that of the parliamentary party. The Conservatives were faced with a leadership contest following the resignation of the Prime Minister, Sir Anthony Eden. There were two candidates, Harold Macmillan and R. A. Butler. The retiring prime minister favoured Butler for the succession.[15] But a head-count of the Cabinet, carried out by Lord Kilmuir, the Lord Chancellor, and Lord Salisbury (grandson of the prime minister), showed that at most three cabinet members, and perhaps only one, favoured Butler for the succession, the rest supporting Macmillan. MPs were also given some opportunity of making their views known; it has been suggested that 'There was a ground-swell of opinion among the back-benchers for Macmillan, and there was a small minority who were implacably opposed to Butler at any price.'[16] If that view is correct, then Macmillan would certainly have been chosen under an electoral procedure.[17]

The Conservative leadership struggle of 1963 is the one that has caused the most controversy, and there is still considerable disagreement among historians in interpreting it. Iain Macleod, in an article in the *Spectator* in January 1964, coined the phrase 'the magic circle' to describe the machinations by which Harold Macmillan, aided by other influential Conservatives, is supposed to have foisted Lord Home upon the party, in order to prevent Butler, whom Macmillan thought ill qualified for the Premiership, succeeding to it.

The leadership contest of 1963 had two novel aspects. The first was that the vacancy occurred in the middle of the annual Party Conference, so that, inevitably, party activists were drawn into the process of selection, the very situation which the party grandees had striven to avoid in 1911. Secondly, in place of the rather haphazard arrangements for consulting anyone other than party influentials, there was a more detailed canvass of MPs, peers, and leading members of the party outside Parliament than had ever occurred before.

It was Harold Macmillan who instituted this procedure of consultation, its novelty masked by Macmillan's use of the phrase 'customary processes of consultation' which implied precedents where none existed. But it should be remembered that Macmillan instituted this procedure only after discovering that the party was unclear as to how it should set about choosing a successor; and the procedure was, it appears, accepted by the Cabinet.[18] The procedure was, however, highly complex. It appears, from evidence presented by A. W. Bradley, a former professor of constitutional law at Edinburgh University, that not one but three questions were asked of MPs.[19] These questions were:

1   Who should succeed Macmillan?
2   Who should be the second choice?
3   Who among the contenders would you least like to see leader?

In Professor Bradley's words, 'account was taken both of the positive and negative standing that the various contenders enjoyed within the party'. What we cannot know is whether in the exigencies of the improvised consultation process, the three questions were in all cases posed without refinement, distortion or the suggestion of names by the questioners.

The procedure may well have been applied defectively. At least one MP complained that his views had never been sought, while others claimed that the questions were slanted. Reginald Bevins, the Postmaster-General, gave the Chief Whip his preferences – Maudling and Bulter – and was then met with a long pause. 'We looked at each other. "What about the peers – Alec and the other one." No pause. I said, "Not at any bloody price." That was an unfortunate answer, all carefully recorded on Martin Redmayne's [the Chief Whip] foolscap.'[20] It seems clear that the whips, on occasion, asked a fourth question, in addition to the three mentioned by Bradley, and that this fourth question mentioned Home by name. As Bevins indicates, MPs might fear that an answer unsympathetic to Home would be reported back, and reflect adversely on their future prospects of advancement. Further, the very procedure of multiple questions, together with references to a hypothetical deadlock, maximized the chances of a compromise candidate, a least unacceptable candidate, such as Home.

The procedure might best be described as one of 'guided democracy'. Some of the guidance was exercised by Harold Macmillan from his hospital bed. He saw members of the Cabinet on 15 and 16 October, and, when Edward Boyle indicated that he was anti-Hailsham and pro-Butler, Macmillan declared, 'I can quite see that you would like someone like *Alec* or *Rab*' (emphasis added). It was, Boyle reminisced in 1979, 'like one of those detective novels where the author has carefully concealed the identity of the culprit, and the reader can only guess at what is meant'.[21] But perhaps more important than Macmillan's intervention was the guidance exerted by the back-bench leaders of the party, and especially by Martin Redmayne, the Chief Whip, and Major John Morrison, chairman of the 1922 Committee.

Major Morrison, who had served longer than anyone as chairman of the 1922 Committee, had already approached R. A. Butler, seemingly the favourite for the succession, at the end of June 1963, just over three months before Macmillan's resignation, to give him a message that was 'simple and direct – "the chaps won't have you"'. On his return from the Victoria Falls Conference, Rab Butler naturally asked friends on the Executive [of the 1922 Committee] whether John Morrison's assessment was accurate. The answer was a bleak "yes".'[22] Morrison had already made extensive enquiries as to what back-bench preferences would be should Macmillan decide to retire.

The account of Major Morrison's approach, given by Philip Goodhart in his history of the 1922 Committee, can now be confirmed from the papers of R. A. Butler at Trinity College, Cambridge. On 21 June 1963 Butler was told by members of the 1922 Committee that 'there was a very strong feeling in the Party that on the question of the next leadership they should jump to a younger generation and not have anybody too closely associated with the present regime'. On 31 July Butler was

> visited by John Morrison and Alex Spearman. The burden of their song was that in view of the strong inclination of the younger backbenchers to get somebody of the new age group it was likely that opinion would crystallise like this as representing the greatest common factor. They were both extremely friendly but seemed quite sure of their diagnosis.[23]

Further, on the day that the House of Lords Reform Bill, allowing hereditary peers to disclaim their titles, reached the Statute Book, Major Morrison had consulted Lord Home, the Foreign Secretary:

> Once again the message was simple. Now that it was possible for peers to disclaim their titles and return to the House of Commons, the demands of party unity might make it desirable and even necessary that the Foreign Secretary should become Leader. Lord Home was sceptical. John Morrison was insistent, and in the end the Foreign Secretary gave a reply that left all the options open: 'I will see my doctor'.[24]

The whips certainly sought to guide back-bench opinion in favour of Home. During the party conference, the executive of the 1922 Committee met at a Blackpool Hotel and came to the conclusion

> that Lord Home was the one candidate likely to promote party unity at a time when party unity was thought to be essential. It was not surprising, therefore, that the Executive agreed on a form of consultation within the Party which would be phrased in a way that was most likely to accentuate Lord Home's strengths. Thus, members of the Party in the House of Commons and the Lords would be asked to

give not only their first preferences, but also their second preferences. They were also to be asked whether they felt particularly opposed to any of the four candidates. It was expected that Lord Home would do particularly well on the second preference, and that few Members would express any opposition to him. The formal consultation would also be carried out by men who knew that 'the backbench Cabinet' [i.e. the executive of the 1922 Committee] had plumped decisively for Home.[25]

It is clear that the procedure adopted in 1963 was not as open as it ought to have been. In particular, because Lord Home was thought by many MPs and by most of the press not to be a candidate, he was not scrutinized as carefully as the three declared candidates – Butler, Hailsham, and Maudling. To what extent can an election be meaningful if some members of the electorate do not know who the candidates are? In part, perhaps, Home's popularity was a result of the fact that he was so little scrutinized. Had he been a declared candidate, it might have been that he, like Butler and Hailsham, would have been blackballed by a determined minority.

Moreover, the outcome did not fulfil its declared purpose, for Home was unable to unite the party. There was considerable antipathy to him from a minority in the Cabinet. According to Enoch Powell, no less than seven members of the cabinet – Macleod, Maudling, Hailsham, Boyd-Carpenter, Errol, Boyle, and Powell himself – indicated that they would refuse to serve under Home unless Butler himself agreed to serve. These seven included a Chairman of the Party, Macleod, an ex-Chairman, Hailsham, and the Chancellor of the Exchequer, Maudling.[26] In the event, two cabinet ministers – Macleod and Powell – did refuse to serve, and the outcome gave an impression of disunity which may have contributed to the Conservatives' narrow defeat in the 1964 general election. The choice of Butler, by contrast, would probably not have led to cabinet resignations, and so Butler might well have been able to unite the party more successfully than Home. Indeed, Macmillan himself apparently came to believe that the selection of Home was a mistake, and that Butler might, after all, have proved a wiser choice.[27]

Nevertheless, even allowing for the many criticisms that can be made of the procedure adopted in 1963, and conceding that the outcome did not fulfil the hopes of its proponents, there is no evidence that the result seriously misrepresented Conservative opinion. It seems clear that Lord Home was the popular choice of the peers, that he had at least a narrow plurality of votes among MPs as their first choice, gaining more support when later preferences were taken into account,[28] and that he was the first choice of the Cabinet, enjoying a plurality but probably not an overall majority among his ministerial colleagues.

It is, moreover, barely credible to suppose that those involved in the selection process, which involved consultations among four different groups, would have been allowed to falsify their findings; not that they would have allowed their findings to be falsified by Harold Macmillan without making any public comment. It may be that supporters of other candidates, and particularly supporters of R. A. Butler, were outmanœuvred; but there is no reason to believe that Butler commanded more support than Home. There is, of course, little doubt that Harold Macmillan did not want to be succeeded by Butler; and, contrary to what is often suggested, it was perfectly legitimate for Macmillan to allow his view to be known. Yet, Macmillan was unable to impose his first choice, Hailsham, upon the party, and he could not have stopped Butler had the latter genuinely enjoyed the confidence of the party.

Butler himself has often been accused of weakness for agreeing to serve under Home when the other two candidates for the leadership – Lord Hailsham and Reginald Maudling – together with other senior ministers, had made clear their willingness to serve under him, and their disinclination to serve under Home. Yet Butler already knew, from what Major Morrison had told him in June, that he was not the first choice of Conservative MPs; his supporters 'were not aware that John Morrison had gone out of his way to warn Rab Butler that "The chaps won't have you". It had not been a warning that was meant to be taken lightly – and it was not.'[29] When Home was trying to persuade Maudling to serve in his government, he declared, bravely, that, if he failed to form a government, Maudling himself, rather than Butler, would become Prime Minister. For Butler, according to Home, could not become leader, since he had too many enemies.[30]

At the time, the selection of Home was criticized as a plot by a right-wing aristocratic cabal determined to keep out Butler. This criticism lacks substance. There is no reason to doubt that, as in 1911 and later in 1990, the Conservative Party preferred a unifying candidate to a strong or experienced one; nor did the policies followed by the Home government differ significantly from those followed by Harold Macmillan's administration. On the other hand, the selection of Lord Home seemed almost deliberately to flout the public mood of the day, which, since around 1960, had become convinced that, economically, Britain was falling behind the countries of the Continent. The remedy for this deficiency was widely felt to be a political leadership more professional in its approach to economic problems, and more sympathetic to the contribution which science and technology could make to economic growth. That mood was being tapped by the new Labour leader, Harold Wilson, and it seemed quixotic of the Conservatives to ignore it. Moreover, the selection of Home lacked legitimacy even in its own terms, because the rules seemed *ad hoc*, not having been agreed in advance. The old procedures could work only if there was a gentlemanly consensus to abide by the result. But this was lacking in 1963. The party failed to close ranks after the leadership contest, and this contrasted badly with the success of Labour's leadership campaign earlier that year. The Conservatives seemed, in William Rees-Mogg's words, to have 'ceased to be gentlemen without becoming democrats'.[31]

For these reasons it was widely accepted that a more explicitly democratic procedure was needed. No consultative process, however fair, would any longer be accepted as legitimate. So it was that the Conservatives decided to adopt an electoral procedure to choose their leader, although, when Humphrey Berkeley had suggested this to a meeting of the Chelsea Young Conservatives earlier in 1963, Lord Aldington had asked him incredulously, 'Humphrey, surely you are not advocating one man one vote', and the general reaction was as if 'I had suggested that the Leader of the Party should be elected by the entire adult population of the African continent'.[32]

IV

In developing a new procedure for the selection of a party leader, Conservatives had to resolve two problems. The first was to choose an electoral method to be used by Conservative MPs. The second was to find a role for influential Conservatives outside the Commons – peers and leaders of the party outside Parliament, members of the Executive Committee of the National Union.

In a situation in which Conservative MPs were united upon a candidate, as in 1902, 1921, 1922, 1937, 1940 and 1955, it did not really matter what electoral system was chosen. Under such circumstances, the new procedure would serve simply as a legitimating mechanism for the party's choice. Where there was no such agreement, however, past experience had shown that neither the first-past-the-post system nor a system requiring an absolute majority on a single ballot would be able to 'cope with the problem that in the remainder of the Party in the Commons (the 50% minus who did not vote for the candidate), there may be packets of radical opposition to the candidate chosen by the majority'.[33] It was vital that the candidate chosen was not divisive. 'The choice of the Commons must be clear beyond reasonable doubt. Ideally, the chosen candidate should receive such overwhelming support as to preclude the emergence of factions of determined opposition to his leadership'.[34] A Conservative leader had to command 'great loyalty from virtually every individual in the Parliamentary Party' if he was to be successful.[35] A single-ballot system could easily exclude a compromise candidate, such as Bonar Law, who might prove more able to unite the party than his opponents. The same would be true of a two-ballot system, of the kind used to elect the French President, whose 'main disadvantage is that in a close run contest it makes it more difficult . . . for a compromise candidate to emerge';[36]

similarly, an alternative-vote system would, in 1911, probably have led to the election of Austen Chamberlain, rather than of Bonar Law, who might well have been eliminated on the first ballot despite being the candidate who could best unite the party. Thus the method of election had to meet two desiderata. First, it had to provide for more than one ballot. Secondly, it had to allow, where necessary, new compromise candidates to emerge if it appeared that the front runners were unable to secure consensus.

The procedure adopted in 1965 made provision for a leadership election only when a vacancy arose through the death or resignation of the current leader. Under these circumstances, any two Conservative MPs could propose another MP for the leadership. The names of the proposer and seconder would not be published, but would remain confidential to the scrutineers. Provision was made for three ballots to be held. To win on the first ballot, a candidate would require an overall majority among Conservative MPs, and, in addition, 15 per cent more of the votes than had been cast for any other candidate. If no candidate surmounted this hurdle, a second ballot would be held. Nominations for the first ballot would be void, and new nominations would be needed. Thus new candidates could stand on the second ballot. To win on the second ballot, a candidate would need an overall majority. If no candidate attained an overall majority, a third ballot would be held in which the three leading candidates on the second ballot would be required to stand. The third ballot, unlike the first two, would be preferential, using the alternative vote procedure. If no candidate won an overall majority on the third ballot, the second preferences of the candidate with the smallest number of votes would be redistributed, so giving one of the two remaining candidates a majority.

Electoral systems can be devised to force a majority choice – the exhaustive ballot used by the Labour Party fulfils this function – or, alternatively, they may be designed, as in, for example, papal elections, to elicit a compromise choice. The method chosen by the Conservative Party does not seek to prejudge whether a compromise candidate should or should not be chosen. It allows for such a candidate, but does not force it upon the party. If one candidate is pre-eminent, as, for example, Eden would have been in 1955, and as Margaret Thatcher proved to be in 1975 and John Major in 1995, the method allowed that candidate to be chosen.Otherwise, the second and third ballots could allow either a candidate with the support of a majority or a compromise candidate to be chosen.

V

The second problem which the Conservatives faced when devising a procedure to choose a leader was whether the party outside the Commons should have a role in the process. It was and remains the custom of the party for a newly chosen leader to be endorsed by a party meeting, comprising, since 1937,Conservative MPs and peers, Conservative parliamentary candidates and members of the Executive Committee of the National Union.[37] In theory, the party's choice of leader could be overriden by this meeting, although, in practice, the new leader was invariably endorsed unanimously. But the question now arose of whether the party outside Parliament should play a real part in the selection process, such as it had done in 1963. Some members of the Executive Committee of the National Union felt that the events of 1963 had created a precedent and a presumption that the party outside Parliament would be given a similar role in future contests. After all, the leader of the Conservative Party was not only the leader of Conservative MPs. He was also, and had been since 1922, leader of the party in the Lords, and leader of the party in the country. He stands in fact at the apex of the party, linking the parliamentary party with the National Union. This seemed to make it necessary to find some way of associating other sections of the party with the leadership-selection process.

The difficulty, however, was to determine what precise weighting the party outside Parliament ought to be given. Those who devised the selection procedure of 1965 were worried lest the party meeting be given power to override the choice of Conservative MPs. If this happened, a Conservative leader could be chosen who might enjoy the support of only a minority of the parliamentary party. Yet, it was only Conservative MPs who were responsible to the electorate. Therefore, it was argued, the MPs ought to have the determining say in choosing a prime minister or potential prime minister. Thus the role of other sections of the party in any election could be only a token one. Therefore, it was decided to adopt a different method of obtaining the views of these sections of the party. This method was characterized by James Douglas, one of its architects, as an 'Outside Inside Method',[38] since the view of other sections of the party would be obtained *before* Conservative MPs held their ballot, rather than being brought into play *after* the ballot had been held, to confirm or oppose the choice made by the MPs. Conservative peers together with the party in the country, as well as, in 1990 and 1995, Conservative Members of the European Parliament would be asked for their views, and these would be made known to the officers of the 1922 Committee, who were in charge of the ballot; and, through them, to Conservative MPs. In the event, however, it turned out that the views of other elements of the party could easily be ignored, if MPs wished to do so. In 1975 both the peers and the party outside Parliament were overwhelmingly for Heath, and in 1990 equally overwhelmingly for Mrs Thatcher. They were overriden on each occasion.[39] It is likely, however, that the powerful opposition manifested by many constituency activists against Michael Heseltine in 1990 persuaded some MPs not to vote for him in the second ballot.

The decision to allow the party outside Parliament only a consultative role corresponded with the ethos and history of the Conservative Party. Since its foundation, the National Union had been regarded as a 'handmaid to the party',[40] rather than part of its policy-making machinery. The National Union was a National Union of associations designed to *support* the Conservative Party in Parliament; it was not itself a part of the Conservative Party, which was essentially parliamentary. Therefore, only Conservative MPs could be given a formal role in the procedure for electing a Conservative leader

VI

The new procedure was first used following the resignation of Sir Alec Douglas-Home (as Lord Home had become after renouncing his title upon assuming the Premiership) in July 1965. It worked smoothly and success-fully, in striking contrast to the bitter struggle of 1963. Edward Heath gained an overall majority on the first ballot, but without surmounting the 15 per cent hurdle. Reginald Maudling, however, chose to concede immediately, rather than face inevitable defeat in a second ballot. The party proceeded to unite around Heath and was able to fight the 1966 general election without being harmed by factional disturbances.

A crucial flaw in the new procedure, however, was that it was designed only to fill vacancies in the party leadership. It made no provision for chal-lenging an incumbent leader who had overstayed his welcome. The presump-tion, perhaps, was that, in such circumstances, the leader would appreciate his position, as Balfour had done in 1911 and Douglas-Home in 1965, and take the gentlemanly course of action. Edward Heath, however, by the end of 1974, had lost three out of the four general elections which he had fought, and yet refused to resign, despite widespread dissatisfaction with his leader-ship on the part of Conservative MPs, one of whom, Kenneth Lewis, declared acidly at a meeting of the 1922 Committee after the October 1974 general election that the leadership was held on a leasehold, and not a freehold basis.[41]

In November 1974, therefore, a committee was set up, chaired by Lord Home (as he had once again become), to modify the rules. This committee made two main proposals. First it proposed that there should be a regular, annual election for the leadership. This would be held within 28 days of the opening of a new session of Parliament, except that, in a new Parliament, it would be held not earlier than three months nor later than six months from the date of assembly of the Parliament. In 1991 the period was reduced to

Table 4.2   Conservative leadership elections 1965–95

Year	Ballot		Outcome
1965	*First ballot*		Heath had won an overall majority
	Edward Heath	150	but had not fulfilled the second
	Reginald Maudling	133	requirement of winning 15% more
	Enoch Powell	15	of the vote than any other
	Abstentions	6	candidate; Maudling and Powell
			withdrew and there was no second
			ballot.
1975	*First ballot*		Heath and Fraser withdrew.
	Margaret Thatcher	130	
	Edward Heath	119	
	Hugh Fraser	16	
	Abstentions	11	
	Second ballot		Thatcher was elected as leader.
	Margaret Thatcher	146	
	William Whitelaw	79	
	James Prior	19	
	Sir Geoffrey Howe	19	
	John Peyton	11	
	Abstentions	2	
1989	*First ballot*		Thatcher was re-elected as leader,
	Margaret Thatcher	314	no further ballot being required.
	Sir Anthony Meyer	33	
	Abstentions	27	
1990	*First ballot*		Thatcher had an overall majority
	Margaret Thatcher	204	but failed to secure the 15% margin
	Michael Heseltine	152	(with 372 MPs entitled to vote, she
	Abstentions	16	was 4 short of the required majority
			of 56); a second ballot was needed,
			and Thatcher withdrew.

Second ballot		Major was only 2 votes short of an
John Major	185	overall majority; the other
Michael Heseltine	131	candidates withdrew and there was
Douglas Hurd	56	no third ballot.
Abstentions	0	

1995	*First ballot*		Major was re-elected leader.
	John Major	218	
	John Redwood	89	
	Abstentions	22	

three months. Secondly, the committee proposed that the hurdle on the first ballot should not be, as hitherto, an overall majority plus 15 per cent more of the votes than had been cast for any other candidate, but rather an overall majority plus 15 per cent more of the votes of those entitled to vote. This marginally higher hurdle was widely thought to be damaging to Heath's chances by making it more difficult for him to win a majority on the first ballot.

The new procedure, as proposed by the Home committee, was used in 1975, and it led to the replacement of Heath by Margaret Thatcher. But it was, perhaps, not contemplated in 1974 that the procedure could be used against an incumbent Prime Minister. The challenge by Sir Anthony Meyer in 1989 was resented by many Conservative MPs loyal to Mrs Thatcher. They argued that Meyer was not a serious candidate and that he could not conceivably be elected. He was nominated merely as a demonstration against the leadership. But this demonstration would, it was believed, damage the party by bringing differences out into the open. After Sir Anthony's defeat, it was contemplated raising the requirement for nomination from two MPs to, say, 60, so that no challenge could be made unless there was already very considerable dissatisfaction with the leadership. In the event, however, no such change was made and the only alteration between 1989 and 1990 was that the names of the MPs nominating and seconding candidates would be made public.

The leadership election of 1990 also gave rise to some dissatisfaction, and the 1922 Committee set up a committee to examine whether further changes were needed. In the summer of 1991 the procedure was amended so that, in future, an incumbent leader can be challenged only if, in addition to a candidate being proposed and seconded, 10 per cent of the parliamentary party write privately to the chairman of the 1922 Committee calling for an election. Without this new provision it is likely that John Major would have faced a challenge in 1994. The leadership election of 1995, at which John Major voluntarily resigned the leadership, challenging anyone to run against him, led to further dissatisfaction, and the 1922 Committee decided that there should be no further leadership elections in the parliament elected in 1992. This may presage a further attempt to limit the provision by which the leader may be challenged annually.

VII

The electoral procedure devised in 1965, and then extended and modified in 1974–5 and in 1991, did not, however, fundamentally alter the Conservative approach to political leadership. What it did was to codify the rough-and-ready procedures adopted in 1911 and 1963. This can be seen by looking at the logic of the three-ballot procedure, at the different rules for winning at each ballot, and then comparing them with the logic of the 'customary processes' of 1911 and 1963.

On the first ballot, the leader must secure a majority of the votes plus 15 per cent more of the votes of those entitled to vote than his or her leading competitor. At first sight, this seems an artificially high hurdle for the leader to surmount. Why should Mrs Thatcher be deemed to have lost the leadership election in 1990 when she polled 204 votes to Michael Heseltine's 152 on the first ballot? This objection would be sound if a bare majority were sufficient to give legitimacy to an incumbent leader. It is clear, however, that even the 204 votes which Mrs Thatcher received in 1990 did not amount to a vote of confidence in her leadership, especially as around 80 MPs were members of the government or whips. Had the rules given Mrs Thatcher a victory at this stage, the Conservatives would probably have been severely damaged by the public revelation of the fact that over 45 per cent of their MPs, and over 50 per cent of those MPs outside the government, were unwilling to support their leader. Mrs Thatcher's authority to govern would have been gravely weakened.

If, therefore, an incumbent leader is forced to face a leadership challenge, the first ballot should be seen as a vote of confidence in the leadership, a vote to see whether the leader has sufficient authority to continue. It is natural that more than a simple majority of the parliamentary party should be required as evidence that the leader still enjoys sufficient support to be able to exercise that authority. If the leader cannot secure the special majority in the first ballot, then, of course, he or she can still choose to enter the second ballot, at which an absolute majority is sufficient. But the first ballot may have shown, as it did in 1990, that neither of the candidates can command sufficient unity among MPs. Therefore, new candidates should be allowed to enter the second ballot so that a unifying figure can be found. Indeed, it seems that a number of MPs in 1990 voted for Heseltine on the first ballot to ensure that Mrs Thatcher resigned, but then supported either Major or Hurd on the second ballot.

It was said in 1975 that it was this provision allowing new candidates to enter on the second ballot that struck the decisive blow against Edward Heath. For, it has been argued that if, on the first ballot in 1975, every MP had thought his vote would be decisive, Heath would have won a majority. But that is not the point. It is of the essence of the first ballot that the vote is not to be a decisive one. It is a vote not to choose a new leader, but to consider whether the existing leader retains the party's confidence. That confidence, Heath, by 1975, had clearly lost.[42]

Until 1991, if no candidate achieved an absolute majority on the second ballot, the three leading candidates were to go forward to a third and final ballot, at which, under the alternative-vote system, one candidate would secure an absolute majority and become the new leader. The three leading candidates *had* to go forward to a third ballot. Such a requirement appeared absurd, however, in the light of the 1990 result when John Major was within two votes of victory; in fact, the chairman of the 1922 Committee used his discretion to abandon the third ballot, since Major's two rivals, Michael Heseltine and Douglas Hurd, had both conceded. The provision now is that the third ballot is confined to the top *two* candidates from the second ballot, but that any candidate can withdraw within 24 hours of the conclusion of the second ballot.

The system of multiple ballots is better than a single ballot held under the alternative-vote system for two reasons. First, choices under a multiple-ballot system are actual rather than hypothetical. Secondly, the system of multiple ballots allows the party in the country to make its views known, even though it has no formal role in the process. This was, arguably, crucial in 1990, when evidence from the constituency parties showed that John Major was more popular than Dougals Hurd, and that Michael Heseltine had deeply antago- nized many MPs and constituency activists.[43] Moreover, survey evidence between the first and second ballots suggested that Major was as capable as Heseltine of winning back votes for the Conservatives.

One may contrast this method of electing a leader with that of Labour, which until 1994 employed an exhaustive ballot procedure for its leadership elections, and required no special majority to confirm the leader in office. This could, in certain circumstances, allow a leader to continue even though he had lost the authority to enable him to govern effectively. Moreover, Labour allows no new, compromise candidates to enter on the second ballot, and so the victor in a Labour leadership contest can easily be the representa- tive of a faction – left or right – rather than a figure who can unify the party.

Leadership elections in the Labour Party, with 1935 being the main exception, are generally choices between political attitudes – e.g. MacDonald versus Clynes in 1922, Gaitskell versus Bevan in 1955, Callaghan versus Foot in 1976, Foot versus Healey in 1980, Kinnock versus Hattersley in 1983 and Blair versus Prescott in 1994. In 1955 Aneurin Bevan proposed to his rival, Hugh Gaitskell, that they both stand down in favour of the third candidate, Herbert Morrison; but Gaitskell, reflecting back-bench opinion in the Labour Party, refused, and won the leadership on the first ballot. Labour explicitly declined to follow the Conservative precedent of 1911 and select a consensual leader.[44] Similarly, in 1980, the electoral procedure dictated a choice between left – Michael Foot – and right – Denis Healey. Yet, it might be argued that either of these candidates would have split the party, and that the choice of a compromise candidate such as Peter Shore would have served the party better by uniting it. Leadership elections in the Conservative Party, by contrast, were not, until 1975 at least, choices between ideologically opposed antagonists; and the party's electoral procedure was one devised for a governing party, one broadly united over issues of principle, a party without ideology.

Moreover, it is because of the great priority which Conservatives give to party unity that the tenure of a Conservative leader is so precarious, and that he or she is in so much more danger of losing the leadership than his or her Labour counterpart. In the Labour Party, the main emphasis is put on party policy, and so, when an election is lost, it is the policy which is thought to be at fault. In the case of the Conservative Party, by contrast, as Philip Williams has noticed, ' "fitness to govern" is a value and personal leadership a presumed electoral asset', and so Conservatives 'give their leaders more freedom to act during a more precarious tenure'.[45] That is why Labour leaders can generally decide for themselves when they should retire, while Conservative leaders are granted this luxury rather more rarely. In Robert McKenzie's graphic words, the Conservative 'Leader leads and the party follows, except when the party decides not to follow – then the Leader ceases to be Leader'.[46]

VIII

Before Mrs Thatcher's resignation in 1990, there was much discussion in the popular press of 'the men in grey suits' who would apparently tell the Prime Minister at some point that enough was enough and that she should go. Yet, the perspective of history shows that, in Stuart Ball's words, 'the arrival at No. 10 of a deputation of "men in grey suits" is about as likely as one of little green men from Mars'.[47] There is no evidence of any occasion when a deputation of elders of the party has enforced the resignation of a Conservative leader. Edward Heath had clearly lost the support of the majority of his back-benchers by 1975, although the party establishment continued to support him; while Margaret Thatcher failed to retain the leadership in 1990 because she had forfeited the support, not so much of party influentials, but of around half of her back-benchers.

Stanley Baldwin succeeded in retaining power after the election defeat of December 1923 despite the opposition to him of many Conservative influentials. He survived also after the 1929 defeat, although Neville Chamberlain had 'come to the conclusion that if S. B. would go the whole party would heave a sigh of relief',[48] and Baldwin seemed to have only one supporter in the shadow cabinet, W. C. Bridgeman. Nevertheless, Baldwin was able to hold on by making an explicit appeal to the wider party at two Caxton Hall meetings, in June and October 1930. The first meeting was to comprise those 'who are actively engaged in the constituencies or candidates',[49] while the second comprised Conservative peers, MPs, and candidates. Both meetings endorsed Baldwin's leadership, so preventing his shadow cabinet colleagues, who had the most profound doubts as to his suitability for the role of Leader of the Opposition, from removing him. In March 1931, also, Baldwin survived, although the majority of his front-bench colleagues favoured his resignation.[50]

In 1947 members of the shadow cabinet sought, entirely without success, to remove Churchill from the leadership. The story is told by James Stuart, the Chief Whip:

> at length, it was decided that the time had come to take steps to acquaint Winston with the possibly unpalatable news that in the opinion of a body of his colleagues he had 'had it' politically. . . While no one had any thought of inflicting any sort of hurt or harm on Sir Winston, he should be informed that it was probably in the better interests of the Party that he should seek peace in retirement.
>
> It quickly became clear to me that each of my companions had excellent reasons for not being the person to convey the tidings to Winston, so I was not surprised that it was agreed unanimously (if you don't count me) that the man for the job was the one who had no axe to grind and was, after all, the Party's Chief Whip!
>
> Winston received me alone in his room at the House. I told him at once that I had a difficult task to perform and that I trusted he would bear with me without being annoyed. He assured me that he would not get annoyed and invited me to proceed. I reiterated my view that no other man had done more than he for his country and then told him of the unanimous view expressed by our colleagues at our meeting. He reacted violently, banging the floor with his stick and implying that I too had joined those who were plotting to displace him.
>
> . . . it did take a few days before he could treat me normally again . . . No more

was heard of his retirement for several years and none of the others present at our private meeting repeated to him the views which they had so kindly invited me to convey.[51]

In 1963, despite the considerable anxieties held by many senior Conservatives concerning Harold Macmillan's leadership, there is no evidence that he could not have continued to lead the party before being struck down by illness. Admittedly, his position had been so weakened that he found himself in the position of having to invite his colleagues, at a cabinet meeting on 8 October 1963, to decide whether he should continue. Yet Enoch Powell was, apparently, the only member of the Cabinet to indicate that he thought the prime minister should resign, and it was only when Macmillan was struck down by illness that he felt compelled to go.

In 1911 and 1965 Balfour and Sir Alec Douglas-Home resigned without being compelled to do so. There was considerable pressure upon them, but, as with Baldwin in 1930–1, they could probably have survived had they chosen to fight, although under such circumstances their authority might gradually have been whittled away, as Edward Heath's was in 1974–5. Balfour believed that he could have stayed – 'I know I cannot be evicted', he told the Chief Whip.[52] Douglas-Home, in 1965, was advised by the Party Chairman and the Chief Whip to resign. They were worried by survey evidence which suggested that, while the electoral position of the party was improving, Douglas-Home's personal rating remained low. The implication was that the leader was coming to be an electoral liability. The Chairman and Chief Whip also told Douglas-Home that the party in the country was against him, and that, although the majority of MPs favoured him, there was 'a sizeable element in the Parliamentary Party in favour of a change'. It appears that some of Edward Heath's supporters had seen the Chief Whip, to urge a change of leadership.[53] This meant that a continuation of the Douglas-Home leadership could divide the party. Nevertheless, the 1922 Committee, by contrast with its future attitude towards Edward Heath in 1974, apparently told Home in 1965 that, if he decided to stay, 90 per cent of the Conservative Party would support him.[54]

In 1974, after the second Conservative election defeat, the majority of Edward Heath's shadow cabinet colleagues probably believed that he ought to resign so as to allow William Whitelaw to inherit, and head off the chances of a candidate of the right. Heath, however, refused to resign, and was defeated because he had lost back-bench support, as had Margaret Thatcher in 1990.

In 1922 and 1940 the situation was complicated by the exigencies of coalition politics. Austen Chamberlain was unwilling to preside over the transition from coalition government to single-party government, while Neville

Chamberlain was unacceptable to the leaders of the Labour Party, whose participation in a coalition government was essential for the effective prosecution of the war. In 1922 the party establishment was split. The leading figures in the Cabinet supported Austen Chamberlain, while the leading officials of the party – the Chief Whip, the Party Chairman, and the Principal Agent – aware of the mounting dissatisfaction on the back-benches and in the country, were opposed to coalition. That is why J. C. C. Davidson predicted, just before the Carlton Club meeting, that the outcome would be 'a slice off the top',[55] since the back-benchers and the constituency parties had made up their minds, while many on the front bench still thought that the Coalition could be preserved. In 1940 the Conservative establishment was terrified at the thought of Churchill, and most of those who believed that Chamberlain should retire favoured Halifax as his successor. It was indeed partly to re-assure the party that Chamberlain remained as party leader after Churchill's succession to the premiership, in May 1940, until illness forced him to retire in September 1940.

Thus, with the *possible* exceptions of 1955 and 1957, Conservative leaders have not been dethroned by the machinations of influentials. The most common pattern, noticeable in 1911, 1922, 1965, 1975 and 1990, is for the leader to lose support on the back-benches. This reflected, in 1911, 1965, 1975 and 1990, a feeling that the leader was becoming an electoral liability. It is, after all, generally the back-benchers, rather than the party's grandees, who have to defend the marginal seats upon which the party's electoral success depends. On each of these occasions, moreover, the disintegration of the existing regime began in the constituencies, not so much among constituency activists – the Conservative constituency associations were still five to one for Mrs Thatcher even after the first ballot in 1990 – but among floating voters – former supporters of the party who had deserted it, but could perhaps be weaned back with a change of leadership. The influentials will often be the last to warn the leader of the degree of disaffection, since their position in politics may be dependent upon a continuation of the existing leadership. Enoch Powell, commenting on the disintegration of Harold Macmillan's regime, declared:

> You lose the public, you lose the press, you lose the party in the House, but the men whose heads you can cut off before breakfast you lose last. The most difficult operation there is is for a Cabinet itself to depose a Prime Minister. So it was everything else that slipped around Harold Macmillan before the Cabinet itself.[56]

So also, the shadow cabinet refused to act against Heath in 1975, while the Cabinet failed in 1990 to give Mrs Thatcher a true estimate of her position until the prospect of defeat stared her in the face.

The electoral procedure used by the Conservatives not only codifies the previous practices of the party. It also enables the force of popular opinion to be brought to bear, through back-bench MPs, upon the processes of leadership selection. Even before the procedure was introduced, the party had shown, in 1963, that it had a mind of its own when it refused to allow Harold Macmillan to impose Hailsham upon it. In 1975 and 1990 popular opinion was brought to bear against incumbent leaders who retained the allegiance of the party establishment, but had lost public support. In both 1965 and 1975, the outcome expressed a desire for change, felt inchoately in the country but more strongly among opinion formers. In 1965 there was a desire for a new style of leadership, which could represent the forces of meritocracy that had propelled Harold Wilson to the premiership in 1964. In 1975 there was a desire to detach the Conservative Party from corporatism and to rethink Conservative policy in accordance with new intellectual fashions which declared that inflation should be controlled by monetary methods, rather than through an incomes policy.

The new system thus makes it more difficult for an 'establishment' candidate to succeed, because such a candidate is more likely to be out of touch with the mood in the country in favour of a change. So it was with William Whitelaw in 1975 and with Douglas Hurd in 1990. In 1964 Iain Macleod complained that eight of the nine senior Conservatives involved in the selection of Lord Home in 1963 had gone to Eton.[57] In 1990, by contrast, Douglas Hurd found it a positive disadvantage to have been an Etonian, and was forced to explain that he had attended the school on a scholarship rather than by hereditary right. Thus, the new system makes it easier for a 'populist' candidate to win election against the wishes of the party influentials. In doing so, the procedure allows the Conservative Party to appear more in tune with new facets of social and economic life – the collapse of deference and the desire of individuals to take responsibility for themselves.

IX

Sweeping away the mythology of the 'customary processes of consultation' is an essential precondition of analysing the real problems facing a leader of the Conservative Party, whose task is fourfold. First, he must display competence and efficiency at his task; secondly, he must be perceived as an electoral asset, and have a reasonable prospect of carrying the country in a general election; thirdly, he must retain the allegiance of Conservative back-benchers; and, fourthly, he must retain the support of the party in the country. Above all, a Conservative leader must not split the party. It has been split only once – by Sir Robert Peel, following repeal of the Corn Laws in 1846 –

and following the split it did not form another majority government again for 28 years, by far the longest period that the Conservatives have ever spent in opposition. The example of Peel, therefore, is one to be avoided at all costs. It is for this reason that it could be said that the founder of the modern Conservative Party is not, as Norman Gash would have it, Sir Robert Peel, but rather Peel's ghost.

'I never can hear Peel praised with patience', Balfour told his niece and biographer, Blanche Dugdale. 'He twice split his Party' (on Catholic Emancipation in 1829, and on the repeal of the Corn Laws in 1846); he 'twice committed what seems to me the unforgivable sin'.[58] Balfour, following the 1903 split on tariff reform, must, with the example of Peel in mind, have consciously decided to risk every humiliation provided that the party was kept together. He strained every nerve to prevent a split. On his sickbed in October 1963, Harold Macmillan told Selwyn Lloyd that

> Balfour had been bitterly criticised for not having a view on Protection and Free Trade. Balfour had said the important thing was to preserve the unity of the Conservative Party. He had been abused for that. But now whoever argued about Free Trade or Protection? When was the last time that the conventional arguments had been interchanged – 1923? Whereas the preservation of great national institutions had been the right priority. Lloyd George might have been clear-cut on policy but he had destroyed the Liberal Party.[59]

In 1910, in declining Lloyd George's proposal for a coalition government, Balfour explained that 'I cannot become another Peel in my party.'[60] In 1922, speaking at the Carlton Club, Bonar Law confessed 'frankly that in the immediate crisis in front of us I do personally attach more importance to keeping our Party a united body than to winning the next election'. If the party continued to support Lloyd George as prime minister,

> I will tell you what I think will be the result. It will be a repetition of what happened after Peel passed the Corn Bill. The body that is cast off will slowly become the Conservative Party, but it will take a generation before it gets back to the influence which the Party ought to have.[61]

Later in the twentieth century, R. A. Butler told Elizabeth Longford, when she was writing her biography of the Queen, that 'The story of Sir Robert Peel splitting the Tory Party was for me the supremely unforgettable political lesson of history. It made an absolutely indelible impression. I could never do the same thing in the twentieth century, under any circumstances whatever.'[62]

Because of the importance of unity in the Conservative Party, candidates who are seen as divisive rarely achieve the leadership. The fear that they would be divisive was a powerful argument against Joseph Chamberlain in

1902, Austen Chamberlain in 1911 and 1922, R. A. Butler in 1957, both R. A. Butler and Lord Hailsham in 1963, Michael Heseltine in 1990 and John Redwood in 1995. The two exceptions to this generalization are the election of Edward Heath in 1965 and Margaret Thatcher in 1975, because on these two occasions there was a felt need for a change of direction as well as a change of leadership, and the new electoral procedure allowed this need to be given effect.

X

There are two conventional viewpoints on the Conservative Party leadership. The first is that the Conservative Party is and always has been oligarchical; as compared with other parties in Britain and especially with Labour, that it is a top–down party. The people who matter in the Conservative Party, according to this view, are the influentials – the men in grey suits of journalistic mythology. According to this view, the electoral procedure introduced in 1965 has hardly altered the oligarchical structure of power. Sir Alec Douglas-Home resigned in 1965 because of the opposition of influentials to his continued leadership, while the disintegration of Mrs Thatcher's regime was a disintegration of her cabinet support, rather than a loss of confidence from below.

The argument of this chapter shows, however, that the Conservative Party has, throughout the twentieth century, been a far more democratic party than is generally thought, being susceptible to pressures from back-bench MPs who often reflect the opinions of floating voters, as well as from the party outside Parliament. The electoral procedure has served to strengthen this democratic element by making it easier for popular opinion in the country to be reflected, via back-bench opinion, in the selection of a party leader.

The second conventional viewpoint is that the Conservative Party was once oligarchical, but that the electoral procedures of 1965 and 1975 have changed all this. Certainly, neither Mrs Thatcher, nor perhaps John Major, would have been selected by the old methods. Yet the extent of the change should not be exaggerated. The introduction of an electoral procedure has not fundamentally altered the nature of the party, but rather codified hitherto uncodified but widely accepted assumptions about the nature of Conservative leadership; and it has enabled the party to respond more effectively to the forces of popular discontent in the country. Nevertheless, from the point of view of leadership selection, the party has perhaps changed rather less during the course of the twentieth century than is commonly imagined.

The Conservative Party is the most electorally successful party in Britain, and one of the most electorally successful parties in any democracy. The leadership selection procedures adopted by the Conservative Party have played an important role in the party's electoral success. But, of course, a complete exploration of the party's success would have to take into account its political heritage as well as the skill with which it selects its leaders; it would have to consider the ethos of the party as well as its constitution; or, to put the matter a little differently, it would have to comprehend, not only the ghost of Peel, but also the legacy of Disraeli.

Notes and references

I am grateful to Andrew Adonis, Stuart Ball, Max Beloff, David Butler, Keith Middlemas, Enoch Powell, Michael Steed, Anthony Teasdale, and D. R. Thorpe for their critical comments on an earlier draft. But they are not to be implicated in either my arguments or my conclusions.

1 While valuable, the three books that have been published on the Conservative leadership do not wholly succeed in dispelling this mythology: Nigel Fisher (1991), *The Tory Leaders: Their Struggle for Power*, London; R. Shepherd (1991), *The Power Brokers: The Tory Party and its Leaders*, London; and Alan Watkins, (1991), *A Conservative Coup: The Fall of Margaret Thatcher*, London. The memoirs of Margaret Thatcher (1993), *The Downing Street Years*, London, and of Kenneth Baker (1993), *The Turbulent Years: My Life in Politics*, London, give a cabinet perspective; Alan Clark (1993), *Diaries*, London, adds little. R. M. Punnett (1992), *Selecting the Party Leader: Britain in Comparative Perspective*, Hemel Hempstead, is an important work, although marred by factual mistakes and a failure to consult some important sources, including the Conservative Political Archives (CPA), which describe how the method of electing the party leader was chosen in 1964–5.

2 Memo by Stamfordham, Windsor Castle, Royal Archives, K. 1814/1, in Robert Blake (1955), *The Unknown Prime Minister: The Life and Times of Andrew Bonar Law*, London, 460.

3 As is perhaps implied in R. T. McKenzie (1964), *British Political Parties*, rev. 2nd edn, London, 51.

4 The standard account is Blake, *The Unknown Prime Minister*, ch. 4, but David Dutton (1985), *Austen Chamberlain: Gentleman in Politics*, Bolton, is also worth consulting.

5 Bridgeman to Sanders, 7 Nov. 1911, in *Real Old Tory Politics: The Political Diaries of Robert Sanders, Lord Bayford, 1910–1935*, ed. John Ramsden, London, 1984, 35.

6 Sir Charles Petrie (1936), *Walter Long and his Times*, London, 171–2.

7 Balcarres diary, 9 Nov. 1911, in *The Crawford Papers*, ed. John Vincent, Manchester, 1984, 244.

8 Austen Chamberlain to Mary Chamberlain, 11 Nov. 1911, University of Birmingham Library, Austen Chamberlain MSS, AC/4/1/726.

9 Memo by Sandars, 'A Note of the Events Leading to Mr Balfour's Resignation', British Library, Balfour MSS, Add. 49767, fo. 289.

10 I owe this point to Dr Stuart Ball.

11 John Ramsden (1978), *The Age of Balfour and Baldwin 1902–1940*, London, 91.

12 Blake, *The Unknown Prime Minister*, 85.

13 Davidson to Blake, 19 May 1955, House of Lords RO, Blake MSS, in Cameron Hazlehurst (1974), 'The Baldwinite Conspiracy', *Historical Studies*, **16**, 189.

14 The standard account of how the decision to choose Baldwin was made is in Blake, *The Unknown Prime Minister*, ch. 32; but see also Hazlehurst, 'The Baldwinite Conspiracy'.

15 See Keith Kyle (1991), *Suez*, London, 533.
16 D. R. Thorpe (1980), *The Uncrowned Prime Minister*, London, 208.
17 The standard account of the 1957 leadership struggle can be found in the official biographies of Eden, Macmillan, and Butler: Robert Rhodes James (1986), *Anthony Eden*, London; Anthony Howard (1987), *Rab: The Life of R. A. Butler*, London; Alistair Horne (1988), *Macmillan, i. 1894–1956*, London.
18 Randolph Churchill (1964), *The Fight for the Tory Leadership*, London, 126.
19 See the letter from Prof. A. W. Bradley in *The Times*, 16 Jan. 1987, reporting a talk given at Cambridge by Sir Knox Cunningham, Macmillan's Parliamentary Private Secretary at the time; also Thorpe, *The Uncrowned Prime Minister*, 233, where it is also said that MPs were asked three questions – who was their first choice, who was their second choice, and the names of anyone they would oppose.
20 R. Bevins (1965), *The Greasy Pole*, London, 143.
21 Anthony Teasdale, interview with Lord Boyle, 1979: I am very grateful to Anthony Teasdale for allowing me to use his interview notes.
22 Philip Goodhart with Ursula Branston (1973), *The 1922: The Story of the Conservative Backbenchers' Parliamentary Committee*, London, 191.
23 Memo by Butler, 'Confidential Note', 31 July 1963, Trinity College Library, Cambridge, Butler MSS G40.
24 Goodhart, *The 1922*, 191.
25 Ibid., 195.
26 Enoch Powell, reviewing the final volume of Macmillan's memoirs, in *Spectator*, 13 Oct. 1973, 481.
27 A. Horne (1989), *Macmillan, ii. 1957–1986*, London, 582.
28 See the evidence of Martin Redmayne, the Chief Whip, in 'The Commons in Action', *Listener*, 19 Dec. 1963, 1013.
29 Goodhart, *The 1922*, 196.
30 Thorpe, *The Uncrowned Prime Minister*, 230. Mr Thorpe was told this by Reginald Maudling in 1974; I am grateful to Mr Thorpe for providing me with this information.
31 *Sunday Times*, 13 Oct. 1963.
32 Humphrey Berkeley (1972), *Crossing the Floor*, London, 28. It is often forgotten that Berkeley made his first proposal for a formal electoral procedure *before* Harold Macmillan's resignation.
33 Memo, Block to Fraser, 17 Nov. 1964, CPA CRD/3/22/10.
34 Ibid.; memo by Douglas, 'Selecting a Conservative Leader', 20 Nov. 1964, CRD/3/22/10.
35 Block to Fraser, 17 Nov. 1964, CRD/3/22/10.
36 Memo by Douglas, CRD/3/22/10.
37 Parliamentary candidates had also been present at the meeting in 1922 which chose Bonar Law as leader.
38 Memo by Douglas, CRD/3/22/10.
39 Shepherd, *The Power Brokers*, 75, 84.
40 H. C. Raikes MP, chairman of the Council of the National Union in 1873, in McKenzie, *British Political Parties*, 146.
41 Fisher, *The Tory Leaders*, 155.
42 Some criticized the provision that new candidates can enter the second ballot as a 'cowards' charter', but exactly the same provision had been accepted in 1965.
43 See e.g. Clark, *Diaries*, 368–9.
44 McKenzie, *British Political Parties*, 601 n. 2, draws this comparison.
45 Philip Williams (1982), 'Changing Styles of Labour Leadership', in Dennis Kavanagh

(ed.), *The Politics of the Labour Party*, London, 55.

46   McKenzie, *British Political Parties*, 145.

47   Ball, letter in *Independent*, 15 Nov. 1990.

48   Ramsden, *Age of Balfour and Baldwin*, 311.

49   Baldwin to Salisbury, 23 June 1930, Hatfield House, 4th Marquis of Salisbury MSS, S(4) 135/184, in John Barnes and David Nicholson (eds) (1988) *The Empire at Bay: The Leo Amery Diaries 1929–1945*, London, 27.

50   Stuart Ball (1988), *Baldwin and the Conservative Party: The Crisis of 1929–1931*, London, ch. 7.

51   Viscount Stuart (1967), *Within the Fringe*, London, 145–7; subsequent attempts to persuade Churchill to retire before 1955 also came to nothing.

52   McKenzie, *British Political Parties*, 81.

53   Fisher, *The Tory Leaders*, 121.

54   Private information.

55   J. H. Grainger (1974), 'Between Balfour and Baldwin', in Donald Southgate (ed.), *The Conservative Leadership 1832–1932*, London, 193.

56   Cited in Alan Thompson (1971), *The Day before Yesterday*, London, 196.

57   Iain Macleod (1964), 'The Tory Leadership', *Spectator*, 17 Jan.

58   Blanche Dugdale (1936), *Arthur James Balfour*, London, i. 259, ii. 55.

59   Selwyn Lloyd diary, 16 Oct. 1963, Churchill College, Cambridge, Selwyn Lloyd MSS 61.

60   Dugdale, *Arthur James Balfour*, ii. 54.

61   Blake, *The Unknown Prime Minister*, 457.

62   Elizabeth Longford (1983), *Elizabeth R.*, London, 229.

5 The 1992 General Election and the British Party System

The British General Election, held on 9 April 1992, resulted in a victory for the Conservatives, their fourth successive victory. This was the first occasion in Britain in which a single party had won four successive general elections since the Napoleonic era. At first sight, admittedly, this victory may not seem particularly striking. The Conservatives gained an overall majority of only 21 seats, the lowest Conservative overall majority this century, except for 1951, and the Conservative share of the vote in the United Kingdom – 41.9 per cent – was the lowest gained by any Conservative government this century, with the exception of 1922.

In reality, however, the Conservative victory is more significant than it at first sight appears. For, to look at the outcome solely in terms of seats is to disguise the scale of Labour's defeat. The Conservative lead over Labour was around 7.4 per cent, larger than at any general election since 1950, except for the elections of 1983 and 1987 when the Conservatives gained landslide victories. The Labour share of the vote – 34.5 per cent – was lower than it has ever been since its formation as a national party in 1918, except for 1931, 1983 and 1987. John Major in fact won the largest victory in terms of votes of any Conservative leader since the war with the exception of Margaret Thatcher.

Labour might, in fact, have done even worse in terms of seats, had it not enjoyed the benefit of a slightly higher swing in certain marginals. Had the swing to Labour been uniform, the party would have regained only around half of the 40 seats which it captured from the Conservatives. As it was, the pro-Labour swing was greater in certain marginals, accounting for around 26 of these 40 net gains. Primarily for this reason, the Conservatives did not enjoy the usual winner's bonus which the British electoral system has in the past conferred upon the leading party. In fact, the ratio of Conservative to Labour in seats – 53.5 to 43.2 – corresponds fairly closely with the ratio in votes – 52.2–42.6. It was the Liberal Democrats and the SNP who were disadvantaged by the electoral system, rather than Labour, while Plaid Cymru, because of the concentration of its vote in Welsh-speaking Wales, was actually slightly over-represented, enjoying 0.6 per cent of the seats for 0.3 per cent of the vote.

The Conservative victory, then, was a striking success for a party which had been in government for 13 years, and which went to the country during a time of recession. Its victory was even more striking in the light of trends in electoral opinion on the continent. It is, of course, dangerous to compare regional and local elections with the outcome of a national general election, but, nevertheless, elections on the continent – regional elections in Baden-Württemberg and Schleswig-Holstein, regional and local elections in France, and national elections in Belgium and Italy – seemingly reveal a generalized feeling of dissatisfaction with government, to the advantage either of parties of the radical Right – the Vlaams Blok, *Front National*, Republicans or German National Union – or, in Italy, of the federalist Lombard League. In Britain, of course, such developments are probably precluded by the first-past-the-post electoral system which inhibits political fragmentation, but, nevertheless, it is plausible to argue that fear of Labour outweighed dissatisfaction with the government as the prime motivating electoral force.

The scale of Labour's fourth successive defeat is underlined by the electoral position in which the 1992 election leaves the party. Labour is now second to the Conservatives in 186 seats; in only 42 of these, however, is the Conservative majority less than 4 000. However, even if Labour were to win all 42 of these seats at the next general election, it would still be 13 seats short of an overall majority. The party now needs a swing of just over 4.2 per cent to secure an overall majority, a higher swing than Labour has achieved since 1945, and a higher swing than has been achieved at any general election since 1945 except for the general elections of 1970 and 1979. If Labour no longer has quite such a mountain to climb as it did before the election, it is still some distance from the summit. It was hardly surprising, therefore, that in the immediate aftermath of the election, the question of realignment on the Left, comprising perhaps an electoral agreement with the Liberal Democrats and a reform of the electoral system, was once again raised.

The Labour Party's Winner-Take-All Stance

There is, indeed, a paradox at the heart of the 1992 general election. Seemingly, it revolved around economic management and the relative merits of tax cuts versus higher public spending. In practice, however, the room for economic manoeuvre which any incoming government would be able to enjoy was severely constrained by Britain's membership of the European

Monetary System, and the further fiscal and monetary commitments entered into at Maastricht. In reality, therefore, the deeper significance of the general election may lie in its consequences for the British party system, and perhaps also for the constitution.

For, if the first-past-the-post electoral system serves to inhibit the growth of splinter parties, it grossly exaggerates the support of the winning party in a particular region. Much was made in immediate post-election comment of the improved Conservative performance in Scotland, where there was a 3.5 per cent swing to the party, even though it still holds only 11 of the 72 Scottish seats. What has been insufficiently noticed, however, is the continued almost total absence of Conservative representation in the great industrial conurbations. Of the 54 constituencies within the cities of Birmingham, Bradford, Glasgow, Hull, Leeds, Liverpool, Manchester, Newcastle and Sheffield, the Conservatives hold just five. Conversely, despite securing around 20 per cent of the vote in the South of England outside London, Labour holds only 10 out of 157 seats in this region. In exaggerating the electoral disparity between North and South, the first-past-the-post system serves to emphasize the geographically uneven spread of economic and social advantage in the country, itself in large part a product of British industrial development. The party conflict at Westminster thus reflects deep-seated territorial tensions as much as, if not more than, differences in political philosophy.

The pattern revealed in the general elections of 1987 and 1992 seems a reversion to a pattern noticeable before the First World War, in the two general elections of January and December 1910. In those elections, the Conservatives won 107 and 103 respectively of the 155 seats in the South of England. 'Few Liberal members', one commentator wrote, 'can lead a settled life within an hour or two's train journey from London'.[1] In the North of England, in Wales and Scotland, by contrast, the Conservatives won only 56 and 53 seats respectively, out of 258. J. A. Hobson, the eminent sociologist, declared

> The two Englands to which the electoral map gives substantially accurate expression, may be described as a Producer's England and a Consumer's England, one England in which the well-to-do classes, from their numbers, wealth, leisure and influence, mould the external character of the civilisation and determine the habits, feelings and opinions of the people, the other England in which the structure and activities of large organised industries, carried on by great associated masses of artisans, factory hands and miners, are the dominating facts and forces.[2]

Territorial differences of the kind so apparent in the two general elections of 1910 and of 1987 and 1992, can best be understood in terms of the core/periphery terminology of Lipset and Rokkan.[3] In Britain, the renewal of this cleavage seems to have been the product of slow but cumulative electoral change since 1959, whereby the two major parties gained support in their already existing areas of strength, the Conservatives in the South of England, Labour in the industrial conurbations, Scotland and Wales. Such a pattern of electoral change antedates, therefore, the rise of Margaret Thatcher, but provided a foundation for the electoral triumph of Thatcherism. The general election of 1992 served only to emphasize the mould of electoral politics which had been set in the 1980s. It is a mould which cannot be explained by any of the current sociological or rational choice theories of electoral behaviour, since it rests upon a developmental process whose roots lie deep in the nation's history. Indeed, it would seem to suggest that historical patterns, long formed, are once again coming to determine electoral politics as they did before the First World War. Since the two general elections of 1910 were in fact the last to be held before the introduction of universal male suffrage and the consequent advance of the Labour Party, one might speculate that a class pattern of politics began, in the 1920s, to replace the core/periphery pattern, but that the latter is now once more coming to the fore as the former recedes. This highly speculative suggestion cannot, however, be defended without a considerable amount of further research.[4]

The geographical pattern of British politics, re-established in the 1980s, is bound to exert a profound effect upon the British party system. For it is not easy for Labour on its own to break the political hegemony of the Conservatives by invading their southern heartland. Indeed, one likely alternative to a majority Conservative government remains, as it has been throughout the 1980s, not a majority Labour government but a hung parliament. For Labour, as we have seen, requires a swing of 4.2 per cent to win an overall majority: a swing against the Conservatives of between 0.6 and 4.2 per cent would bring about a hung parliament. With a hung parliament, Labour would probably have to talk to the Liberal Democrats, and perhaps to the nationalists also if it is to be able to govern for more than a very short period of time. One might then ask why Labour should not negotiate with the Liberal Democrats before the election, rather than afterwards, especially if such negotiations might actually improve Labour's chances of winning.

Yet Labour remains a majoritarian party, sharing the presumptions of a winner-take-all system, while living within a political system in which such responses now seem counter-productive. Since 1931, Labour has been dominated by the ghost of Ramsay MacDonald, and has seen any form of power-sharing with another party in peacetime as a species of betrayal. After 1983, when the general election of that year had revealed an even division between the two anti-Conservative forces – Labour and the Liberal/SDP Alliance – much of Labour's efforts was concentrated, not on welding these two forces together so as to overthrow the Conservatives, but on relegating the Alliance to a firm third place, so that Labour could resume its unchallenged position as Her Majesty's Loyal Opposition. Indeed, those who designed the advertising campaign for Labour for the 1987 election congratulated themselves after it was all over, since 'We did achieve our objective of relegating the Alliance to a poor third place; that was the crucial achievement of the campaign. . . . We lost this election but we laid the groundwork for winning the next'.[5] Yet, after the 1987 election, Labour still needed a 6 per cent swing to become the largest party and a swing of 8 per cent to secure an overall majority, swings larger than have been secured by any party at any general election since 1945; and, since the Alliance was, after the 1987 general election, second to the Conservatives in 230 seats, but to Labour in only 31 seats, it might have made more sense for Labour to regard the Alliance as a second anti-Conservative party, an alternative but also complementary to, Labour, not as an antagonist from the 'bourgeois' camp.

Labour's winner-take-all stance lies in great contrast to the experience of the social democratic parties of the continent, living as they do either with systems of proportional representation that require power-sharing and coalition government, or, as in France, with a two-ballot electoral system which required cooperation between Socialists and Communists if the Left was to have any chance of overthrowing Gaullist hegemony. Such electoral systems not only require cooperation between political parties, they also facilitate it either through the two-ballot mechanism which allows the first ballot to be in effect a primary by which the two parties of the Left could, in the 1970s, test their relative strength; or through multi-member constituencies within which parties can share representation; or, as in Germany, through a two-vote system by which, for example, the SPD could ask its supporters in the 1970s to use their constituency vote for the SPD, but to 'lend' their list vote to the FDP, the SPD's coalition partner. It was this arrangement which allowed the social-liberal coalition to govern for 13 years, between 1969 and 1982, even though the SPD vote was lower than the CDU/CSU vote in every election except that of 1972.

The position taken by the Labour Party since 1931 would make sense only if the other political parties and the political system itself were basically antagonistic, as representing the 'capitalist system', rather in the way that the SPD saw the German political system as deeply antagonistic before 1914. At that time, paradoxically, Labour, by contrast, was perfectly prepared to work with other parties. Indeed, its early development was only possible because of a secret pact with the Liberals – the so-called Gladstone–MacDonald pact of 1903. Later, during the 1920s, Ramsay MacDonald sought to drive the Liberals out of the political system, hoping that progressive Liberals would join Labour so that all of the forces of progress would be united within one party. By 1930, however, it was clear that such a project could not succeed;

and MacDonald, perforce, entered into discussion with the Liberals, to whom he was forced to concede the alternative note. But hopes of a new 'Progressive alliance' were dashed by the financial crisis of 1931, which swept Labour from office and gave the party its deep-seated distrust of power-sharing.

In 1977–8, however, Labour was again forced to enter into a power-sharing arrangement with another party – the Lib-Lab pact. But James Callaghan, rather than seeking to make of the pact a basis for a more long-term arrangement, preferred to seek an overall majority on his own in 1978–9, while, during the early 1980s, Labour's shift to the Left made any contemplation of power-sharing arrangements with another party a form of heresy.

More recently, however, voices have been heard within the Labour Party suggesting that Labour's policy of isolation was self-defeating. Such voices have on the whole been heard at the grassroots, rather than among the Labour leadership and also in journals such as the *New Statesman*. They have been assisted by developments both in local government and in Scotland.

The local elections of 1985 rendered the majority of county councils in England and Wales hung. A number of Labour councils soon forced a modification of the party's official policy of 'no deals, no pacts, no coalitions', and the years after 1985 saw the development of an 'expanding common ground between Labour and Liberal Democrat groups over policy priorities and expenditure levels rooted in a shared antipathy to Thatcherism. . .'[6] This policy cooperation even seems to have led to informal pre-election pacts between Labour and the Liberal Democrats in the 1989 county council elections, a development to which John Cunningham, Labour's Shadow Environment Secretary, turned 'a Nelsonian blind eye' – 'if local parties want to make deals, it is a matter for them. But there is no question of encouraging them'.[7]

In Scotland, a Constitutional Convention was established in March 1989, to press for a Scottish parliament within the United Kingdom. Labour was prepared to work with the Liberal Democrats in the Convention, and was even prepared, in the interests of acquiring the support of a wide swathe of Scottish opinion, to depart from the first-past-the-post system for elections to a Scottish parliament. It was, indeed, largely as a result of the attitudes of the Labour Party in Scotland that the Plant Committee came into being to review electoral systems for the Scottish parliament, as well as for the reformed second chamber which Labour was proposing, and for the House of Commons.

Unsuccessful Liberal Democrat Strategies

Labour, then, having made the mistake of acting as a potentially majoritarian party during a period in which the assumptions of the political system were working against it, has been coming to question these assumptions, albeit at a glacially slow rate. But the Liberal Democrats also, despite their commitment to proportional representation and coalition government, failed to understand the significance of the changed party system of the 1980s.

Since the time of the Liberal revival in the late 1950s, many Liberals have understood realignment as a means by which they might replace Labour as the main party on the Left, rather in the way that Labour, in the 1920s, had replaced the Liberals. Liberals tended to think of themselves, indeed, not as belonging to a minority party taking their place within a multi-party system, but rather as belonging to a potentially majoritarian party, temporarily displaced from its rightful place in the party system. For this reason, they tended to be sceptical of power-sharing or coalition. In his *Memoirs*, Jo Grimond complained that, in the 1960s, 'The prospect of coalition . . . scared Liberals out of their wits', and, paradoxically, those who cried the loudest for electoral reform were 'also the most adamant against any coalition with other Parties' although 'if electoral reform led to the results for which Liberals hoped and which statistics foretold, that is fifty to seventy MPs to which our vote entitled us, then if government was to be carried on, coalitions of some sort would often be essential'.[8] Jeremy Thorpe, Grimond's successor, refused to countenance discussion of coalition between the general elections of February and October 1974, while in 1977, David Steel had to exert all his influence to persuade Liberals to accept even the very limited parliamentary arrangements involved in the Lib-Lab pact.

The Liberal strategy of replacing Labour was dealt a crushing blow when Harold Wilson succeeded, albeit narrowly, in winning the 1964 general election. By 1977, the Liberals were propping up a Labour government rather than seeking to replace it. But the realignment strategy surfaced again with the formation of the Liberal/SDP Alliance in 1983, and, with the Conservatives benefiting from the Falklands effect while Labour remained in turmoil, it appeared for a while quite plausible. The aim of replacing Labour was revived, even after the collapse of the Alliance, by Paddy Ashdown during his campaign for the leadership of the Liberal Democrats in 1988. Yet, by then, this strategy had no chance of success.

For the outcome of the general election of 1987 showed that Labour was impregnable in its areas of electoral strength. Not only did Labour succeed in raising its vote to 31 per cent, while the Alliance fell back to 23 per cent, but the Alliance did worst electorally in the Labour heartland, which was where Labour's recovery was strongest. The general elections of 1983 and 1987 showed that the combination of the first-past-the-post electoral system and the distribution of its electoral support entrenched Labour within its heartland, so that it could not be broken even when, as in 1983, its vote fell to 27 per cent. After the 1992 general election, the Liberal Democrats had become, even more than the Alliance after 1987, an anti-Conservative party. A 4 per cent swing from the Conservatives to the Liberal Democrats would bring the Liberal Democrats an extra 14 seats, while an equivalent swing from Labour to the Liberal Democrats would bring them no extra seats at all, the most marginal Labour/Liberal Democrat seat being Chesterfield, where a 5.2 per cent swing is needed.

Electoral Pacts

The opposition parties, therefore, find themselves deadlocked. Labour, although it cannot be broken, needs a large swing to defeat the Conservatives. The Liberal Democrats can, at best, make minor incursions into the Conservative heartland; they can no longer hope to replace Labour, much less 'break the mould' of British politics, the hope of the Alliance in the early 1980s. Conceptually, the Liberal Democrats may be as much anti-Labour as they are anti-Conservative. The British electoral system, however, is a geographical system, not a conceptual one; and, for as long as geography remains fundamental, that is, for as long as Britain refuses to adopt proportional representation, the Liberal Democrats find themselves positioned inevitably as an anti-Conservative party, complementary to, and not competitive with, Labour. The Liberal Democrats are complementary to Labour, although much weaker electorally, and may be able to win support which Labour is unable to attract. As Heath, Jowell and Curtice have suggested, the Liberal vote, far from representing 'a rather amorphous collection of individuals, without any particular unifying beliefs', has come to be an ideologically structured vote, whose supporters adhere to a different set of beliefs from those of Labour.[9] It this suggestion is correct, then the facts of psephology point unequivocally to an electoral pact between the two anti-Conservative parties. Yet it is unlikely that an overall national pact between Labour and the Liberal Democrats will be achieved before the next general election, even if psephological logic points in that direction.

An alternative outcome would be a series of local arrangements, perhaps within a regional framework, negotiated by constituency associations with the encouragement of party headquarters. That was what seems to have occurred between the Conservative and Liberal Parties in 1951. There was no national pact, but Conservative constituency associations were encouraged to make deals with Liberals where these would assist the anti-Labour cause. On 28 September 1950, Lord Woolton, Chairman of the Conservative Party, had written to Lord Teviot, leader of the National Liberals:

I have had two long talks with Clement Davies [leader of the independent Liberals] who is firmly of the opinion that it would be inadvisable that the head-quarters of our parties should seek to enter into any agreement. He thinks that such efforts should be conducted on the constituency level, and it would be best if they arose spontaneously. That is also very emphatically the view of most of those who hold office in the Conservative Party who have discussed this problem with me.[10]

Following the 1951 general election, Churchill offered the Ministry of Education to Clement Davies, a signal perhaps of the extent of cooperation in the period immediately preceding the election.

In the general election of 1951, seven Liberal candidates, and five of the six Liberal MPs elected in 1951, faced no Conservative opponent. Indeed, when the Conservatives issued their first list of prospective candidates on 1 October 1951, these included the Liberals in all seats in which they were unopposed by Conservatives![11] In two seats – Dundee W. and Greenock – there were 'taking turns' pacts in 1950 and 1951, by which one party was allowed to represent the anti-socialist cause in 1950, and if it failed to win, the other party was to have its turn in 1951. It is arguable indeed that the Conservatives would not have secured an overall majority in 1951 without such local arrangements with the Liberals. The median swing in seats where there were straight fights both in 1950 and 1951 was 0.4 per cent, insufficient to secure an overall majority for the Conservatives. It may be that one of the factors ensuring that the 1950 Liberal vote went disproportionately to the Conservatives was in fact the known existence of local arrangements, whose effects could have been felt well beyond the constituencies in which they operated.

A limited pact of the 1951 type, but this time between the Liberal Democrats and Labour, was to be advocated shortly after the 1987 general election by the psephologist Michael Steed, who believed that it should cover '30 or so carefully selected seats on either side' which 'could be presented as a form of insurance, thus not inhibiting or damaging a Labour thrust for outright victory'. Such a limited pact, Steed argued, would have little effect with a Conservative vote of over 40 per cent, but if the Conservative vote 'came down to about 40 per cent, it would decide whether or not we had a Conservative government in the mid-1990s'.[12] In fact, it may be that Steed was too cautious in his estimate of the effect of a pact. For its consequences might have been felt not just in the constituencies in which it operated, but also in other constituen-cies, particularly neighbouring ones, where it might have had the effect of per-suading Liberal Democrats to transfer their votes disproportionately to Labour, and Labour to transfer their votes to the Liberal Democrats in con-stituencies where their own party candidates were lying a poor third.

Europe: The Achilles' Heel of the Conservatives?

Faced with a divided opposition, and an opposition, moreover, accepting rules of the game which handicap its chances of achieving power, a continuation of Conservative hegemony can by no means be excluded from consideration. Nor indeed is such one-party hegemony unusual among democracies. On the contrary, as R. M. Punnett showed in 1981, it was the alternating governments of the 1960s and 1970s which were unusual in terms of the comparative experience of democracies in different parts of the world. 'In experiencing life without a dominant party', Punnett then wrote, 'Britain is unique among European and Anglo-American democracies'.[13] In 20 of 21 democracies studied, with Britain being the only exception, one party had held power either alone or in coalition for a least two-thirds of the post-war period and in all but six of the countries studied, for over three-quarters of the period.[14] It should not be assumed, therefore, that there is any natural force, any automatic 'swing of the pendulum' likely to propel the opposition parties back into power. The experience of the 1980s and 1990s is more natural in terms of democratic experience than was that of the 1960s and 1970s.

In such a situation, opposition is as likely to come from within the dominant party as from the parties comprising the opposition. One likely source of conflict within the ruling Conservative Party looks to be the European Community. The Community has already been responsible for seismic shifts in British politics. It was responsible for a major constitutional innovation, Britain's first nationwide referendum, in 1975. It was one of the main issues behind the split in the Labour Party in 1981 which led to the formation of the SDP; and it was a prime factor in the resignations of Nigel Lawson in 1989 and Sir Geoffrey Howe in 1990, this latter resignation precipitating the fall of Margaret Thatcher from the premiership.

Until the late 1980s, it was the Labour Party whose internal cohesion seemed most in danger from the development of the Community; in the 1990s, by contrast, it may be the Conservatives, the party, since Disraeli, of English nationalism, which suffers more acute strains. It is the Conservative Party which has always seen itself as the guardian of the British constitution, whose ethos is that of parliamentary sovereignty and adversarial politics. The ethos of the Community, by contrast, is quite different; it is one of power-sharing, proportional representation and consensual politics. Moreover, under Margaret Thatcher, the Conservative Party abandoned the policies of interventionism which had characterized it during the years of Macmillan and Heath, and moved in the direction of free market policies and deregulation. This stance seemed to align the Conservatives more with the Republicans in the United States than with their Christian Democrat counterparts in the Community.

A growing divergence of view between Conservatives and Christian Democrats culminated in the conflict over the European Community's Social Charter, which became the Social Action Programme, and is now, following the Maastricht Treaty, referred to as the social chapter. For Christian Democrats and Social Democrats alike, the Social Charter was designed to complement the free-market, deregulatory measures, which would produce the Single Market, thus ensuring that those excluded from the benefits of the Market – for example, the low-paid, part-time workers and pensioners – would also achieve gains. As Jacques Delors told the TUC Conference in September 1988, 'It is impossible to build Europe only on deregulation . . . The internal market should be designed to benefit each and every citizen of the Community'; while, speaking the same month to German trade unionists and business executives in Cologne, he called for a 'new Keynes or Beveridge' to draw up Community plans for social welfare, redistribution and employment. Thus the Social Charter was, in the words of David Martin, the British Labour MEP, an attempt 'to turn the European *Economic* Community into a European Community where all citizens would benefit from the Single Market'.[15] The social chapter was, however, rejected by the Conservatives, both under Margaret Thatcher and under John Major, and became at Maastricht the subject of a separate protocol on social policy, by which, in formal terms, the other eleven members of the Community, excluding Britain, 'opted in' although the political reality, of course, is that it is Britain which has 'opted out' of the chapter.

Such an approach carries with it, however, the danger of marginalizing the Conservatives within the Community. In March 1989, James Elles, a Conservative MEP, declared that 'At a time when the Iron Curtain is beginning to come down between East and West, an iron drawbridge is being drawn up between Britain and Europe.'[16] In the European Parliament, the Conservatives remained detached from the main groups of the centre-right, and in particular, from the European People's Party (EPP), the Christian Democrat grouping whose constitution commits it to a federal Europe. After the elections to the European Parliament of 1989, when the Spanish Partido Popular left the European Democratic Group (EDG) for the EPP, the EDG consisted solely of 32 British Conservatives and 2 Danish Conservatives. It was a national party grouping seeking to operate within a supranational parliament.

The views of Conservative MEPs, exposed as they were to the working of Community institutions, came increasingly to diverge from their Westminster counterparts. In particular, Conservative MEPs sought alliance with the EPP, the second largest political group in the European Parliament, so that they could play a larger role in the Parliament's activities. On 28 February 1992, Sir Christopher Prout, leader of the European Democratic

Group, sent a letter on behalf of members of the Group to the chairman of the EPP Group, seeking to join it as allied members, in which the EDG accepted the EPP's 'basic political views'. Largely unnoticed during the British electoral campaign, the EDG was accepted *provisionally* by the EPP. Leo Tindemans, president of the EPP Group, said that the members of the Conservative Group in the European Parliament had accepted the EPP's programme which, it must be remembered, involves a commitment to a federal Europe as well as to the social chapter. The German Christian Democrat, Bernhard Saelzer, declared that the accession of the EDG would reinforce the pro-European forces in the United Kingdom. 'He felt that the Conservatives would now also adopt pro-European positions concerning the Social Charter and Europe's future role'. The EPP decided, however, to look again at the arrangement agreed between it and the EDG, 'at the end of Parliament's current term of office and in the light of experience and of the election programme'.[17]

It is doubtful if the full implications of this agreement have been understood by Conservatives in Britain. Indeed, on the very same day, 7 April, that the EDG requested accession to the EPP group, British Conservatives in the European Parliament were abstaining on the vote reaffirming the Maastricht Treaty, since the resolution criticized the British government for its failure to commit itself to monetary union and to the Community's social policy. Conservatives in the European Parliament did not wish to be seeming to dissociate themselves from John Major's government at the end of a hard-fought election campaign when the outcome was still very much in doubt. Moreover, speaking at Cambridge on 7 February 1992, the Foreign Secretary, Douglas Hurd, had defended Maastricht in terms which the EPP would have found wounding, as a significant 'check for federalist ambitions'.

The commitments made by British Conservatives in the European Parliament, and, more generally, the ongoing development of the European Community, whose culture is so strongly opposed to the ethos of the Conservative Party, is likely to offer a far greater challenge to the cohesion and hegemony of the party than anything that the opposition parties will be able to provide. Until the freezing of party politics in the 1920s, dominant parties in Britain lost their hegemony through party splits as much as through electoral defeat – the Home Rule split of 1886 rendered the Liberals ineffective as a governing party for 20 years, the Tariff Reform split of 1903 did the same to the Conservatives, while the Asquith/Lloyd George split of 1916 finally destroyed the Liberal Party as a governing force. It would be foolish to speculate on how the development of the Community might affect the internal cohesion of the Conservative Party. Europe, after all, was a subject conspicuous by its absence from the electoral campaign; the two major parties tacitly agreed not to discuss it, since each was split on the issue.

Seemingly, therefore, Europe is now a dormant issue in British politics; and yet, in the long run, might not the future of the British party system depend more upon the logic of our membership of the Community than upon the vicissitudes of internal politics?

Notes and references

1   E. N. Mozley (1910), 'The Political Heptarchy: An Analysis of Seven General Elections', *Contemporary Review*, 405.
2   J. A. Hobson (1910), 'The General Election. A Sociological Interpretation', *Sociological Review*, 112–13.
3   S. M. Lipset and S. Rokkan (1967), Introduction to Lipset and Rokkan (eds), *Party Systems and Voter Alignments: Cross-National Perspectives*, Collier-Macmillan.
4   See Chapter 6.
5   Philip Gould, Peter Herd and Chris Powell (1989), 'The Labour Party's Campaign Communications', in Ivor Crewe and Martin Harrop (eds), *Political Communications: The General Election Campaign of 1987*, Cambridge University Press, 86.
6   Steve Leach and Chris Game (1992), 'Local Government: The Decline of the One-Party State', in Gareth Smyth (ed.), *Refreshing the Parts: Electoral Reform and British Politics*, Lawrence and Wishart, 153. See also Steve Leach and Chris Game (1989), *Cooperation and Conflict*, London, Common Voice.
7   February 1989, quoted in Leach and Game, op. cit., 154.
8   Jo Grimond (1979), *Memoirs*, London, Heinemann, 211–12.
9   Anthony Heath, Roger Jowell and John Curtice (1985), *How Britain Votes*, Oxford, Pergamon Press, 142.
10   Woolton Papers, Bodleian Library, Oxford.
11   David Butler (1952), *The British General Election of 1951*, London, Macmillan, 94.
12   Michael Steed (1987), 'How to Nobble the Thatcher Vote', *New Stateman*, 27 November.
13   R. M. Punnett (1981), 'Alternating Governments: the Inefficient Secret of British Politics?', *Studies in Public Policy*, No. 93, Centre for Studies in Public Policy, University of Strathclyde, 1.
14   Punnett, *op. cit.*, 11, 12.
15   David Martin (1992), 'Somebody Does it Better: PR in the Building of the EC', in Gareth Smyth (ed.), *Refreshing the Parts: Electoral Reform and British Politics*, London, Lawrence and Wishart, 137–8.
16   Cited in *Agence Europe*, 26 March 1989.
17   *Agence Europe*, 9 April 1992.

6 Lessons of History: Core and Periphery in British Electoral Behaviour, 1910–92

(with William H. Field)[1]

Most theories of electoral behaviour rest on models of voter socialization, the impact of the external economy, or some combination of the two. They range from long-term models based on party identification and tradition to short-term economic models in which rational voters evaluate economic performance as a prelude to making a *de novo* choice at each general election. Each group of models contains a major flaw, however: party identification models have found it difficult to explain abrupt changes in party support; while economic models, whether predicated on unemployment, inflation, house prices, economic optimism, or any number of other indicators, have seemed to need revision after each general election. Furthermore, neither of these types of explanation has successfully accounted for the growing north/south divide in recent British general elections. Any analysis of recent electoral change in Britain must take into account the existence of a specific core–periphery dimension, a product no doubt of the historical expansion of the British state and the impact of that expansion on the territory of modern Britain.

After the British general election of 1987, a number of commentators drew attention to the key role played by socio-geographical factors operating across groups of constituencies. The most striking of these contrasts was that between north-west and south-east Britain, with Devon and Cornwall appearing to behave rather differently from either.

But, even before the 1987 election, Steed had argued in a prescient article that the core–periphery cleavage between south-east and north-west Britain was 'the most significant simple dichotomy in political Britain today' (Steed, 1986: S99). Indeed, socio-geographical factors seem to have operated in a cumulative fashion in Britain since the late 1950s; at almost every general election since 1959, the Conservatives have done better in the south-east, i.e.

Table 6.1   Mean change in percentage share of the vote, 1983–7

	Conservative	Labour	Liberal/SDP Alliance	No. of seats
NW Britain	−2.7	+6.5	−4.2	273
SE Britain	+1.2	+1.6	−2.5	344
Devon and Cornwall	−3.1	+2.6	+0.7	16

Source: Curtice and Steed, 1988, p. 320. The south-east region includes the whole of the South of England and the Midlands, excluding Devon and Cornwall.

the Midlands, East Anglia, and the south-east and south-west regions, excluding Devon and Cornwall. For its part, Labour has done better in the north-west, i.e. elsewhere in Great Britain, again excluding Devon and Cornwall. Moreover, this effect was particularly marked in the recent elections of 1979, 1983 and 1987. The net effect of this cumulative change has been a decline in the Conservative vote in the north-west from 50.4 per cent in 1955 to 33.8 per cent in 1987 while Conservative support in the south-east has declined much more modestly, from 52.5 per cent to 46.7 per cent over the same period.

The general election of 1992 saw a partial reversal of this pattern, the swing against the Conservatives being smaller in the north-west than in the south-east (Curtice and Steed, 1992). A number of different explanations for this partial reversal have been offered. The most natural explanation relates it to the contrast in the economic experiences of the two halves of Britain between 1987 and 1992, the recession and the collapse of the housing market affecting the south-east more severely than the north-west. There are powerful arguments against such an explanation, however, and the reasons for the partial reversal of the long-term pattern since 1959 will, no doubt, form a topic of psephological debate for some time to come (for an overview of the debate on the north-south divide, see Curtice and Steed, 1992; R. J. Johnston *et al.*, 1988; Curtice, 1988; Heath *et al.*, 1991; and Pattie *et al.*, 1992).

Even after the 1992 general election, however, the distribution of seats in the House of Commons between north-west and south-east Britain was highly skewed. In north-west Britain, the Conservatives had 70 seats to Labour's 183; in the south-east, by contrast, the pattern was reversed: 254

Conservative seats to 87 Labour seats.

What has been little noticed is the extent to which the geographical pattern established in the 1980s replicates that of the years before the First World War and, in particular, the two general elections of 1910. In the two 1910 elections, the Unionists (i.e. Conservatives and Liberal Unionists) gained roughly the same number of seats as their main opponents, the Liberals. In the January election they won 273 seats compared with the Liberals' 275; in the December election both parties gained 272 seats with the remaining seats in each election won by Labour and Irish Nationalist candidates. As Table 6.2 shows, the Unionists won the bulk of constituencies in south-east Britain in both elections but less than a quarter of the seats in the north-west.

Table 6.2   Seats won by Conservative and Unionist candidates, 1910–92

	NW Britain	*SE Britain*	*Devon/ Cornwall*
January 1910	56 (22%)	182 (65%)	7 (35%)
December 1910	62 (24%)	170 (60%)	13 (65%)
1951	110 (40%)	189 (59%)	13 (87%)
1955	117 (43%)	205 (62%)	12 (93%)
1987	81 (30%)	280 (82%)	14 (88%)
1992	70 (26%)	254 (74%)	12 (75%)

This striking similarity in the geographical pattern of elections over a period of 80 years deserves more attention than it has so far received. It suggests, as does the work of André Siegfried and his school in France, that, behind the processes of short-term electoral swing, there are long-term spatially distributed factors in voting behaviour that condition the electoral framework within which the parties operate. Figures 6.1, 6.2 and 6.3 show that there is some similarity in the geographical distribution of the Unionist/Conservative vote in the general elections of January 1910 and 1992, where support was greatest in the south-east of the country. In 1951, by contrast, when class polarization was at its height, Conservative support was much more widespread, with Lancashire, southern and eastern Scotland, and much of Yorkshire voting Conservative. In this election, the Conservatives captured 40 per cent of the seats in the north compared to 22 per cent in

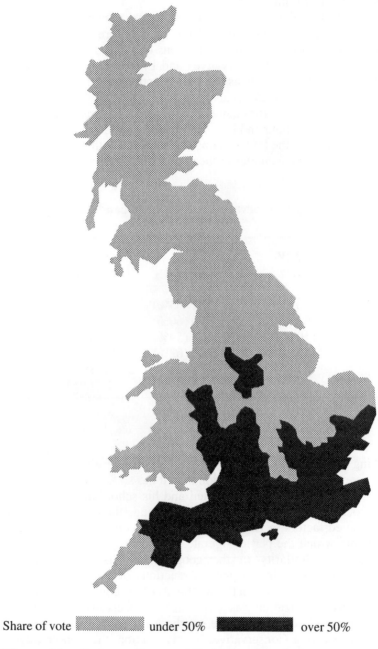

Share of vote [under 50%]   under 50%   [over 50%]   over 50%

Figure 6.1   Conservative and Unionist vote, January 1910

Share of vote ░░░░░░ under 50% ████████ over 50%

Figure 6.2 Conservative vote, 1951

Share of vote ░░░░░░ under 50% ████████ over 50%

Figure 6.3   Conservative vote, 1992

January 1910 and 26 per cent in 1992 (see Table 6.2). The maps also hint that, both in 1910 and 1992, there was a core–periphery cleavage at work. Thus, our basic hypothesis is that the similarity between the geographical distribution of the vote for right and left between the two general elections of 1910 and the general elections of 1987 and 1992 indicates the persistence of a cleavage of the core–periphery type. (For discussion of the core–periphery cleavage, see Lipset and Rokkan (1967); Rokkan and Urwin (1983); Mény and Wright (1985); and Bogdanor (1987, 85–7). Moreover, the two general elections of 1910 were the last to be held before the introduction of universal male suffrage in 1918 and the advance of Labour to major party status. Thus it may be that in the 1920s and 1930s a class pattern of politics replaced the core–periphery pattern of previous years but that the former pattern is once more coming to the fore as the class cleavage loses its hold on the British electorate.

The evidence suggests a core–periphery cleavage rather than a cleavage based on ethnicity and a cultural division of labour because northern England seems to share the same electoral pattern as Scotland – anti-Unionist in 1910, balanced between Labour and the Conservatives in the 1950s, but once again strongly anti-Conservative in 1987 and 1992. Thus Hechter's (1975) approach which confines the periphery to the 'Celtic fringe' is hardly adequate. The approach offered by Steed (1986) which puts northern England, Devon and Cornwall in the periphery, as well as Scotland and Wales, and of course Ireland, has far more explanatory power. Although ethnicity is not a dividing line between the core and the periphery in England, survey data suggest that residents of the English periphery share many of the same attitudes towards London as do their Scottish and Welsh neighbours (Miller, 1977; Steed, 1986).

Electoral behaviour in Britain has been influenced, therefore, not only by immediate sociological or economic factors, but also by older historical and developmental cleavages first analysed by Seymour Martin Lipset and Stein Rokkan.

Britain and the Lipset–Rokkan Freezing Hypothesis

Stein Rokkan's model of European political development suggests that mass politics in modern European democracies has been structured by four fundamental cleavages (Lipset and Rokkan, 1967). Two of these four cleavages derive from the national revolutions as the central nation-building élites came into conflict both with peripheral cultures and with the power and privileges of the church. The second pair of cleavages derives from the industrial revolution. The struggle between landed interests and industrial and urban interests emerged before the mobilization of the mass electorate, but the class cleavage between the owners and workers did not find political expression until universal male suffrage became a reality. In almost every country in Western Europe, this occurred in the first two decades of the twentieth century; in Britain, it came in 1918.

In the latter part of nineteenth-century Britain, the Liberal/Conservative battle had been fought primarily along the religious and land-capital cleavages without substantial class mobilization (Blewett, 1972; Wald, 1983). In 1886, the hitherto dominant Liberal party had split on the Irish Home Rule issue. This gave increasing salience to the core–periphery cleavage as electors in south-east England, Lincolnshire, and the Midlands rejected Home Rule. Excluding the aberrant Liberal landslide of 1906, Unionists won between 61 per cent and 81 per cent of the English seats south of a line from the Humber to the Dee between 1886 and 1910, far more than they were able to win elsewhere in Britain. However, the resolution of many of the religious issues during the First World War reduced the salience of the cleavage, and, during the 1920s, the structure of party competition came to be dominated by class (Miller, 1977). To be sure, geographical differences persisted after 1922, particularly in Scotland and Wales, but these were much reduced from the earlier period (Miller, 1983).

In 1967, Lipset and Rokkan argued that political parties mobilize new electors around existing cleavages. Once the entire adult population could vote there were no new groups to mobilize around new cleavages. Consequently, 'the [European] party systems of the 1960s reflect, with few but significant exceptions, the cleavage structure of the 1920s' (Lipset and Rokkan, 1967: 50). In Britain, the freezing of the party system followed the replacement of the Liberals by Labour as the main party of the left and led to a party system in the 1950s and early 1960s characterized by two overwhelmingly dominant parties almost evenly matched vying over a very stable electorate with a high level of party identification.

Many observers have argued, however, that there has been an unfreezing process in operation since the 1960s. There has been a fall in the very high levels of party identification characterizing the 1950s and early 1960s, and this is held to signify dealignment (Särlvik and Crewe, 1983; Alt, 1984). Moreover, the lack of substantial regional electoral distinctiveness characteristic of the 1950s has increasingly given way to a geographical polarization, with important consequences for the electoral system (Miller, 1983; Curtice and Steed, 1982; 1986; 1992; Johnston *et al.*, 1988). Inglehart (1984) has gone so far as to suggest that a new electoral alignment has emerged to complement if not replace the class cleavage.

From the perspective of 1992, however, the evidence for dealignment looks increasingly weak. The surge in voting volatility of 1974 has receded and looks now to have been a by-product of the rebirth of the Liberal party rather than a decomposition of the class cleavage *per se* (Bartolini and Mair, 1990: 116; Field, 1992). As an alternative to the hypothesis of dealignment, therefore, Heath *et al.* (1991) have suggested that a change in the structure of society – the rise of a new class of primarily left-leaning service employees – has led to a partial realignment of the left. Heath *et al.* argue that this realignment has been aided by the 1981 split in the Labour party. But the persistent and stable electoral strength of the Conservatives since 1979 suggests that there has not been a realignment *across* the class cleavage.

Although Heath *et al.* have done much to challenge the unfreezing or dealignment argument, their approach is unable to explain the variation between north and south. Using the three-level model of social class and adding controls for social origins, union membership, housing tenure, the 'neighbourhood effect' and income and unemployment measures, they are able to reduce the regional effect on the vote, but not to eliminate it.

A general study of net volatility across European electorates from 1885 to 1985 finds that volatility has not increased since the Second World War, and that in fact volatility across the class cleavage line has been decreasing (Bartolini and Mair, 1990). Bartolini and Mair conclude that, far from there having been dealignment, there has been a hardening of the class cleavage over the last 50 years that fits very neatly into Lipset and Rokkan's freezing hypothesis: 'there has been no substantial and sustained growth in electoral mobility across the class-cleavage boundary; in these terms at least, the cleavage remains frozen' (Bartolini and Mair, 1990: 119). The authors generalize this conclusion to suggest that there has been little change in the cleavage structures of European democracies. Their discussion ignores the changing geography of the vote in Britain, and so they are unable to explain the growth of the north/south divide. Other explanations, such as those by Johnston *et al.* (1988), Pattie *et al.* (1992), or McAllister and Studlar (1992) are not successful in explaining the divide either.

The focus on the class cleavage in the literature is understandable, since the freezing hypothesis concerns itself primarily (but not exclusively) with the development of party systems following mass mobilization across this cleavage. However, in presenting aggregate data on successive elections at the national level, Bartolini and Mair ignore two potential challenges to their contention that cleavages remain frozen. The first challenge is creeping change: their calculation of net volatility between successive elections measures changes in electoral support but not the direction of change or the trend across several elections. If, for example, over the course of several elections, support for the left had waned (or waxed) at a rate equal to the average net volatility of the preceding period and then stabilized at a level substantially different from its previous level, it would be difficult to assert that the cleavages had remained frozen. Indeed, were the rate of change slow enough, support for the left could increase to 100 per cent or fall to zero without affecting the volatility calculation. In Britain, the combined level of support for the left (Labour and Liberal) has increased from around 45–50 per cent in the 1950s to 50–60 per cent in the 1980s. Some form of realignment across the cleavage may have occurred.

A second challenge comes from breaking national results down to the regional or constituency level and examining the geographical dimension of the cleavage pattern. Rokkan (1970) suggested that geographical stability was a key indicator of the freezing hypothesis. Curtice and Steed (1988: 330–3) have shown that there has been a dramatic shift in the regional distribution of support for left and right in Britain since 1955. Within the framework of continued stability of the class cleavage, neither Heath *et al.* nor Bartolini and Mair are able to explain this shift in electoral strength. These changes in the regional distribution of support again suggest that a realignment that does not fit into the class cleavage model has taken place.

In this chapter we seek to test whether a core–periphery cleavage, similar to that before the First World War, has re-emerged. We do this by examining the geographical distribution of the vote in the general elections of 1987 and 1992, and comparing them to two elections that were held at the height of uniform national swing and two-party dominance – 1951 and 1955. We then compare them to the two elections of 1910. Our methodology is presented in an appendix.

Data Collection

Geographical continuity of party support is an essential element of the Rokkan model: parties renew their core clienteles from generation to generation by recruiting in the same social milieux from which they have gained preponderant support in the past (Lipset and Rokkan, 1967: 50; Rokkan, 1970). For this reason, a major alteration in the geography of support would suggest that there has either been an alteration in the geography of the socioeconomic characteristics of the population or that the alteration has been in the relative importance of a particular cleavage.

In terms of the six general elections under study here, high levels of correlation in the geographical distribution of the vote across different elections would suggest the persistence of the same cleavage patterns; conversely, lower levels of correlation would suggest that the salience of cleavage patterns has changed. Our method is similar to that of Pomper (1967), where a correlation matrix is presented to show stable, persistent voter coalitions across a series of consecutive elections.

We divided Britain into 42 county-equivalent units (Table 6A.4) with approximately equal boundaries over the elections in our sample. The basis of the division was the county since constituency boundary changes are by law required to respect county and London borough lines (Butler, 1992; Mortimore, 1992). The major redrawing of counties in 1972 complicated our efforts to create exact geographical units over the time period, but we finally emerged with 42, units with minor boundary problems in Yorkshire and between Lancashire and Cheshire. In selecting this number of units we have compromised between the 25 regional units used by Pelling (1967) and Dunbabin (1980) and the 161 constant units in Miller (1977). While we were unable to reproduce Miller's units across the 1972 county boundary changes, we felt that increasing the observations over 25 would make the correlations more valuable. We have, however, excluded Ireland from our analysis entirely.

For each of the 42 county-equivalent units, we gathered data on the percentage of votes cast and seats won for the Conservative and Unionist parties. We then examined the stability of voting patterns across time at this county-equivalent level. We also sought to characterize the geography of each election through a principal components analysis.

The national election results over the period show remarkable stability for the Conservative and Unionist parties. In Great Britain in the two 1910 elections, the Unionists polled 47.4 per cent and 47.5 per cent, in 1951 48 per cent, in 1955 49.6 per cent, in 1987 43.3 per cent, and in 1992 42.8 per cent of the vote. These minor changes in support, however, mask much more dramatic changes within the core and periphery areas as Table 6.2 shows.

Our initial analysis consists of calculating simple Pearson r's correlating the percentage of votes won by Unionists in the 42 county-equivalent units for each pair of elections – see Table 6.3. The December 1910 election poses problems for our analysis because of the large number of uncontested constituencies – 87 of the 570 constituencies in Britain containing 16 per cent of the electorate. As this inevitably distorts the geographic pattern of party support and so limits the utility of the results as a base for comparison, the December 1910 election is presented as corroboration for the January 1910 election and as part of the principal components analysis. There is a further discussion of the December 1910 elections in the appendix. Table 6.3 shows that, not surprisingly, the results from the first two 1910 elections correlate strongly with each other, as do the pairs 1951 and 1955 and 1987 and 1992. The second election of each pair broadly confirms the geographical distribution of the vote in the first.

The normal processes of economic growth and social change reduce the geographic stability of most electoral patterns. Industrialization leads to the expansion of cities and the relative depopulation of agricultural areas. It is

Table 6.3   Correlation matrix percentage votes won by Conservatives and Unionists in the general elections of 1910, 1951, 1987 and 1992 weighted by 1951 representation

	Dec. 1910	*1951*	*1955*	*1987*	*1992*	*Core/ periphery**
Jan. 1910	.953	.606	.659	.736	.743	.727
Dec. 1910		.666	.704	.702	.711	.646
1951			.942	.620	.651	.325
1955				.583	.611	.392
1987					.994	.732
1992						.728

*Dummy variable scored 1 for core areas, 0 for periphery.

therefore not surprising that the correlations of the January 1910 election with 1951 and 1955 are much lower than those of the 1910 elections. Clearly the rise of class and the advance of industrial society have altered the electoral geography. Contrary to expectations, however, but in line with our hypothesis, the correlations do not continue to fall over time: the elections of 1987 and 1992 are more similar in their geographical pattern to January 1910 than they are to 1951 and 1955. They are also more similar to January 1910 than are the elections of the 1950s.

It is clear that the 1987 and 1992 elections show a reversion to the pattern of 1910 and do not simply indicate a continuing decay of an earlier pattern through social change. The lowest correlation is between 1987 and 1955, not between the most distant elections. 1987 and 1992 correlate better with January 1910 than do 1951 and 1955. This correlation matrix shows that the geographical distribution of support for the Conservative and Unionist parties is much more similar between the first and last pairs of elections than the elections of the 1950s were to either pair.

Correlating the election results with a dummy variable scored 1 for the core area of south and east Britain and 0 for north and west Britain, including Devon and Cornwall, shows the varying electoral impact of this cleavage. Table 6.3 shows that the dummy variable for the core correlated highly with the Conservative and Unionist share of the vote in 1910, 1987, and 1992, but not in 1951 or 1955. These two elections show only a small regional effect. In terms of the percentage of variance explained (i.e. as an r^2), the dummy variable for each region explains 46 per cent to 54 per cent of the geographical variations in votes won in the first and last pairs of elections but only 11 per cent to 15 per cent in the 1950s.

To control for the distribution of uncontested constituencies, correlations of seats won by the Conservative and Unionist parties are presented in Table 6.4. The results are broadly similar to the correlations of shares of the vote; the basic pattern in terms of inter-election correlations and regional variation remains the same.

Table 6.4 Correlation matrix percentage seats won by Conservatives and Unionists in the general elections of 1910, 1951, 1987 and 1992 weighted by 1951 representation

	Dec. 1910	1951	1955	1987	1992	Core/ periphery*
Jan. 1910	.963	.540	.587	.774	.706	.689
Dec. 1910		.580	.631	.791	.728	.635
1951			.968	.762	.813	.349
1955				.755	.798	.342
1987					.973	.730
1992						.663

*Dummy variable scored 1 for core areas, 0 for periphery.

Similar results are obtained through a principal components analysis (PCA). PCA extracts from a set of variables subgroups of variables which correlate with each other but not with other variables. These subgroups, called components, are generally held to reflect unmeasured but underlying processes that caused the correlations (Tabachnik and Fidell, 1989: 597). From an examination of the scatterplot of the factor scores for each observation it is usually possible to detect the underlying concept which the factor is modelling. For our purpose the PCA analysis will measure how different the three pairs of elections are (see Johnston *et al.*, 1987).

The PCA confirms the results of the correlation matrix in that all six elections are moderately to highly correlated. Due to this, the PCA initially extracted only one component which accounted for 80 per cent of the variance of the vote across the county-equivalent units. However, the scree plot of eigenvalues against the factors, which aids the identification of the number of factors needed to define the data, suggested that a second component, much less explanatory than the first, might still be useful. A transformation of the dataset using the varimax rotation technique (Tabachnik and Fidell, 1989: 610) to maximize the variance of factor loadings produced two components which, when combined, explained 91.7 per cent of the variance of vote. Table 6.5 indicates the factor loadings. The first component encompassed the first and last pair of elections and could be called the 'geographical' component as it correlates highly ($r = 0.5380$) with our dummy variable for core and periphery in Table 6.6.

Table 6.5   Factor loadings varimax rotation

	Factor 1	Factor 2
Jan. 1910	.760	.526
Dec. 1910	.688	.618
1951	.386	.887
1955	.311	.929
1987	.926	.295
1992	.916	.333

Table 6.6   Factor score correlations with class and regional variables

	Factor 1 'geography'	Factor 2 'class'
Region	0.5380	–0.0727
% Employer and manager	0.3253	0.2129
% Semi-skilled manual	–0.2622	–0.2186
% Males in mining	–0.2350	–0.3333

Source: Class variables from 1966 census.
Region: Scale is 1 = core, 0 = periphery.

The second component includes the two elections from the 1950s and shows a different voting pattern from the geographical dimension of factor one. This factor does not correlate strongly with any class measure. There are three possible reasons for this. Factor two only explains 11 per cent of the variance in the distribution of the vote across the six elections while the first factor explains 80 per cent of the variance. Furthermore, the factor only loads highly on two of the six elections. Since all the elections correlated with a minimum r of 0.583, any correlations with this less powerful factor must of necessity be low. Second, the Conservative vote has never been as class-based as the Labour vote; correlations of the Conservative vote with class are therefore low. Third, region itself correlates with class measured as the percentage of employers and managers in each county-equivalent unit in 1966; see Miller and Raab, 1977. Factor two could therefore describe the correlations of class and election results once the correlation with region has been removed. This second factor could thus be called the 'class' component of voting. Table 6.6 summarizes the relationships of the factors to class and regional variables.

'Class is the basis of British party politics; all else is embellishment and detail' (Pulzer, 1967: 98). While Pulzer's famous statement describes perfectly well the elections of the 1950s, class cannot be given the same predominant role for the general elections of 1987 or 1992; nor does it apply to the elections of the Edwardian period. Wald (1983: 154–9) has shown that, while class was gaining in electoral importance, religion dominated the electoral alignment in the period 1885 to 1910. He also showed that the core–periphery cleavage, independent of both religion and class, emerged strongly between 1900 and 1910 in Scotland, Wales and peripheral England. The core–periphery cleavage modified the religious alignment without supplanting it; in 1910 religion remained dominant, but geography was also important.[2]

Between the wars, the importance of religion declined as the newly enfranchised electorate mobilized around the class cleavage. By 1951, the Conservative party could claim only a small benefit from the Anglican community while the Liberals had lost their base in the Nonconformist churches (Miller and Raab, 1977: 248). The class cleavage was now dominant with only small regional deviations that were not rooted in social structure.

Rose (1974: 510) and Miller (1978) develop the idea of the core class as the class which has the strongest affinity for a particular party. The core class for the Conservatives consists of employers and managers (census socio-economic groups 1, 2, and 13). A regression analysis of the 1951 election using 1966 census data shows the percentage of employers and managers as the best predictors of the Conservative vote ($R = 0.61$; see Table 6.7).[3] The effect of the dummy variable for core and periphery at this election was minimal; it reduced the Conservative vote by just under two per cent in the periphery and increased the R from 0.61 to 0.65.

By 1987, however, the dummy variable had increased substantially as an influence on the pattern of the vote. While the percentage of employers and

Table 6.7   Correlation coefficients (multiple R): Conservative vote and core class 1951–5 and 1979–92

	Class only[a]	Class and region[b]
1951	0.61	0.65
1955	0.54	0.62
1979	0.78	0.84
1983	0.78	0.84
1987	0.74	0.84
1992	0.75	0.85

[a] Class: % economically active and retired males from social economic groups 1, 2 and 13 (employers, managers, owner-farmers). Data for 1955 are from 1966 census; data for 1979–92 are from 1981 census.
[b] Region: Scale is 1 = core, 0 = periphery.

managers correlates with the 1987 Conservative vote at 0.74, the multiple R rises to 0.84 when region is added. The same relation holds for 1992: the correlation of the Conservative vote with class alone is 0.75 but rises to 0.85 with class and region. Further, the regional effect reduces the Conservative share of the vote by 10 per cent in the peripheral parts of the country in 1987 and 1992. Table 6.7 shows the increasing importance of the core–periphery divide since 1979 and compares it to 1951 and 1955. Admittedly, the correlation coefficients for the 1950s are not strictly comparable with the coefficients for later years since class data were drawn from different census years (1966 and 1981) using slightly different definitions of the socioeconomic groups. The importance point to note is the increase in the multiple R associated with the core–periphery dummy variable that is not present in the 1950s.

Conclusion

These data provide persuasive evidence for the existence of a core–periphery cleavage operating in the two general elections of 1910 and the general elections of 1987 and 1992. In these general elections there was also an explicit core–periphery element to the main election issues of the day. The 1910 general elections were dominated by constitutional issues, i.e. the reform of the House of Lords and Irish Home Rule, and the latter had an explicit core–periphery dimension. There was also the issue of the disestablishment of the Welsh Church, which was a core–periphery issue as well as a religious one, since it pitted the core religion (Anglicanism) against the beliefs, practices, and language of the periphery (McLean, 1983). Moreover, these core–periphery issues had been at the very centre of politics since 1886 when Gladstone had first espoused Irish Home Rule.

The issues of 1951, by contrast, were overwhelmingly class-based: nationalization, the future of the welfare state, and so on. The manifestos of the two main parties said nothing about Wales and Scotland, while the now-shrunken Liberal party offered just one paragraph promising Scottish and Welsh Parliaments. When, in 1959, the core–periphery dimension began once again to emerge, there was no immediate change in the political agenda at the national level. By 1974, however, core–periphery issues, such as devolution, had re-emerged in tandem with changes in voting behaviour and in particular an increase in support for the SNP. In 1992, the major parties published separate manifestos for Scotland and Wales, and both Labour and Liberals supported devolution for the English regions, as well as for Scotland and Wales. All of the parties promised support for the Welsh language; even the Conservatives, the party most hostile to devolution, called attention to their record of making Welsh part of the school curriculum in Wales and a near-requirement for public employment in the principality (Conservative Party, 1992).

It would, however, be misleading to suggest that the main electoral issues in 1992 were, as in 1910, of the core–periphery type. What has occurred since the late 1950s has been the gradual and steady emergence of a new cleavage which was initially unaccompanied by any change in the political agenda at national level. By 1992, admittedly, issues of constitutional reform, devolution and nationalism were playing an important if subordinate part in the general election campaign. But this, by contrast with the pre-World War I period, had occurred *as a result* of a change in voting behaviour. It was not itself a cause of that change. And the victorious Conservatives fought the general elections of the years 1979–92 on the basis that the core–periphery cleavage was fundamentally irrelevant to British politics.

Nevertheless, a major issue in the general elections of 1987 and 1992, as in the two general elections of 1910, was the geographical distribution of political power. In each of these elections, the Conservative and Unionist parties supported the status quo while the Liberals, Labour and the nationalists sought to devolve power away from Westminster. Thus the outcome of these elections decided the future shape of the polity as well as which party would win power at Westminster.

In 1910, it was the Liberals, buttressed by their electoral understanding with Labour, whom the core–periphery cleavage seemed to favour. Since 1979, by contrast, the core–periphery cleavage has made possible

Conservative dominance, a dominance which will not be broken until the parties of the left are able successfully to invade the Conservative heartland.

In the general elections of 1910, despite winning 47 per cent of the vote in Great Britain, the Unionist parties remained on the opposition benches at Westminster. By 1992, however, although their share of the total vote in Great Britain had fallen to 43 per cent, the Conservatives managed to win an absolute majority of the seats in the Commons for the fourth successive occasion.

Part of this difference may be due to the electoral understanding between Liberals and Labour in 1910, an understanding which was absent in 1992. In 1910, voters in Great Britain faced a bi-polar choice between the Liberals, supported by Labour, and the Unionists. In 1992, by contrast, there was no such understanding. Voters were faced, not with a two-bloc party system, but with a three-fold choice. Thus, the alternative to the Conservatives was not a Liberal government with assured support from Labour and the Irish Nationalists, as in 1910, but a Labour minority government, resting perhaps upon uncertain Liberal Democrat support, with a second election within a short period of time, as had occurred in 1974, being a distinct possibility. It was hardly surprising therefore that, following Labour's fourth defeat, there was once again talk of a new understanding or pact with the Liberal Democrats.

But, whatever the merits of these speculations, it is clear that there is considerable scope for the study of long-term historical patterns in voting behaviour. In the analysis of electoral change and also of party strategies, there are lessons to be learnt from history.

Appendix

Methodology: Data Problems and Solutions

There are several structural problems with comparing election results across multiple changes in constituency boundaries over long stretches of time. This appendix addresses the following concerns: changes in party strength and labels, problems of uncontested returns, changes in the electoral system, boundary changes, and population movements.

The period under study encompasses political upheavals, three expansions of the suffrage – in 1918, 1928, and 1969 – and changes in party support. The territory of the United Kingdom shrank in 1922 with the secession of the Irish Free State. Labour replaced the Liberals as the major anti-Conservative party among the electorate and in the House of Commons. The Liberal party itself split, part of it uniting with the Conservatives while the remainder limped on, a shadow of its former self. Minor parties from all parts of the political spectrum offered candidates from time to time. In these circumstances the project of defining the two sides of the core–periphery cleavage is not an easy one.

It was the Unionist parties – the Conservatives and their Liberal Unionist allies, together with various independent candidates or small parties advocating a strengthening of the Empire – which represented the centralizing force in the political system. Opposing them are the Liberal and Labour parties, Celtic nationalist parties, prohibitionists, socialists, communists and various anti-Conservative independents. In dividing the political spectrum in this way we follow the schema set out by Bartolini and Mair (1990) and the labelling guidelines of Craig (1971, pp. xii–xviii; 1974, pp. xii–xviii).

One problem in comparing aggregate election returns lies in the statistical distortions created by uncontested seats. The December 1910 election is especially difficult in this regard: the Conservative and Liberal Unionist coalition presented only 436 candidates for the 456 seats in England while the Liberals and Labour combined fought only 404 constituencies. This resulted in the uncontested election of 54 Conservative or Liberal Unionist and 16 Liberal or Labour MPs. For Britain as a whole (excluding university seats), 93 members were returned unopposed in this election. As a result, 17.8 per cent of the English electorate, 29 per cent of the Welsh electorate and 11.6 per cent of the Scottish electorate were unable to vote. Table 6A.1 shows the number of unopposed returns for 1910 and 1951. All seats were contested by Conservatives and non-Conservatives alike in the 1955, 1987 and 1992 elections.

Uncontested returns distort the measurement of party support because there is no way of knowing who would have won a contested election, nor by what margin. There is no measure of relative support. Rather than extrapolating a winning margin (as is done in *The Times House of Commons, 1911* for the December 1910 general election), we presented similar analyses based on seats won and votes cast at each election. Broadly similar results in the correlations suggested that the distortions were rather small.

Changes in the electoral system since 1910 also demand attention. University seats are ignored in this study as they did not represent a geographical entity and cannot be included in the constant units used in this investigation. Moreover, university seats were abolished in 1948 so no time comparison of them as a special unit is possible. The issue of two-member seats, of which there were 23 in 1910, is somewhat more complex. An analysis by Craig (1974, pp. 595–626) shows that well over 95 per cent of voters cast their two votes for candidates from the same party or at least the same alliance (Lib-Lab or Conservative-Liberal Unionist). The level of party support among voters can be estimated by dividing the total vote for each group

Table 6A.1   Candidates returned unopposed

	Conservative and Lib. Unionist	Liberal and Labour
Jan. 1910	7	1
Dec. 1910	57	28
1951	4	0

Source: Lloyd, 1965; Craig, 1983; Butler and Butler, 1986.

Table 6A.2   Correlation matrix percentage seats won by Conservative and Unionist candidates in the general elections of 1910, 1951, 1987 and 1992 unweighted and weighted by 1910, 1987

	Weight	*Dec. 1910*	*1951*	*1955*	*1987*	*1992*
Jan. 1910	unw.	.948	.697	.689	.779	.795
	1910	.957	.544	.594	.709	.709
	1987	.953	.641	.585	.761	.768
Dec. 1910	unw.		.751	.745	.742	.762
	1910		.598	.646	.672	.674
	1987		.703	.658	.733	.742
1951	unw.			.936	.658	.686
	1910			.936	.587	.618
	1987			.887	.638	.664
1955	unw.				.590	.619
	1910				.530	.562
	1987				.693	.710
1987	unw.					.990
	1910					.992
	1987					.994

by two. The number of voters who divided their vote between Conservative and non-Conservative candidates was inconsequential.

Boundary changes are the most difficult obstacle. The most important changes came into effect in 1918, 1948, 1955, 1974 and 1983 (Butler, 1992 gives an overview). The number and variety of changes make it extremely difficult to compare constituency-level results except within a period of constant boundaries . Some degree of aggregation was needed to create constant or near-constant units for this analysis. Since county boundaries remained quite stable (with only minor changes) between 1885 and 1972, these form the basis for the 42 units used in this paper. 1983–92 constituencies have been fitted into the pre-1972 county boundaries as much as possible. Where the discrepancy is too large, as in the old convoluted border between Gloucestershire, Herefordshire, and Worcestershire, counties have been combined. There are 35 county-equivalent units in England, 3 in Wales, and 4 in Scotland.[4]

One result of the aggregation procedure is an imbalance in the parliamentary representation of the different units. In 1910, for example, Bedfordshire and Buckinghamshire each contained 3 seats while Lancashire contained 55 seats and Inner London contained 59 seats. In 1987 and 1991, the smallest county unit, Dorset, represented 4 seats while the largest, Outer London, had 56 seats. This imbalance might have considerable consequences by magnifying the effect of a change in party support in small county units and minimizing the effect in large county units.

To assess the impact of this, the correlation analysis has been performed in two different ways. The body of the paper presents analyses of the data weighted by the number of seats in each county unit in 1951. For example, the mean level of Conservative support in Bedfordshire, 4 seats in 1951, expressed as a percentage of total votes cast or total seats won, is treated as if it had been entered into the data matrix as four observations with the same value. Outer London, with 59 seats, is treated as if it had been entered 59 times.

The varying sizes of the county units suggested the utility of weighting them according to their parliamentary representation. Due to differential population growth rates in Britain during this century, however, more than one weighting system could be used: Inner London had 59 seats in 1910, 43 seats in 1951, and 29 seats in 1987. As the choice of weight was likely to make a difference in the analysis, we tried several different systems. Weighting by 1910 representation would minimize changes in party strengths in urban areas while weighting by 1987 or 1992 representation would minimize changes in rural areas. An unweighted correlation would similarly minimize change in large county-equivalent units.

Because 1951 is the approximate mid-point of the period we are analysing,

we felt that such a weighting would minimize the many possibilities of distortion resulting from population changes and the varying sizes of the
county-equivalent units. To show the extent of these distortions, Tables 6A.3
and 6A.4 present correlation matrices for per cent votes and per cent seats
won, respectively, in an unweighted condition and weighted by representation in 1910 and 1987. The addition of one seat in 1992 does not affect the
analysis in any material way.

The choice of weighting does not seem to have an effect on the goodness
of fit between 1951 and other years. The difference between the unweighted
correlation of 1951 with January 1910, and the 1987/1992 correlations for
votes is much smaller than when the 1951 weighting is used. The difference
is also smaller when weighting for representation in 1987. The difference

**Table 6A.3   Correlation matrix percentage seats won by Conservative
and Unionist candidates in the general elections of 1910,
1951 and 1987**

	Weight	Dec. 1910	1951	1955	1987	1992
Jan. 1910	unw.	.948	.519	.612	.730	.691
	1910	.952	.474	.532	.739	.663
	1987	.964	.571	.619	.788	.733
Dec. 1910	unw.		.518	.618	.725	.685
	1910		.536	.600	.770	.701
	1987		.600	.654	.796	.745
1951	unw.			.944	.749	.793
	1910			.962	.739	.789
	1987			.969	.772	.822
1955	unw.				.747	.779
	1910				.725	.771
	1987				.767	.810
1987	unw.					.973
	1910					.970
	1987					.975

when weighting is based on 1910 representation is much larger than weighting for 1951. This suggests that the degree of electoral stability is greatest in high growth areas, and especially the south-east.

Table 6A.4   Data aggregation: constituencies per county-equivalent unit

The 42 county-equivalent units are listed below with the number of constituencies in each in 1910, 1951 and 1987. Note the additional constituency in Buckinghamshire due to the new constituency in Milton Keynes in 1992.

Bedfordshire (3, 4, 5)
Berkshire and Oxfordshire (9, 9, 12)
Buckinghamshire (3, 5, 7/8)
Cambridgeshire and Huntingdonshire, and Northamptonshire (13, 9, 12)
Cheshire (13, 17, 17)
Cornwall (7, 5, 5)
Cumberland, Westmoreland, and Barrow in Furness (10, 7, 6)
Derbyshire (9, 10, 10)
Devon (13, 10, 11)
Dorset (4, 4, 4)
Durham (15, 17, 15)
Essex (7, 10, 16)
Gloucestershire, Herefordshire, and Worcestershire (21, 19, 21)
Hampshire and Isle of Wight (12, 14, 19)
Hertfordshire (4, 7, 10)
Kent (13, 12, 16)
Lancashire (55, 60, 56)
Leicestershire and Rutland (7, 9, 9)
Lincolnshire (11, 8, 9)
Inner London (59, 43, 29)
Outer London (16, 59, 56)
Norfolk (10, 8, 8)
Northumberland (8, 10, 10)
Nottinghamshire (7, 10, 11)
Shropshire (5, 4, 4)
Somerset (10, 7, 9)
Staffordshire (18, 19, 21)
Suffolk (8, 5, 6)
Surrey (4, 8, 10)

East and West Sussex (9, 11, 15)
Warwickshire, including Birmingham (14, 22, 23)
Wiltshire (6, 5, 5)
Yorkshire East Riding (6, 6, 6)
Yorkshire North Riding (13, 12, 13)
Yorkshire West Riding (34, 41, 37)
North Wales (10, 8, 9)
Dyfed and Powys (10, 6, 6)
Industrial South Wales (14, 22, 23)
South Scotland and Edinburgh (16, 13, 14)
Glasgow/Lanarkshire (23, 33, 32)
Highland and Islands (8, 6, 6)
Northeast Scotland (23, 19, 20)

Notes

1   The authors wish to thank David Butler, Iain McLean, Anthony Heath, Susan Field, Michael Steed and Bruno Paulson for comments on earlier drafts of this chapter. We are also grateful for data (Crewe, 1977; McAllister and Rose, 1987) kindly provided by the ESRC.
2   Wald actually says that by 1910 class and religion had achieved rough parity in their electoral importance, but goes on to say that, given the high quality of the data on the class composition of constituencies, and the poor quality of data on their religious composition, it is clear that class did not become important until after 1918 (Wald, 1983: 159).
3   The 1966 census was the first to be published on the basis of parliamentary constituencies. The 1955 to 1970 period is thus the first to combine ecological and electoral data without boundary mismatches. As the 1955 election was already matched to the 1966 census, the authors concluded that the regression coefficients would be more comparable if the 1951 election were matched to that census rather than to another census year. Miller (1977) suggests that the distortion caused by the long time lag is minimal.
4   This aggregation runs the risk of burying pockets of Conservative strength in areas such as the Lancashire cotton towns, but the frequent redrawing of constituency boundaries makes this unavoidable. Where county boundaries have been radically redrawn, as in Lancashire, Yorkshire and Lincolnshire, they have split some constituencies at one or another of the elections we are studying. We have chosen to place such constituencies in the county-equivalent unit that contains more than half the land mass of the seat in question. Analyses of alternative aggregation procedures, i.e. placing the constituencies in different county-equivalent units, suggest that the correlation matrices are not materially affected.

References

Alt, James (1984), 'Dealignment and the Dynamics of Partisanship in the British Electorate', in Russell Dalton, Scott Flanagan, and Paul Allen Beck (eds), *Electoral Change in Advanced Industrial Democracies: Realignment or Dealignment?*, Princeton: Princeton

University Press.
Bartolini, Stefano and Peter Mair (1990), *Identity, Competition, and Electoral Availability: The Stabilisation of European Electorates, 1885–1985*, Cambridge: Cambridge University Press.
Blewett, Neal (1972), *The Peers, the Parties and the People: The General Elections of 1910*, London: Macmillan.
Bogdanor, Vernon (ed.) (1987), *The Blackwell Encyclopedia of Political Institutions*, Oxford: Basil Blackwell.
Butler, David E. (1992), 'The Redrawing of Parliamentary Boundaries in Britain', *Journal of Behavioural and Social Sciences*, **37**, 153–63.
Butler, David E. and Gareth Butler (1986), *British Political Facts, 1900–1985*, 6th edn, London: Macmillan.
Conservative Party (1992), 'The Best Future for Wales: The Conservative Manifesto for Wales 1992', Cardiff: Conservative Central Office for Wales.
Craig, F. W. S. (1983), *British Parliamentary Election Results, 1950–1973*, Chichester: Political Reference Publications.
Craig, F. W. S. (1974), *British Parliamentary Election Results, 1885–1918*, London: Macmillan.
Crewe, Ivor (1977), *British Parliamentary Constituencies, 1955–1974* [computer file], Colchester: ESRC Data Archive.
Curtice, John (1988), 'One Nation', in Roger Jowell and Sharon Witherspoon (eds), *British Social Attitudes 1988*, Aldershot: Gower.
Curtice, John and Michael Steed (1982), 'Electoral Choice and the Production of Government: The Changing Operation of the Electoral System in the United Kingdom Since 1955', *British Journal of Political Science*, **12** (3), July, 249–98.
Curtice, John and Michael Steed (1986), 'Proportionality and Exaggeration in the British Electoral System', *Electoral Studies*, **5** (3), December, 209–28.
Curtice, John and Michael Steed (1988), 'The Results Analysed' in David Butler and Dennis Kavanagh, *The British General Election of 1987*, London: Macmillan.
Curtice, John and Michael Steed (1992), 'The Results Analysed' in David Butler and Dennis Kavanagh, *The British General Election of 1992*, London: Macmillan.
Dunbabin, J. P. D. (1980), 'British Elections in the Nineteenth and Twentieth Centuries, A Regional Approach', *The English Historical Review*, **325**, April, 241–67.
Field, William H. (1992), 'Electoral Volatility in Britain: A Reassessment of Voting Patterns 1959–1992', *Joint Unit for the Study of Social Trends, Working Paper no, 14*; Social & Community Planning Research and Nuffield College.
Heath, Anthony, John Curtice, Roger Jowell, Geoff Evans, Julia Field and Sharon Witherspoon (1991), *Understanding Political Change: The British Voter, 1964–1987*, Oxford: Pergamon Press.
Hechter, Michael (1975), *Internal Colonialism: The Celtic Fringe in British National Development 1536–1966*, Berkeley: University of California Press.
Inglehart, Ronald (1984), 'The Changing Structure of Political Cleavages in Western Society', in Russell Dalton, Scott Flanagan and Paul Allen Beck (eds), *Electoral Change in Advanced Industrial Democracies: Realignment or Dealignment?*, Princeton: Princeton University Press.
Johnston, R. J., A. B. O'Neill and P. J. Taylor (1987), 'The Geography of Party Support: Comparative Studies in Electoral Stability', in Manfred J. Holler (ed.), *The Logic of Multiparty Systems*, Dordrecht: Kluwer Academic Publishers.
Johnston, R. J., C. J. Pattie and J. G. Allsop (1988), *A Nation Dividing? The Electoral Map of Great Britain, 1979–87*, London: Longman.

Lipset, Seymour Martin and Stein Rokkan (1967), 'Cleavage Structures, Party Systems, and Voter Alignments: An Introduction', in Seymour Martin Lipset and Stein Rokkan (eds), *Party Systems and Voter Alignments*, New York: The Free Press.

Lloyd, Trevor (1965), 'Uncontested Seats in British General Elections, 1852–1910', *The Historical Journal*, **7** (2), 260–5.

McAllister, Ian and Donley T. Studlar (1992), 'Region and Voting in Britain, 1979–87: Territorial Polarization or Artifact?', *American Journal of Political Science*, **36** (1), February, 168–99.

McAllister, Ian and Richard Rose (1987), *United Kingdom Ecological Data 1983, 1987* [computer file], Colchester: ESRC Data Archive.

McLean, Iain (1983), *The Legend of Red Clydeside*, Edinburgh: John Donald.

Mény, Yves and Vincent Wright (1985), *Centre-Periphery Relations in Western Europe*, London: George Allen & Unwin.

Miller, William L. (1977), *Electoral Dynamics in Britain Since 1918*, London: Macmillan.

Miller, William L. (1978), 'Social Class and Party Choice in England: A New Analysis', *British Journal of Political Science*, **8** (3), July, 257–84.

Miller, William L. (1983), 'The Denationalisation of British Politics: The Re-Emergence of the Periphery', *West European Politics*, **6** (4), October, 103–29.

Miller, William L. and Gillian Raab (1977), 'The Religious Alignment of English Elections Between 1918 and 1970', *Political Studies*, **25** (2), June, 227–51.

Mortimore, Roger (1992), *The Constituency Structure and the Boundary Commission: The Rules for Redistribution of Seats and their Effect on the British Electoral System 1950–87*, Oxford, D. Phil Thesis.

Pattie, Charles, Ed Fieldhouse, Ron Johnston and Andrew Russell (1992), 'A Widening Regional Cleavage in British Voting Behaviour, 1964–87: Preliminary Explorations', in Ivor Crewe, Pippa Norris, David Denver and David Broughton (eds), *British Elections and Parties Yearbook 1991*, New York: Harvester Wheatsheaf.

Pelling, Henry (1967), *Social Geography of British Elections, 1885–1910*, London: Macmillan.

Pomper, Gerald M. (1967), 'Classification of Presidential Elections', *Journal of Politics*, **29** (3), August, 536–66.

Pulzer, Peter (1967), *Political Representation and Elections in Britain*, London: Macmillan.

Rokkan, Stein (1970), 'Nation Building, Cleavage Formation and the Structuring of Mass Politics', in Stein Rokkan (ed.), *Citizens, Elections, Parties*, Oslo: Universitetsforlaget.

Rokkan, Stein and Derek W. Urwin (1983), *Economy, Territory, Identity: The Politics of West European Peripheries*, London: Sage.

Rose, Richard (1974), 'Britain: Simple Abstracts and Complex Realities', in Richard Rose (ed.), *Electoral Behaviour: A Comparative Handbook*, New York: Free Press.

Särlvik, Bo and Ivor Crewe (1983), *Decade of Dealignment: The Conservative Victory of 1979 and Electoral Trends in the 1970s*, Cambridge: Cambridge University Press.

Steed, Michael (1986), 'The Core–Periphery Dimension of British Politics', *Political Geography Quarterly*, **5** (4), October, S91–S103.

Tabachnik, Barbara G. and Linda S. Fidell (1989), *Using Multivariate Statistics*, Cambridge: Harper & Row.

The Times Guide to the House of Commons 1911 (1911), London: The Times Printing Office.

Wald, Kenneth D. (1983), *Crosses on the Ballot: Patterns of British Voter Alignment Since 1885*, Princeton: Princeton University Press.

7 Electoral Pacts in Britain since 1886

I

An electoral pact is an agreement between two (or more) distinct and separate parties to co-operate electorally. Such pacts frequently occur in the multi-party systems of the Continent, but they have been much less frequent in Britain, especially since 1931. The purpose of this chapter is to explain why national electoral pacts have become so rare, and to argue that they perform an important function in giving elasticity to the party system, and in making it adaptable to social change.[1]

On the Continent, pacts are frequent since most democracies are both multi-party and bipolar, with the main cleavage lying between parties of the Left and parties of the Right. This means that, to maximize its influence, a party does well to co-operate with like-minded parties from the same bloc, so as to defeat the greater enemy which lies on the opposite bloc. This co-operation is often assisted by particular features or mechanisms of the electoral system.

It is, in fact, precisely because the majority of democracies – with Switzerland being the most notable exception – possess bipolar party systems, in which a Left party or bloc of parties confronts a Right party or bloc of parties, and yet are also multi-party, that most electoral systems make provision for co-operation between two or more like-minded parties. The type of provision made will differ with the electoral system.

The German electoral system allows the voter to distribute his or her first and second votes between two different parties, thus indicating the political colour of the coalition which the voter favours. This has proved a crucial factor in creating an electoral basis, first for the Social Democrat–Free Democrat coalition in the years 1969–82, and then for the Christian Democrat–Free Democrat coalition which has ruled West Germany, and then Germany, since 1982. Without the willingness of electors to cast their first votes for the Christian Democrats and their second votes for the Free Democrats, this coalition might well not have been possible, since the Free Democrats might not have been able to surmount the 5 per cent threshold. Moreover, the pact enables Free Democrat voters, knowing that their party was unlikely to win a constituency seat, to cast their first vote for the party to which it was allied, the Christian Democrats. In the 1983 election, for example, no less than 58 per cent of those who had voted Free Democrat on the second vote supported the Christian Democrats on the first vote, as compared with only 29 per cent voting Free Democrat on the first vote (Bogdanor, 1984: 66).

The single-transferable vote system allows the voter to signal a coalition through the way in which preferences are distributed; this was a crucial factor in the construction of the National Coalition of Fine Gael and Labour which governed the Irish Republic between 1973 and 1977. Fine Gael voters, hitherto a conservative force in Irish politics, showed through their pattern of transfers that they were prepared for their party to co-operate with Labour; while supporters of Labour, whose party had abandoned the politics of isola-tion for co-operation with a 'bourgeois' party, proved willing to use their later preferences to secure the election of Fine Gael candidates.

Other proportional systems may allow *apparentement*, a provision by which separate parties can declare themselves linked for the purposes of vote-counting and seat allocation. The votes of these separate parties are then counted together, as though they had been cast for a single list (Williams, 1964: ch. 2). A further possibility is *panachage*, as employed in the electoral systems of Switzerland and Luxembourg, by means of which the voter can distribute his or her votes in a multi-member constituency system across more than one party list.

The majoritarian electoral systems – the alternative vote and the second ballot – also provide for co-operation. The alternative vote is, in this respect, analogous to the single transferable vote, while the second ballot emphasizes the importance of co-operation by allowing for bargaining amongst parties between the first and second ballots. In Fifth Republic France, the second-ballot electoral system has proved of considerable importance in encourag-ing agreements between the parties of the Left – Socialists and Communists – and, to a somewhat lesser extent, the parties of the Right – Gaullists and Giscardians – particularly for presidential elections.

All of these mechanisms serve to reward co-operative parties and penalize the intransigent. Other things being equal, a party which is prepared to ally itself with others is likely to secure more seats for a given percentage of the vote than an extremist party which avoids co-operation with others, and with which others do not wish to co-operate. It is for this reason that, in the multi-party systems of the Continent, pivot parties such as the German Free

Democrats enjoy such tremendous influence. Proportional representation can ensure that each vote carries the same weight; but it cannot ensure that each vote will carry the same weight in the process of government formation. Votes cast for parties which are prepared to co-operate together will carry more weight than votes cast for intransigent parties.

Under the plurality system, however, co-operation is much more difficult, for it can only be achieved by reciprocal withdrawal of candidates on the part of the parties which seek to co-operate. The candidates of party A must withdraw from constituencies *p*, *q*, *r*, etc. in exchange for the candidates of party B withdrawing from constituencies *u*, *v*, *w*, etc. This gives rise to two main problems.

The first problem is that, in a political system such as that in Britain, where local constituency parties are autonomous, a headquarters agreement between the leaders of the two parties, A and B, although it might influence the stance of the constituency parties, cannot determine them. In pre-democratic times, before parties existed as mass organizations, the stance of a party could be largely determined by its leaders. This would make it relatively easy to construct an alliance. The shifts and manœuvres of the Peelites between 1846 and 1859, when they finally cast their lot with the Liberals, would not be possible today, since the leaders would, at every stage, have to convince their members in the country of the correctness of the stance they were taking. The more parties have developed as mass organizations, the more their freedom of manœuvre to form electoral alliances has been limited.

The essential pre-condition of a pact – the reciprocal withdrawal of candidates – cannot, therefore, under modern conditions, be decided upon by the leaders of a party alone. The decision as to whether or not to run a candidate lies with local constituency parties, and national headquarters cannot force a constituency party to withdraw its candidate. Indeed, a constituency party will often regard the running of a candidate as part of its very *raison d'être*, and will be loth to ask its candidate to stand down, even in the wider interests of the party. The candidate, also, will often be unwilling to make the supreme sacrifice. The following *cri de coeur* of a Liberal candidate, who had been asked to stand down in the interests of a candidate from the Social Democratic party, made at the SDP's Council for Social Democracy, at Great Yarmouth in 1982, is perhaps not untypical:

> Seven years ago, when I became prospective parliamentary candidate for this constituency, we sold a home we all dearly loved to move to live in the constituency, our youngest left her school and all three children eventually went to school locally. My wife changed her job to teach in the local comprehensive school and we accepted the upheaval because we both believed that for me the only way to nurse the constituency was to live in it and become part of it. (Josephs, 1983: 155).

Moreover, even if a constituency party can be persuaded not to put up a candidate, and the candidate can be persuaded to stand down, the purpose of the exercise might still be frustrated by an independent candidate of the same political tendency, a John the Baptist figure, channelling away votes which would otherwise be given to the other party in the pact. That, in fact, was what happened in a number of constituencies in Britain in 1918, when, despite the existence of the coupon determining the allocation of Conservative and Lloyd George Liberal candidatures, 83 uncouponed Conservatives stood, of whom 50 were successful. One of these successful uncouponed Conservatives defeated the former Liberal Prime Minister, H. H. Asquith, in East Fife. Asquith had been granted the coupon, but opposition to him was so strong that local Conservatives insisted upon putting up a candidate. Similarly, in 1931, local Conservatives were much more willing to stand down for Simonite Liberal Nationals than for Samuelite Liberals, who continued to support Free Trade. (Simon himself had not been opposed by a Conservative in either the 1924 or the 1929 general elections.) For this reason there were contests between Conservatives and Liberal Nationals in only four constituencies, but 79 contests between other Liberals and Conservatives (Thorpe, 1991: 177). In 1951 there was no national electoral pact, but Conservative constituency associations were encouraged to make deals with Liberals, where these would assist the anti-Labour cause. Seven Liberal candidates, and five of the six MPs elected, faced no Conservative opposition; and, when the Conservatives issued their first list of prospective candidates, these included the Liberals in all the uncontested seats (Butler, 1952: 94). But Conservatives were more willing to stand down for Liberals who had opposed the Labour government than for those who had supported it. Indeed, of those who had opposed Labour, only Jo Grimond faced Conservative opposition. A pact, if it is to be successful, therefore, must go with the grain of local constituency opinion; it cannot be imposed by party head-quarters.

Secondly, even when a pact has been agreed and approved by party head-quarters, and accepted by the constituencies, it does not follow that it will have a determining influence upon party supporters and electors. A party is not like a disciplined army which can order its supporters to transfer their votes in accordance with decisions made by a party organization. There must be some overriding reason – defeating Home Rule in 1886, preserving financial stability in 1931 – which persuades voters to follow the advice of their parties. A pact, if it is to be successful, must go with the grain, not only of local constituency opinion, but also of local electoral opinion.

II

It is perhaps surprising, given the difficulties attending the formation of an electoral pact under a plurality electoral system, that they have played so important a part in British politics since 1886. There have, in fact, been five national electoral pacts during this period.

1 The pact between Conservatives and Liberal Unionists in 1886, a pact which lasted through seven general elections until the two parties merged in 1912.
2 The pact between the Liberal party and the Labour Representation Committee (LRC), forerunner of the Labour party, in 1903, often known as the Gladstone–MacDonald pact. This pact was operative only during the general election of 1906, but it continued in the shape of an informal understanding during the two general elections of 1910.
3 The pact between the Conservatives and the Coalition Liberals, during the 'coupon' election of 1918. This pact would, it was hoped by the party leaders, encourage fusion between the two parties, but fusion was rejected, probably to the relief of the Conservative party in the country, by the Coalition Liberals in March 1920.
4 The pact between the parties comprising the National government – the Conservatives, Liberal Nationals, Liberals, and National Labour – during the general election of 1931. The National government also fought a second general election in 1935, by which time the Liberals had left the government, and the Liberal Nationals and National Labour, with whom the Conservatives maintained an electoral pact, had become almost indistinguishable from the Conservatives.
5 The pact between the Liberals and the Social Democratic party, creating the Alliance, in 1981–2. This pact held for the general elections of 1983 and 1987.

These pacts have been of considerable importance in British politics. Each of them, except the last, secured a period of electoral hegemony for the dominant party in the pact. The 1886 pact ensured the dominance of the Unionist alliance for a period of 20 years, and the defeat of Home Rule. The Gladstone–MacDonald pact of 1903 gave the Liberal party a period of electoral dominance until the outbreak of the First World War. The 'coupon' election of 1918 prefigured the period of Conservative dominance between the wars, by confirming the split in the Liberal party; while the arrangements made in 1931 ensured that Labour would be faced, in the vast majority of constituencies, with a single National government candidate, so that it would be unable to benefit, as it had in 1929, from a split vote amongst the parties opposing it. Only the pact forming the Liberal–SDP Alliance failed to achieve its object, which was to 'break the mould' of the political system, although it came nearer to doing so than any party or grouping since the Liberal party under Lloyd George in the years 1929–31.

It is noticeable that the Liberal party has been involved in each of these pacts. That ought not to be particularly surprising. Since the end of the First World War the Liberals have been the centre party in British politics; and, in a three-party system, it is the party in the centre which is most likely to be sought as a coalition partner, or a partner in an electoral pact. In 1886, also, it was the Whig element of the Liberal party, the most centrist group in the political constellation, which formed the dominant element in the Liberal Unionist party. Not only is a centrist grouping in a plurality electoral system ideally placed to pursue an electoral pact; but, because the plurality system discriminates so severely against it, such a pact may well be the only way in which it can survive as an electoral force.

Labour has participated in only one pact at national level – the Gladstone–MacDonald pact of 1903. Its attitude towards pacts, or indeed any form of co-operation with other political parties, has been deeply conditioned by the trauma of 1931. The most powerful figure in modern Labour politics is the ghost of Ramsay MacDonald; and the events of 1931 have led Labour to take the view that any leader who seeks to co-operate with other parties in peacetime is guilty of a form of betrayal.

Were Labour's attitude to change, this would do no more than put the party in line with other European Social Democratic parties. In 1933, one year after they had begun their long period of electoral hegemony, the Swedish Social Democrats, in a minority in the lower house of the Rikdsdag, reached an agreement with the Agrarian, now Centre, party to combat unemployment in exchange for the introduction of price supports on agricultural products – the so-called 'Red–Green Coalition'. In Germany, as we have seen, the Social Democratic Party was able to come to power in 1969 with the aid of the Free Democrats; while the hegemony of the French Socialists was made possible by co-operation with the Communists, co-operation which was, of course, facilitated by the second-ballot electoral system.

If Labour's attitude towards electoral pacts must remain in some doubt, there can be no doubt that the predominant tendency of electoral pacts in Britain since 1886 – with the Gladstone–MacDonald pact of 1903 being the main exception – has been to benefit the Conservatives, enabling them to gain power with the aid of satellite parties, splinters from their opponents such as the Liberal Unionists, Liberal Nationals, and National Labour. Indeed, it can be argued that, between 1886 and 1951, the only general elections won by the Conservatives as an independent party were those of 1922 and 1924. As late as 1975 Harold Macmillan was able to declare:

the last purely Conservative Government was formed by Mr Disraeli in 1874 – it is the fact that we have attracted moderate people of Liberal tradition and thought into our ranks which makes it possible to maintain a Conservative government today. A successful party of the Right must continue to recruit its strength from the centre, and even from the Left Centre. Once it begins to shrink into itself like a snail it will be doomed . . . (1975: 18–19)

The electoral pacts of 1886, 1918, and 1931 each prefigured long periods of Conservative hegemony, a hegemony granted to them by political leaders – Joseph Chamberlain, Lloyd George and Ramsay MacDonald – who were anything but Conservative in the traditional sense, who never saw themselves as Conservatives, and who were never comfortable working with the Conservative party. Yet they helped ensure that the Conservatives remained the natural party of government in Britain.

III

The Gladstone–MacDonald pact of 1903 was drawn up primarily because the Liberal party, having lost the two previous general elections, did not believe that it could win the next without an ally in the form of the support of the Labour movement. Labour, especially in Lancashire, the stronghold of the 'Tory working man', could secure votes for the 'Progressive alliance' which the Liberals would not be able themselves to win. The LRC for its part realized that it could not survive in a world of three-cornered fights, without an agreement. It badly needed an ally if it was ever to establish a foothold in the inhospitable environment created by the plurality electoral system. The pact was greatly assisted by the fact that the 1884–5 settlement, establishing the single-member constituency as the norm, had nevertheless retained 46 double-member boroughs. In these constituencies it was possible for an LRC candidate and a Liberal to fight in tandem, just as Whigs and Radicals had been able to fight together in double-member constituencies before 1885. Indeed, of the 29 seats won by the LRC in 1906, no less than 11 were in the double-member constituencies.

In the 1906 general election the pact fulfilled its function for both parties. Of the fifty LRC candidates, all but 18 enjoyed a straight fight with a Conservative opponent; and all but three of the LRC MPs in England and Wales (the pact did not operate in Scotland) were elected without Liberal opposition. Thus, the pact both enabled Labour to gain a secure foothold in the Commons, and allowed the Liberals to contain Labour within areas where it was already naturally strong. Although there was no explicit renewal of the pact for the two general elections of 1910, there was a tacit understanding, on the part of the two-party leaderships at least, that they would do their best to avoid splitting the 'Progressive' vote. In January 1910 Labour fought just 27 seats against Liberal opposition, and in December 1910 a mere 11 (Blewett, 1972: 241, 262). In this latter election the only Labour candidates elected were those without Liberal opponents. The understanding was assisted by the fact that Labour was finding itself unable to win seats against Liberal opposition; indeed, in every three-cornered by-election in a Liberal-held seat between December 1910 and 1914, Labour came bottom of the poll. For so long as the two parties co-operated, however, the hegemony of the Left was assured, and it is difficult to see how the Conservatives could have broken it. One cannot, of course, know whether the understanding between the two parties could possibly have survived the expansion of the franchise and the massive changes induced by the First World War; but the fact that it did not survive enabled the Conservatives to dominate the inter-war period.

The other four electoral pacts have been the result of party splits, and they have served to confirm those splits. When the first meeting of the Liberal Unionist party was held in the House of Commons in May 1886, the Marquess of Hartington, who was in the chair, was able to harden the resolve of MPs to oppose Gladstone's Home Rule Bill, 'by reading a message from the Conservative Chief Whip giving an absolute undertaking on behalf of that party not to contest at the next election the seat of any Liberal member who voted against the Bill' (Chilston, 1961: 77).

The pact of 1886 determined the shape of British politics for the next 20 years. By giving the Liberal Unionists a free run against Gladstonian candidates, the Conservatives allowed the Liberal Unionist party to survive, confirmed the Liberal split, and made Liberal reunion extremely difficult. The Liberal Unionists were crucial to the success of the Unionist alliance, because there were voters opposed to Home Rule who would, nevertheless, not be prepared to vote for a Conservative candidate. Nearly ten years after the pact, in 1895, Joe Chamberlain could write to his son, Austen, 'No one who has not worked among the electors can be aware how strong are old prejudices in connection with party names and colours and badges. A man may be a good Unionist at heart, and yet nothing can persuade him to vote "blue" or give support to a "Tory" candidate' (Blewett, 1972: 15).

The Conservatives thus gained considerably from the pact of 1886. They helped to engineer a split in the Liberal opposition with the aid of a party which could never aspire to more than satellite status, and whose seats were largely in areas which Conservatives could not hope to win. The Liberal Unionists were confined to their 1886 position, and would not be allowed to expand from their bridgehead into Conservative territory. Thus, the number of seats which they won in 1886 — a total of 77 — represented their ceiling.

They never succeeded in winning so many seats again. The Liberal Unionists were to prove a most valuable adjunct, but never a competitor, to the Conservatives; and in 1912 the two parties formally merged.

In 1918 the 'coupon' election actually helped to *create* a new political identity, for the differences between Asquithian and Lloyd Georgian Liberals were not crystallized until the machinery of the coupon arrangements forced them to stand in opposition to each other. Indeed, part of the purpose of the electoral agreement was to assist in the creation of a new political identity in the post-war world, an identity which would be neither Conservative nor Liberal, but a fusion of the two. The old issues which divided the parties – Home Rule, Tariff Reform, Church disestablishment – would, hopefully, be submerged under this new dispensation. Bonar Law, the Conservative leader, went so far as to confess to A. J. Balfour in 1918 that he was 'perfectly certain, indeed I do not think anyone can doubt this, that our party on the old lines will never have any future again in this country' (Bonar Law, 1918). Austen Chamberlain, who succeeded Bonar Law as Conservative leader in 1921, hoped that the Conservatives and Coalition Liberals would merge, as the Conservatives and Liberal Unionists of his father's generation had done. Yet, in March 1920 the Coalition Liberals had already rejected 'fusion', and it is doubtful if Conservatives in the country could ever have been persuaded to accept it, even if their leaders had pressed it upon them with more tact than Austen could summon. In the event, the Coalition collapsed, through a revolt by local Conservative constituency associations who were already choosing candidates to oppose Coalition Liberals, and through the hostility of back-bench Conservative MPs and junior ministers. When the Conservative leaders sought to overcome these objections by summoning a meeting of Conservative MPs at the Carlton Club in 1922, they were soundly defeated, and the Coalition came to an end.

In October 1931 the National government, composed of the Conservative, Liberal National, Liberal and Labour parties, formed just two months previously, fought the general election as a government, in striking contradiction to the pledge made at its formation, that 'The election which may follow the end of the Government will not be fought by the Government but by the parties' (Samuel, 1931). By contrast with 1918, however, no formal 'coupon' was issued endorsing particular candidates with the imprimatur of the government. Instead, there were negotiations between party headquarters, which sought to influence their respective constituency parties. These methods of informal persuasion left just 88 constituencies out of 615 in which there were contests between candidates supporting the National government (Thorpe, 1991: 177). As Andrew Thorpe, the historian of the 1931 general election has remarked, 'Given the poor relations which often prevailed, the wonder is perhaps not the number of constituencies in which National candidates ultimately stood against each other as the number of straight fights achieved' (ibid.: 166). That there were not more clashes is probably due to the overriding fear of a Labour victory and the financial instability to which it was thought a Labour victory would give rise.

The National government's decision to go to the country as a government confirmed and finalized the splits in the Labour and Liberal parties. It made reunion between MacDonald and his former colleagues impossible, while it showed that the Liberals were split three ways – between the newly formed Liberal National party, willing to support the National government unconditionally even if this meant abandoning Free Trade; the Samuelite Liberals, offering conditional support to the National government, provided that it made no serious departures from Free Trade; and the Lloyd George family group, which came out in root-and-branch opposition to the National government, and advocated support for Labour. From this threefold split, the Liberal party never recovered.

In 1981 the formation of the Social Democratic party confirmed the split in the Labour party. Indeed, David Steel, the Liberal party leader, has confessed that he persuaded potential defectors *not* to join the Liberal party, but to form a new party, precisely in order to maximize the number of Labour defectors and widen the Labour split. Labour MPs would, it was thought, be willing to defect to a party calling itself 'Social Democratic', even if it was to be virtually indistinguishable from the Liberal party, but not to a party called 'Liberal'. Steel admitted this strategy in an article written for the Liberal journal, *New Outlook*, entitled 'The Alliance: Hope and Obligation', published in September 1981.

> I do not deny that my role, as I saw it, in encouraging a social democratic breakout from the Labour Party and the formation of a new party was, and is, a high-risk strategy. But I also believe that it is the approach which provides us with the only chance to break the existing two-party system and present the electorate with a credible alternative government, in one move, at the next General Election.
>
> I know that some will argue that my job a year ago should have been solely to encourage Labour dissidents to join the Liberal Party as the only agency capable of change. Had I pursued that line I do not believe that the Labour Party – and British politics – would have been shaken to anything like the same degree by the earthquake caused by those willing to quit the Labour Party.
>
> The possibility of a new Social Democratic grouping maximised the numbers of those prepared to cross that divide. The presence of an SDP, whose leaders and membership recognise an ally and friend in the Liberal Party, maximises the potential appeal of the forces of realignment' (quoted in Bogdanor 1983: 278–9).

The Alliance, formed of the Liberal and Social Democratic parties, followed the precedent set by Lloyd George and Bonar Law, in 1918, in allocating seats by means of a signed agreement, negotiated by the two parties. These are, in fact, the *only* two occasions on which the allocation of constituencies has been decided in this way (Hart, 1990: 34–5). Guidelines were drawn up by party headquarters as principles to help determine a fair allocation of seats, and an independent arbitrator was called in at the end of the process to sort out contentious cases (Josephs, 1983: Appendix B). The whole process proved long drawn out and difficult, but, eventually, success was achieved. In the 1983 general election there were only three constituencies in which candidates from the Liberal and Social Democratic parties stood against each other.

IV

In Britain, electoral pacts have proved to be essentially temporary arrangements. They have led either to merger or to separation. The Liberal Unionists merged with the Conservatives in 1912; the National Labour party wound itself up shortly before the 1945 general election, while the Liberal National party signed, with the Conservatives, the Woolton–Teviot agreement in May 1947, urging the merger of Conservative and Liberal National constituency associations. In 1948 the Liberal Nationals, by now indistinguishable from the Conservatives, renamed themselves the National Liberal party, and in 1966 became an integral part of the Conservative party. The Social Democratic party agreed, by majority vote, to merge with the Liberals in 1987, although the minority, led by Dr David Owen, the party leader, formed a 'continuing' SDP, which, however, wound itself up in 1990. Thus, one wing of the SDP merged, while the other separated only to find itself extinguished by the iniquities of the electoral system.

The Gladstone–MacDonald pact of 1903 did not lead to a merger between the Liberal and Labour parties, nor did Labour ever intend that it should. After 1918 it proved impossible to recreate the prewar arrangements. Labour proposed to run candidates over the whole country, refusing any longer to be confined by a pact with the Liberals. Arthur Henderson hoped that co-operation with the Liberals could still be secured and declared in December 1917 that 'he would depend on the alternative vote and on a friendly understanding between Liberalism and Labour to give each other their second choice' (Wilson, 1970: 317). With the defeat of the alternative vote in 1918, however, there was no machinery to help secure co-operation between the Liberal and Labour parties, and Labour's refusal to co-operate with the Liberals ensured that the Conservatives were in power, either alone or with allies, for all but three years of the interwar period.

The 1918 'coupon' election was seen by the party leaders, if not by the rank and file, as a step toward merger, but this, as we have seen, failed to come about. In 1931 the components of the National government eventually merged with the Conservatives, except for the Samuelite Liberals, who, unlike their former colleagues, the Simonites, refused to countenance any departure from Free Trade, and resigned from the National government in September 1932 in protest at the Ottawa agreements which established a protective tariff.

Electoral pacts, then, have either proved a means to party realignment, or have not lasted. Where, as in 1886 and 1931, an electoral pact has made possible the survival of a splinter party, that party has proved short-lived. It has been little more than a satellite or client party, performing the function of a resting-place for MPs who would eventually cross the floor, but were unwilling to do so immediately. These satellite parties – the Liberal Unionists, National Labour, and the Liberal Nationals – made it easier for both MPs and voters to swing towards the Conservatives without feeling that they were sacrificing their political identity. But the impression which these parties gave of having an independent identity of their own was deceptive. Parties such as the Liberal Unionists, the Liberal Nationals, and the National Labour party could never be regarded as serious competitors for power in the way that the Conservative, Liberal, and Labour parties have been. None of these satellite parties was ever able to put up a full slate of candidates. They would never have been able to increase their representation in the Commons, and the effect in each case of the electoral pact was to ensure their survival at the cost of confining them to a narrow bridgehead. British politics, under the plurality electoral system, is inherently dualistic in nature. No third choice is possible. In 1886 one either supported Home Rule or opposed it, in which case one had no alternative but to sustain a Conservative government. Similarly, in 1931, one either supported the National government or opposed it. In each case, what seemed like a third choice, of supporting a Conservative-dominated government but preserving a separate political identity, proved illusory.

The only way in which electoral pacts could have proved permanent would have been if the electoral system had been altered. This would have enabled co-operating parties to survive as independent entities. In retrospect, it is perhaps surprising that electoral pacts did not give rise to stronger pressure for reform of the electoral system.

There is some evidence that support for proportional representation among Liberal MPs in 1884 corresponded with incipient Liberal Unionism. Fifteen of the 23 Liberal members of the Proportional Representation Society who remained in the Commons in 1886 voted against the Home Rule Bill, while another 15 members of the Society were to emerge, after 1886, as Liberal Unionists (Jones, 1972: 103). Yet, neither Hartington nor the other

Liberal Unionist leaders ever showed much interest in proportional representation.

After 1903 the Gladstone–MacDonald pact would have been assured of permanence if the electoral system had been changed to either proportional representation or the alternative vote. Yet the Liberals, while not wholly unsympathetic to the alternative vote – the first draft of the abortive franchise bill of 1912 provided for its adoption – were nevertheless unwilling, without pressing necessity, to allow Labour to extend its organization into Liberal territory; and, until 1914, the danger from Labour did not seem so great as to make electoral reform an urgent matter. Labour, on the other hand, under MacDonald's leadership, believed that it could eventually become the dominant party in the state. When that stage had been reached, the plurality system would work to Labour's advantage and enable it to obtain power without having to share it with other parties. So Labour, almost uniquely among European socialist parties, continued to support the plurality system.

After 1918 the Coalition Liberals could have retained their independent existence by means of proportional representation, but Lloyd George hoped and believed that the coalition would lead to fusion. In April 1917 Lloyd George had told C. P. Scott, editor of the *Manchester Guardian*, that proportional representation was a 'device for defeating democracy . . . and for bringing faddists of all kinds into Parliament, and establishing groups and disintegrating parties' (quoted in Wilson, 1970: 274); and he had been instrumental in ensuring that the unanimous recommendation of the Speaker's Conference in 1917, calling for proportional representation in borough constituencies, was defeated. By November 1925, however, Lloyd George was telling Scott that 'Some one ought to have come to me . . . in 1918 and gone into the whole matter. I was not converted then. I could have carried it then when I was prime minister. I am afraid it is too late now' (quoted in ibid.: 484).

In 1931 the formation of the National government actually frustrated the chances of electoral reform. Earlier in the year an electoral reform bill, providing for the introduction of the alternative vote, had been introduced by the minority Labour government and passed by the Commons. It was, however, rejected by the Lords; and, under the Parliament Act procedure as it then stood, two further sessions were required before it could be passed into law over the Lords' veto. Samuel, the Liberal leader, sought to persuade the leaders of the National government to persist with the alternative vote, but was brushed aside; while the Liberal Nationals, identifying their future with the Conservatives, felt no interest in proposing a measure which was anathema to their coalition partners.

V

The pact between the Liberals and the SDP, which was in large part intended to secure proportional representation, is the only postwar example of a national pact in British politics. The failure of the Liberal–SDP Alliance to 'break the mould' of British politics, and the ending of the political careers of the Labour MPs who defected in 1981, will probably ensure that it is a long time before a similar party split takes place. In the 53 years before the Second World War, by contrast, there were four national electoral pacts, as well as a number of proposed pacts which failed to materialize – such as a pact between Liberals and Unionist Free Traders in 1903–4, a pact between Liberals and Labour in the 1920s, and a 'Popular Front' between opponents of the Baldwin–Chamberlain governments in the 1930s. Why is it that pacts have become so rare a phenomenon in British politics?

One part of the answer has already been hinted at. The growth of party organization has made it impossible for party leaders to negotiate a pact without the support of the grass roots of the party. Yet, to party activists, any suggestion of an agreement with another party which involves the withdrawal of candidates will seem like a confession of defeat, an acceptance that their party cannot win an election on its own. This attitude has been widespread, in postwar Britain, even in the Liberal party, although members of the party cannot seriously have ever entertained any prospect of being able to win a general election on their own.

There is a further aspect of modern party organization which explains why electoral pacts have become rare. Under modern conditions, political parties feel, if they are to be national parties, that they have to contest every constituency. Until the Reform Act of 1832, by contrast, 'the *preponderant tradition* in English electoral practice was probably *the tradition of uncontested elections*' (Edwards, 1964: 185; emphasis in original) and even between 1885 and 1922 an average of 138 seats at each general election remained uncontested (Craig, 1974: 584–5; see also Butler and Butler 1986: 224). To fight every constituency was not then, as it is today, a virility symbol for a political party. The Conservatives, therefore, were perfectly willing to withdraw candidates in 1886 or 1918 if it were to their political advantage; while the Liberals did not feel fearful that, if they stood down in a few constituencies for LRC candidates in the general election of 1906, they would be accused of lacking confidence in their electoral prowess. On the contrary, the psychological effect of the pact, secret though it was, would, they believed, boost their prospects of electoral success. 'The main benefit', declared Jesse Herbert, private secretary to the Liberal Chief Whip, in 1903, of a pact 'would be the effect on the public mind of seeing the opponents of the Government united. It would give hope and enthusiasm to the Liberals, making them vote and work. It would make the Tories fearful and depressed and rob them of energy and force' (Poirier, 1958: 189).

Today, however, a corollary to the claim that a political party is a national party is the further claim that there is no type of seat which it is unable to win, even if the psephological facts suggest otherwise. The only exception to this – and the exception to almost all generalizations about UK politics – is Northern Ireland, where Conservatives, Labour and Liberals have been content, with rare exceptions, not to compete. Until 1972, the Ulster Unionist party took the Conservative whip at Westminster. Northern Ireland, however, is the exception which proves the rule. Parties from the mainland do not fight there so as to be able to distance themselves from its problems. To involve themselves too directly in Northern Ireland's affairs would be to risk taking sides on the issue of the border and alienating voters on the mainland. In every other part of the United Kingdom, by contrast, the major parties feel that they are unable to make any similar declaration of disinterest.

The success of the arrangements between the Conservatives and Ulster Unionists resulted from a perfect compatibility of interest. Such a compatibility is more likely to be achieved if the parties co-operating in a pact have electorally distinctive constituencies, as, to a large extent, the Liberals and the LRC had in 1903. It is at least arguable that the Alliance between the Liberals and the SDP would have been more successful if the SDP had, from the beginning, sought to emphasize that it could tap electoral support which was spatially distinctive from that of the Liberal party, even at the cost of concentrating its efforts upon particular regions, rather than fighting across the whole country. This would have involved making an explicit appeal to the Labour electoral constituency in the north-east, from which a number of the Labour defectors came, and also in London, where the activities of the extreme Left were leading to widespread disaffection, to be tapped later in the 1980s by the Liberals. To have made such a strategic decision, the SDP would have had consciously to see itself as a predominantly regional party, as the early Labour party had done, and sought to fight intensively on a narrow front, rather than unsuccessfully on a wider front. Such a strategy would have avoided squabbles with the Liberals, since the two parties would no longer have been competing for the same electoral market; and, in retrospect, it might have offered a better chance of success than the strategy actually adopted, which was, in effect, to create a second Liberal party under another name.

VI

Developments in modern party politics – primarily the tightening of party organization and the nationalization of party politics – have made party lines in Britain more rigid, militating against both realignment and its concomitant phenomenon, the electoral pact. This is in many respects a pity. Until the Second World War, periodic realignments brought fluidity to the political system as new issues stimulated new political cleavages. Realignment proved the means by which the political system could adapt itself to new conditions. The 1903 Gladstone–MacDonald pact enabled politics to accommodate itself to the growth of the Labour interest and the politics of social reform. The Lloyd George coalition sought to overcome the sterile disputes of the prewar period and to enable Britain to adapt to fundamental structural change, both at home and on the international stage. Under the National government of 1931, the free trade–protection debate finally disappeared from British politics, and constitutional progress in India was achieved more easily than would have been possible under a purely Conservative government. In each of these cases, realignment proved a means of bringing new blood into governing parties, and putting new issues on to the political agenda.

Since 1945, by contrast, the British party system has become rigid and frozen, and the absence of any successful realigning movement has contributed to a remarkable loss of elasticity in the party system. It is in large part because of this inelasticity that the call for reform of the electoral system and for constitutional reform has arisen. Yet, in all the questioning of our constitutional arrangements over the past two decades, the party system itself has largely escaped critical scrutiny. Few have been willing to ask whether the party system serves the common good as effectively as its beneficiaries would have us believe. This is a matter for some surprise, given that the major parties are, in effect, the custodians of the British Constitution. For this reason, any discussion of constitutional reform which fails to address the facts of party domination will be unrealistic.

Yet it is the inelasticity and rigidity of the party system which is, in the author's opinion, the prime source of Britain's failure to resolve its social and economic problems. The party system which, until 1939, proved, on the whole, a means of accommodating politics to social change has now become a barrier to such accommodation. That barrier is likely to remain until it is swept away by a reform of the electoral system.

Notes

I owe a great deal in the preparation of this chapter to Michael Steed, with whom I have enjoyed many stimulating discussions on electoral pacts. I am grateful also to Andrew Adonis for commenting on a first draft of the chapter. They are not, however, to be implicated in either my arguments or my conclusions.

1   This chapter does not deal with local pacts, nor with pacts in Northern Ireland.

References

Blewett, N. (1972), *The Peers, the Parties and the People: The General Elections of 1910*, London: Macmillan.

Bogdanor, V. (ed.) (1983), *Liberal Party Politics*, Oxford: Clarendon Press.

— (1984), *What is Proportional Representation? A Guide to the Issues*, Oxford: Martin Robertson.

Bonar Law, A. (1918), Bonar Law MSS, House of Lords Record Office, 95/1, 5 Oct.

Butler, D. (1952), *The British General Election of 1951*, Macmillan.

— (1978) (ed.), *Coalitions in British Politics*, London: Macmillan.

— and Butler, G. (1986), *British Political Facts, 1900–1985*, London: Macmillan.

— and Ranney, A. (eds) (1979), *Referendums*, Washington DC: American Enterprise Institute.

Chilston, 3rd Viscount (1961), *Chief Whip: The Political Life and Times of Aretas Akers-Douglas, 1st Viscount Chilston*, London: Routledge & Kegan Paul.

Craig, F. W. S. (1974), *British Parliamentary Election Results, 1885–1919*, London: Macmillan.

Edwards, Sir G. (1964), 'The Emergence of Majority Rule in English Parliamentary Elections', *Transactions of the Royal Historical Society*.

Hart, M. (1990), 'Electoral Pacts', *Contemporary Record*, 2/3, (Feb.).

Jones, A. (1972), *The Politics of Reform, 1884*, Cambridge: Cambridge University Press.

Josephs, J. (1983), *Inside the Alliance: An Inside Account of the Development and Prospects of the Liberal/SDP Alliance*, London: John Martin.

Macmillan, H. (1975), *The Past Masters*, London: Macmillan.

Poirier, P. (1958), *The Advent of the Labour Party*, London: Allen & Unwin.

Samuel, Sir H. (1931), Memorandum in Samuel MSS, House of Lords Record Office, A/77, 24 Aug.

Thorpe, A. (1991), *The British General Election of 1931*, Oxford: Clarendon Press.

Williams, P. (1964), *Crisis and Compromise: Politics and the Fourth Republic*, 2nd edn, London: Longmans.

Wilson, T. (ed.) (1970), *The Political Diaries of C. P. Scott: 1911–1928*, London: Collins.

PART III
THE CONSTITUTION UNDER STRAIN

8   Britain and European Union

Introduction

When the United Kingdom joined the European Community in 1973, she was committing herself to membership of an organization whose constitution was likely to be both unfamiliar and uncongenial. For the constitutional and political practices of the founding member states were very different from those to which the United Kingdom was accustomed. The institutional differences between Britain and her Continental partners may seem of a merely mechanical nature. Yet they reflect deep-seated psychological factors rooted ultimately in history. They flow in the last resort from the fact that our historical experience is so profoundly different from that of our Continental neighbours.

Among the most important dates in British history are 1066, the last occasion on which Britain was successfully invaded; 1660, the year in which the monarchy was restored; and 1688/9, the year of the Glorious Revolution. Since then our political regime has remained basically unchanged. On the Continent, by contrast, the key dates are 1789, when the French Revolution began; 1848, the year of the failed liberal revolutions; and 1917, the year of the Russian Revolutions. Britain succeeded in avoiding all of these revolutions.

Experience of the Second World War served to widen the gap between Britain and her Continental neighbours. For the six founder members of the Community suffered either from Fascism, from enemy occupation, or both. Britain alone among the European belligerents suffered neither. The European Community was founded by political leaders such as Adenauer, Schuman, and De Gasperi as a direct result of their wartime experience. The impulse to European unity was kindled in the ashes of the Resistance as a reaction against the idea of nationalism of which Fascism and National Socialism seemed but perverted forms. In Britain, by contrast, the war symbolized the triumph of nationalism, or rather of patriotism. Winston Churchill was accustomed to speak of 'our island home', the fortress which had kept us safe from invasion. There was no reason for us to crib or confine British nationalism nor to submerge it in supranational institutions.

Even when Britain joined the European Community in 1973, her basic attitudes did not change. She remained as far as ever from sharing the psychology of the other Member States. In particular, she found it difficult to grasp the importance of the principle of power-sharing, the very leitmotif of the Community. For the Community exemplifies the separation of powers both within its own institutions, and also between its own institutions and the Member States.

The Continental democracies all have enacted constitutions prescribing what their legislatures can and cannot do and so power-sharing appears natural to them. The United Kingdom, by contrast, almost alone among democratic states, lacks a codified constitution. This is because the central, if not the only, principle of the British constitution has been, and perhaps still is, the sovereignty of Parliament. For, if Parliament is able to do anything, there is little point in having a constitution which purports to limit its power; and the British constitution can be summed up in just eight words: 'What the Queen in Parliament enacts is law.'

Furthermore, the United Kingdom is a profoundly unitary country lacking any regional or provincial layer of government; and this makes it even more difficult for her to understand the principle of the division of powers. It is noticeable that those countries such as the German Federal Republic which are familiar with federalism in their internal arrangements find it easier to cope with the division of powers within Community institutions than a country such as Britain whose Parliament is seen as the centre of the political universe.

In these two spheres, then – the division of power between the legislature and other institutions, and the territorial division of power – the Community was bound to impose great strains upon the British political system. Moreover, because the Community could not easily be fitted into the Left/Right divisions of British politics, it has given rise to a new cleavage in British politics, one which has proved to be intra-party rather than interparty. Indeed this new cleavage played a large part in disrupting the Labour Party in the years 1970–81, and by the 1990s, it threatened to exert a similar disruptive impact upon the Conservatives.

Thus the European Union poses a triple threat to British institutions – first to the centrality of Parliament in the country's constitutional arrangements, second, to the primacy of central government in central–local relations, and third to the lines of division between the parties. This chapter examines each of these threats in turn. First, it is necessary to examine how Parliament has sought to come to terms with the reality of a new legal order which limits its sovereignty.

Parliament and the European Communities

The European Communities Act 1972 gives the force of law to existing Community legislation and also provides for future Community legislation to have direct effect in Britain. Westminster has no formal constitutional role at all in this process. It cannot amend Community legislation, and is not required to approve it, although it may be required to legislate to incorporate Community legislation into domestic law, or to make supplementary provision for the application of Community legislation.

Parliament, then, has only a secondary legislative role in the European Union. In the Community political system, the normal functions of legislatures are given by the Treaty of Rome to national executives, acting collectively. The governments of the Member States, in the Council of Ministers, assume the function of Community legislators, a function which they are coming increasingly to share with the European Parliament. But the British Parliament, if it cannot be a legislator in so far as European Community law is concerned, can nevertheless scrutinize Community legislation in advance of its adoption by the Council of Ministers, and lobby other Community institutions – the Commission and the European Parliament – so that the British point of view is heard.

Although Community law comprises a distinct legal order and the Community legislative process is quite different from that of the United Kingdom, they cannot be treated as two entirely separate and isolated legal systems. Increasingly, British law is coming to be influenced by Community legislation, especially, although not exclusively, in such areas as agriculture, trade, industry, employment, immigration, and the environment. While the prediction made by Jacques Delors in 1988, that 80 per cent of key economic and social decisions would be taken at European level within ten years, may be exaggerated, there can be no doubt of the increasing importance of Community legislation for the Member States. For example, users of water are now paying higher water charges as a result of the Water Act 1989, a precursor to the Water Acts 1991, the form of which was deeply influenced by EC Directives. The Criminal Justice Act 1993, which appears to be a purely English criminal law reform, in fact also enacts the Insider Dealing Directive. Therefore, no study of legislative processes in Britain would now be complete without taking account of Community legislation.[1]

Because of her different constitutional traditions, however, Britain finds it difficult to comprehend and operate a legislative division of powers between two levels of government. Instead, it seems natural to conceive of the Council of Ministers and the European Parliament as in *competition* with Parliament, rather than being complementary to it. This attitude was expressed in its most extreme form by Enoch Powell, a fervent opponent of British membership of the Community, for whom the two parliaments, Westminster and Strasbourg, were 'involved in a duel which only one of them can survive . . . It follows that all devices for linking the UK element of the European Assembly to Parliament, still more for subordinating them to Parliament, are contrary to the essential implications of direct elections and would break down if attempted.'[2] The conception here is of two entirely separate political systems competing with each other; and on this view, the notion of a division of powers makes no sense.

The three main institutions of the Community, apart from the Court of Justice, are the Commission, the Council of Ministers and the European Parliament. The Commission, whose members are appointed by agreement among the fifteen member governments for a five-year renewable term (four years before the Maastricht Treaty), initiates and implements policy. It is the Council of Ministers, however, comprising ministers from the governments of the Member States, which takes the major policy decisions.

Formally, the European Parliament is primarily a consultative rather than a legislative body which must be consulted on all major issues and has the right to dismiss the Commission by a vote of censure. Under the Single European Act which came into effect in July 1987, the Parliament was given additional powers over the bulk of legislation concerning the single internal market. The Maastricht Treaty increased the powers of the Parliament still further and, under Article 158 of the Treaty of Rome, as amended, Parliament must approve the President and the other members of the Commission.

The European Parliament, however, as well as the Council of Ministers as a legislative body (and even, in some ways, the domestic parliaments of the Continental Member States) are parliaments of an entirely different sort from Westminster, and British legislators find it difficult to understand them. For Westminster is dominated by the executive, while the European Parliament is able to carry on a dialogue with other Community institutions – the Commission and the Council of Ministers. Until the Maastricht Treaty, there was a considerable 'democratic deficit' in the Community, since powers had been transferred from the Member States where they were, in theory, under the supervision of parliaments, to a Community whose executive – the Commission and the Council of Ministers – was not, in the same way, under the supervision of the *European* Parliament. Maastricht helped to resolve this deficit by increasing the powers of the European Parliament, a process which had been begun by the Single European Act. The Maastricht Treaty was, however, perceived as a threat by British policy-makers for whom the only acceptable form in which the Community should be governed was through a confederal Council of Ministers, a Council operating under rules of unanimity and secrecy so as to secure a *'Europe des patries'* after the style of the late General de Gaulle.

The House of Commons is fundamentally a debating chamber, dominated by the binary dialogue between Government and Opposition. The standing committee procedure for the scrutiny of legislation is in essence an extension of the process of debate; indeed, it has been suggested that these committees could be more accurately termed 'debating committees'.[3] Parliament is, as Bernard Crick once put it, a continuous election campaign.[4] Its procedures are geared to informing the electorate of issues in dispute between Government and Opposition, and it implies the existence of two disciplined armies in the House of Commons articulating two quite different philosophies. Community legislation, however, is not being promoted by a government, nor attacked by an opposition. Most Community legislation does not fit in to the binary conception of politics dominant at Westminster; it departs from the normal pattern of a series of measures to which the government is committed and which it has an interest in defending. Community legislation, therefore, is bound to impose a strain upon the House of Commons as it struggles to assimilate an entirely different legislative process into its traditional procedures.

Turning from legislative activity to democratic institutions, it should be noted that the European Parliament, by contrast with Westminster, is, like most Continental legislatures, a multi-party parliament, operating through carefully constructed coalitions. Since the implementation of the Single European Act in 1987, its driving force has been a coalition between the Christian Democrats – the European People's Party – and the Socialists: in other words, between a party group of the moderate Right and a party group of the moderate Left. It was, for example, this coalition which in the 1989 Parliament secured the election of the Spanish Socialist, Enrique Baron Crespo, as President of the Parliament for the first two and a half years, in exchange for an agreement that there would be a Christian Democratic president for the second half. Such coalitional politics are quite unfamiliar to British politicians. In Britain, coalitions occur either in wartime – 1915–16, and 1940 – or at a time of economic emergency – 1931 – but they are seen as essentially *temporary*, as involving a *suspension* of normal adversarial party politics. On the Continent, by contrast, coalitions, in political systems characterized by multi-party politics and proportional representation, are generally seen as involving a *continuation* rather than a suspension of party politics. The parties engaged in a governmental coalition, e.g. the Christian Democrats and Free Democrats in the Federal Republic, continue to argue out their differences, but within government rather than outside it. Such a conception of politics is almost wholly alien to British experience.

The European Parliament, like a number of other Continental legislatures, is horseshoe-shaped rather than rectangular after the manner of Westminster; and, like other Continental legislatures, it is essentially a working legislature, rather than a debating one, devoted primarily to legislative scrutiny rather than to adversarial politics or the general scrutiny of the executive. There is in the European Parliament an absence of confrontation when compared with Westminster. That is partly because there is no party-supported government at Strasbourg seeking to promote its legislation or to secure support for its policies.

As compared to the European Parliament, Westminster is geared to consider legislation only when it reaches a fairly final form, rather than to scrutinize draft legislation. By the time that legislation reaches Parliament, it will generally have been drafted and redrafted many times, following consultation with various interested parties, and the backing and prestige of the government will normally be behind it. A legislative proposal put forward by the Commission and a subsequent decision taken in principle by the Council of Ministers, on the other hand, although already the subject of consultation with interested parties before formal presentation, is subject to considerable amendment as it goes through the legislative process until the negotiations in the Committee of Permanent Representatives of the member states prior to the meeting of the Council of Ministers. This method is quite unknown in British constitutional experience.

In contrast to the House of Commons, the European Parliament has strong specialized committees whose function is both legislative and investigatory. In the Commons, standing committees do not begin to scrutinize legislation until after Second Reading, i.e. after the principle of the legislation has been agreed. The Commons, unlike the European Parliament, has no committee whose role is that of pre-legislative scrutiny of domestic legislation, nor do its standing committees hear oral evidence or receive written evidence. The European Parliament is thus a legislature of a very different kind from the House of Commons. It is not surprising that the two Parliaments find it difficult to communicate with and understand each other. Their attempt to do so resembles a dialogue between two incompatible computers.

Scrutiny of Community Legislation

When the United Kingdom joined the European Community in 1973, she was faced with the problem of how she was to scrutinize and exert influence over a political system quite different from that to which MPs were accustomed.

Parliament's involvement with Community matters takes place under three different procedures. Legislative scrutiny is undertaken by Select Committees on the European Communities in the Commons and Lords. Debates take place on the floor of the House, and, in the Commons, in two new standing committees set up in 1991. Thirdly, Community issues are often considered in the departmentally related select committees established in 1979. The first two of these procedures will be described in turn.

Following the reports of the Foster Committee in the Commons and the Maybray-King Committee in the Lords, both Houses in 1974 established select committees to scrutinize Community legislation. The Commons Committee was set up as the Select Committee on European Secondary Legislation, but in 1976 was renamed Select Committee on European Legislation. In the Lords, the Committee was named Select Committee on the European Communities. The Commons and Lords Committees have different terms of reference and ways of working which have turned out to be complementary.

The Commons Select Committee, which comprises 16 MPs, is primarily a sifting body. It sorts through all documents on draft legislation and other matters submitted to the Council of Ministers or the European Council. It reports weekly to the House, sifting documents into one of four categories:

1 those of sufficient legal or political importance to justify debate;
2 those of legal or political importance, but not warranting debate;
3 those of no legal or political importance;
4 those of legal or political importance, in respect of which the Committee is not yet in a position to decide whether debate would be justified.

In addition to sifting, the Committee carries out the valuable function of publishing, with its reports on documents, its recommendations for debate, and departmental memoranda giving the views of the British government and evidence from affected parties.

In 1990, two new specialist standing committees were established in response to criticisms that too many Community debates were held on the floor of the House after 10 p.m. with only a short time being available for debate. They remain deliberative committees, and, unlike the departmentally related select committees, they have no investigative role.

The House of Lords Select Committee is a more influential body than its Commons counterpart. It is chaired by a salaried office-holder of the House, who, as Principal Deputy-Chairman of Committees, ranks third in the Lords after the Lord Chancellor and the Chairman of Committees. Whereas in the Commons, the Committee before 1991 sifted legislation for the *House* as a whole to consider, in the Lords it is the Chairman of the Select Committee, assisted by a legal adviser and the Clerk, who sifts legislation for the *Select Committee* and its sub-committees to consider. This sift is later endorsed by the Select Committee itself. On average, around one-third of the Community documents received are selected for further consideration, and around one-tenth are the subject of reports to the House.

The Select Committee itself comprises 24 peers and meets on a fortnightly basis when the House is sitting. By contrast to its Commons counterpart, however, it conducts most of its work in six subcommittees, five of which operate in particular policy areas, while the sixth, chaired by a Law Lord, considers Community institutions and the legal implications of Community legislation.

In addition to considering draft Community legislation, the House of Lords Committee also establishes *ad hoc* subcommittees from time to time to consider wider topics, such as, in the 1989–90 session, Economic, Monetary, and Political Union, or proposals which cross subcommittee boundaries such as the European Company Statute.

The House of Lords Select Committee calls upon a wide range of sources, including MEPs, for both written and oral evidence. MEPs giving evidence to the House of Lords Committee are not confined to those representing Britain, but will include members of other nationalities, so enabling the House of Lords Committee to establish links with the Rapporteur of the relevant Committee of the European Parliament. Moreover, the House of Lords Committee also takes evidence from Commission officials, and representatives of interest groups, academics, etc. in all the countries of the Community.

Around one-half of the reports from the House of Lords Committee are debated in the House. Since the government does not enjoy control over the order paper in the House of Lords as it does in the Commons, the Select Committee could always, in the last resort, *insist* upon a debate. These debates are in no way dominated, as those in the Commons have been, by the division between pro- and anti-Europeans, and a leading part is played in debates on the floor of the House by members of the Select Committee and the subcommittees. At the same time, the debates are of less importance in the Lords than in the Commons, for the reports of the Commons Select Committee are on limited and technical matters, and not wide-ranging as is the custom with the Lords Committee. In the Lords, it is the reports which are important, not least because they attract a wide readership throughout the Community and its institutions, and not the debates.

In the Commons, the European Committee was primarily a *sifter* of Community legislation for the House as a whole. Its function was that of gatekeeper, and it was the whole House which was supposed to consider the implications of legislation in its debates and standing committees. In the Lords, on the other hand, there was never any pretence that the whole House could consider the implications of Community legislation; that is the Committee's function.

There is widespread agreement that the scrutiny procedures adopted by the Lords are among the most effective in the Community. In 1977, a Committee established by the Hansard Society for Parliamentary Government was 'struck by the relevance and businesslike nature of the results of the Lords' work in this field, and think it significant that the Commons, who are meant to represent the people of this country, have taken in contrast to the Lords, a largely inward-looking and conservative attitude where the opposite was required.' And in 1982 a Report of the Study Group of the Commonwealth Parliamentary Association on 'The Role of Second Chambers' concluded that the Lords offered 'the only really deep analysis of the issues that is available to the parliamentary representatives of the [then] ten countries in the Community . . . . The Lords' reports are far more informative and comprehensive than those produced by the Commons committee on European legislation.'[5] The Study Group attributed this to the greater specialist knowledge of peers and comparative absence of partisanship.

The scrutiny of Community legislation and policy now forms a major part of the work of the House of Lords. After the House of Commons in the 1960s declined to agree to any reform of the Lords, the peers sought a role for themselves. In the evolutionary fashion typical perhaps of British institutions, they seized the opportunity of British entry into the Community and the consequent need to scrutinize Community legislation. Far less divided over Community membership than the Commons – the Lords approved membership by 451 votes to 58 in October 1971 – the process of scrutiny was not bedevilled, as it had been in the Commons, by the issue of whether British membership of the Community was or was not 'a good thing'.

The work of the House of Lords Select Committee is enormously time-consuming. Few MPs would be willing 'to take on a commitment of anything like the scope implied by the House of Lords model'.[6] For the Commons is composed primarily of professional politicians who would obtain little political advantage from the relatively unglamorous work involved in the scrutiny of Community instruments, while the House of Lords is composed almost wholly of those who have put thoughts of political advancement behind them. Further, it has the advantage, because of the system of nominating to life peerages men and women of eminence, of containing experts in almost every field covered by Community activity. Whether the subject-matter be agriculture, law, or economics, some of the leading authorities in the country will be found in the Lords; and since much Community legislation is technical, this means that the Lords is peculiarly suited to considering it. A disproportionate part of the work of the Select Committee and its subcommittees is in fact played by the life peers who comprise around one-third of the membership of the House as a whole, but around two-thirds of those serving on the Select Committee.[7] Thus the scrutiny procedures of the House of Lords owe their effectiveness to factors which it would be difficult to replicate in any legislature dominated primarily by party politicians. They depend upon the peculiarities of a chamber whose members are there either by hereditary right or by nomination.

Majority Voting in the Community and Parliamentary Accountability in the UK

Until the coming into force of the Single European Act in July 1987, the British position in the Community was defended by the so-called 'Luxembourg Compromise' which provided for use of the veto in the Council of Ministers to protect vital national interests. Before 1987, it had been tacitly accepted that, even where the Treaty prescribed majority voting, unanimity would be required. The extension of majority voting provided for under the 1987 Act has, however, had the effect of nearly eliminating use of the veto,which has become politically unacceptable in areas where the Treaty prescribes majority voting. The Maastricht Treaty has extended majority voting still further into areas where, in the past, unanimity was required.

If a Member State can now be readily outvoted, this has fundamental consequences for the way parliamentary accountability operates. Ministers remain accountable to Parliament for how they act and vote in the Council of Ministers, but if the voting strength of individual ministers in the Council of Ministers has been weakened, this means that Parliament's residual influence over Community legislation has also been weakened. For Parliament exercises no influence over Community legislation other than through the voice and vote of ministers in the Council of Ministers. Thus the inability of British ministers to veto legislation in the Council of Ministers is bound to weaken the influence that can be exercised by Parliament. For this reason, both the Single European Act and the Maastricht Treaty have had the effect of further eroding the direct influence of national parliaments over Community legislation. Thus, if Parliament wishes to retain influence, it may have to exercise it in other ways.

The position of Parliament is protected by the so-called scrutiny reserve, a government undertaking not to agree in the Council of Ministers to any proposal for European legislation which has been recommended by a select committee for debate before that debate has been held, unless special reasons obtain. The effect of this provision is in theory to allow the select committees to insert themselves into the Community decision-making process by requiring the Council of Ministers to wait before coming to a decision until Parliament has debated Community legislation. This scrutiny reserve was not part of the Treaty of Rome, but a convention accepted by the Council of Ministers to respect British parliamentary procedures. Its effectiveness depends, however, upon the possibility of a veto by a British minister until

Community legislation has been discussed in Parliament. With the removal of the veto, the scrutiny reserve is likely to become less effective.

Moreover, legislation, especially when it concerned completion of the internal market, has been moving much faster through the European Parliament and the Council of Ministers, and each Presidency of the Council is eager to secure passage of as many proposals as it can during its six-months period of office so as to increase its prestige within the Community. British ministers have, as a result, become much less willing to use the scrutiny reserve to delay a measure supported by the member state which holds the Presidency of the Council of Ministers. This speeding-up of the Community legislative timetable poses a challenge to the procedures adopted in the Commons to scrutinize Community legislation.

Parliamentary procedures in Britain are geared to checking the activities of ministers in the Council of Ministers. But the Council when it operates by majority voting, as is now frequently the case, can no longer be checked by Westminster or indeed by any other national parliament. For Westminster, like the other parliaments of the member states, can no longer in these cases formally insert the outcome of the scrutiny procedure into the Community legislative process.

Therefore the traditional method of scrutinizing Community legislation needs reappraisal. The Single European Act and the Maastricht Treaty have fundamental consequences which are undermining Britain's traditional approach based upon the influence of national ministers in the Council of Ministers. In future, this channel will be weaker, and influence will have to be exerted at an earlier stage if it is to have any effect. There are two possibilities. The first is to seek to influence the Commission before a Commission proposal is finalized. The second is to seek to persuade the European Parliament before the First Reading debate at Strasbourg. In order to achieve this, the UK Parliament, through its appropriate committees, must seek to persuade, inter alia, the European Parliament, through *its* appropriate committees, of the need for Community legislation to be amended. But this in turn involves a change in the central focus of Commons procedures – away from the emphasis on debates and standing committees, and towards the more investigatory and forensic procedures associated with the select committees.

The House of Commons and the Community

The role of debates on the European Community was considered by a wide-ranging report of the House of Commons Procedure Committee on *The Scrutiny of European Legislation*, published in November 1989, 'the first major enquiry into the way in which the House deals with European legislation since the Procedure Committee's Report of 1978'.[8] It painted a depressing picture of debates in the Commons. The Clerk of the House of Commons referred to 'a predictable group of Members' attending debates. 'Whatever the subject matter it seems to be the same Members who have put down the amendments.'

> MR. WINNICK.   What you are saying, in effect, is that the Members who turn up re-fight the pro- and anti-argument over membership of the EC, to a large extent, and perhaps more of the antis turn up, understandably, than those in favour?
> CLERK OF THE HOUSE.   I think, if it is not going beyond my role to say that, that seems to be my observation and I think that it is missing an opportunity for Members who are expert on the issue before the House to be taking part in these important debates.[9]

Often debates were held too late to influence Community decisions. In one extreme case, in June 1989, the Commons began a debate on a draft directive on broadcasting at 1.08 a.m. on the day on which it was due to be considered by the Council of Ministers! In the past, vital matters failed to be debated at all. There was, for example, no advance debate in the Commons on the fateful 1989 Madrid summit at which Stage One of European Monetary Union was approved. Thus, Commons discussion of a host of consequential legislative measures was pre-empted. The way in which the House was treated over the Madrid summit represented, according to the Procedure Committee, 'a serious breakdown in the scrutiny system' (para. 46).

The Procedure Committee therefore recommended, and the government accepted, a proposal that, in place of the legislative debates, general debates be instituted every six months on the Foreign Office paper on the development of the Community, at least three weeks before the twice-yearly European Council summit. This has been a beneficial change. For example, the debate before the Summit in the second half of 1991 convinced ministers that the social protocol to the Maastricht Treaty would not be acceptable to the vast majority of Conservative MPs. Thus, the government knew that it had to secure an opt-out if the Treaty was to win the approval of Parliament.

Nevertheless, the central weakness in the role of the Commons *vis-à-vis* the Community remains. It was pointed out in 1989 by John Biffen, a former Leader of the House, in evidence to the Procedure Committee. Biffen argued that because the House had no effective control over the minister, and the minister had only limited leverage over his colleagues in the Council of Ministers, the debating procedure was but 'a symbolism'. Parliament retained 'the trappings of more formal and adversarial politics' in a situation in which it was more important to learn 'to operate by influence and consensus'.[10]

'The Select Committee', according to Biffen, 'with its consensual tradition, could become a more effective way of influencing Ministers'. Since Westminster cannot any longer exercise very much influence over the Council of Ministers, Biffen asked, why not acknowledge this, and 'In return for surrendering an ineffective power . . . seek an arrangement which offered a greater prospect of influence'.[11] Mr Biffen, however, proposed that the Commons create a Select Committee for European Affairs on the model of the House of Lords Select Committee. But the trouble with this proposal is that it would only serve to reinforce the separation of 'European' business from other business before the House. Sir Leon Brittan, Vice-President of the Commission, speaking to the Coningsby Club on 13 July 1989, declared that such a separation made no sense. 'It is now increasingly appreciated', he said, 'that the Community's proposals cover a vast range of subjects. They cannot be kept in some sort of ghetto, separate from the mainstream of political debate.'

It is one of the basic faults of Parliament's approach to Community issues that it tends to treat 'Europe' as an insulated policy area, separate from other policy areas. Yet Community law will increasingly blend with British law in such areas as trade, industry, agriculture, employment, and environment. Parliament tends to divide its activities in terms of procedures, with different procedures being brought into play according to whether a matter involves, for example, finance, legislative scrutiny, administration, or Europe. Yet, the consumer of legislation is not concerned with procedures, but rather with the question of how legislation, whether deriving from Parliament or from the Community, is likely to affect him or her personally.

The obvious way of recognizing the interconnectedness between British and Community law is for the Commons to rely more upon the investigatory procedures of the departmentally related select committees established in 1979, rather than upon a separate European Select Committee and standing committees. Thus, instead of a single committee having the sole responsibility for scrutinizing Community legislation, the task of examining draft Community legislation 'should pass to the Select Committees of the House responsible for different policy areas'. Each departmentally related select committee should examine its structure to see how it might best equip itself for the task. Indeed, the Procedure Committee in 1990 gave a very broad hint that the departmentally related select committees were the right bodies to undertake this kind of work.[12] 'We believe that European legislation is an area in which the House can benefit from the detailed, forensic examination of policy issues and practical implications which Select Committees are particularly well equipped to carry out. Certainly, this is a task which the House as a whole cannot perform properly, since it has no real mechanism for the sustained and effective questioning of Ministers.' Debates on the floor of the

House or in standing committees would come to the better informed if they had been preceded by select committee investigations. Developments along these lines are already coming to be seen. The Foreign Affairs Select Committee now has regular sessions in which it takes oral evidence from Foreign and Commonwealth Office ministers on the future programme of the Council of Ministers and the European Council, 'including particular priorities of the current and future Presidencies and the Commission'; while the Select Committee on European Legislation began, in October 1989, regular evidence sessions with FCO ministers, 'the purpose of which is to identify Presidency priorities'.

The select committees could, according to the Procedure Committee, play a particularly important anticipatory role at an earlier stage of the Community legislative process, i.e. before legislation reaches the Council of Ministers. This would involve discovering what new developments and new thinking were taking place, both in the Commission and in the European Parliament.

Recognition of the role of the departmentally related select committees would indicate that Parliament had appreciated that its main function *vis-à-vis* the Community, following the Single European Act and Maastricht, was not so much to scrutinize legislation as to lobby Community institutions so that Community legislation takes full account of British interests. If the select committees were given earlier warning of forthcoming legislative proposals, particularly in the form of working texts, they could seek to exert influence upon the Commission. Therefore, they should 'press for regular access to the various documents by the Commission indicating its future programme' and 'seek to establish links with the Commission' with a view to obtaining working texts of draft legislation going through the Council of Ministers, being amended by working groups and by the Committee of Permanent Representatives of the Member States. Following the Single European Act and the Maastricht Treaty, the European Parliament, having a greater role in Community legislative procedure through the co-operative and co-decision procedures, will be in a much stronger position to help Westminster obtain this information. The select committees could, in the view of the Procedure Committee, also play a lobbying role *vis-à-vis* the European Parliament by cultivating 'informal contacts with Members of the European Parliament with an interest or expertise in relevant subjects, including Rapporteurs'.[13]

If the select committees were also able to involve MEPs in their work, perhaps by employing them as specialist advisers, this would greatly improve the scrutiny procedures of the Commons. For MEPs can act as an early warning system to the House, since they are dealing with Community issues in a more systematic fashion and on a daily basis. Further, MEPs often have earlier access to information, since they can ask questions of Commissioners and cross-question them on the implications of Community legislation. Moreover, they can, if they wish, propose amendments in the European Parliament based upon the opinions of MPs in the Commons.

At present, however, the expertise of MEPs seems insufficiently used. One MP on the Procedure Committee, David Winnick, asked the leader of the Conservative MEPs Christopher Prout:

> Q. 308. Do you have a feeling that perhaps the expertise of members of the European Parliament from other national states is being drawn upon, whereas Britain is not?
>
> MR PROUT. Yes, there is no doubt about that.[14]

Co-operation between the two Parliaments has been hindered because, in the words of the Procedure Committee, 'A large body of opinion in the House of Commons has tended to regard the European Parliament with a degree of condescension' (para. 105). Membership of the European Parliament has sometimes been seen as a consolation prize for those who have failed to be selected for the Commons; while any increase in the power or influence of the European Parliament is seen as a threat to Westminster. Unless the Commons can bring itself to regard Strasbourg as a body with its own distinct powers which are *complementary* rather than *competitive*, it will continue to fail to use the expertise of MEPs effectively. At present, mutual resentment between the two Parliaments threatens to fragment scrutiny at the expense of the Commons just at a time when greater co-ordination is essential and could prove enormously fruitful.

Parliamentary Sovereignty and the Community

Parliament adapted itself to British membership of the Community, under-standably perhaps, in an evolutionary fashion so as to change its procedures as little as possible. 'It is quite remarkable', John Biffen has commented, 'the extent to which we have not undertaken any fundamental alteration in our procedures to take account of what I think to be something almost without precedent in significance over the last generation or so.'[15] 'Europe' was seen as a discrete and separate issue which could be tacked on to Parliament's traditional business as a kind of optional extra. It was seen as something extraneous, as a separate and insulated political system whose points of con-tact with the UK Parliament would be very few.

It is, in the last resort, the principle of parliamentary sovereignty, the idea of Westminster as the only sun which provides light and around which other institutions move and have their being, which forms the main conceptual block to appreciating a new division of power. For the concept of sovereignty implies that there must somewhere be a supreme political authority in the Community – either the member states, which means that Community decisions can be nothing more than the product of intergovernmental agreement; or the Community itself, and that would mean, as Hugh Gaitskell, the British Labour leader once put it, the end of a thousand years of history, the end of the nation-state. Yet, there is a third alternative, a genuine division and sharing of powers between the Community and the Member States, so that each complements but neither controls the other. Indeed the whole *raison d'être* of the Community is that power can be shared and sovereignty divided so as to create a political entity capable of carrying out common policies without compromising the identity of the component units.

The undivided sovereignty of Parliament was emphasized by the Glorious Revolution in Britain, over 300 years ago, in 1689. Perhaps the time has now come to cease emphasizing it.[16]

Europe, Subsidiarity and Central–Local Relations in the UK

The European Community, as well as requiring fundamental alterations in the procedures of Parliament, is likely also to require a redefinition of the relationships between central and local government. For local authorities have been developing links with the Community which will have important implications for their constitutional position. This is so for two main reasons.

The first is that Community legislation is bound to impinge upon local government responsibilities. Even before the Maastricht Treaty, the Community had competence over such matters as economic development, transport, energy, and environmental health, all of which are in Britain in part the responsibility of local authorities. Maastricht considerably widens the scope of the competences of the Community, adding to this list education, culture, consumer protection, and tourism. Moreover, the Treaty gives the Community for the first time authority to approve measures relating to town and country planning, land use, and management of water resources (Art. 130s).

Secondly, Community law makes the member states, not local authorities, legally responsible for ensuring compliance with its provisions, even where the actual responsibility for carrying out the policies lies with local government. Local authorities, however, are responsible for *implementing* Community legislation on such matters as, for example, trading standards and consumer protection, and if they do not, they can, so it appears, be liable in civil proceedings.[17]

Thus, in addition to the traditional central–local relationship, and the relationship between member states and Brussels, there is a third intergovernmental relationship, that between local authorities and the Community. Indeed, one authority has argued that, with regard to 'the 1992 process' alone, the completion of the internal market, 'no area of local government activity will be unaffected by this major shift towards closer European integration'.[18]

At first sight, however, because it is member states and not local authorities which are responsible for compliance with Community legislation, it would seem that the extension of Community competences will exert a constraining effect upon local government through a process of creeping centralization.

The Community, however, is naturally concerned with the distribution of power between central government and local authorities within the Member States, even though it has no authority over the structure of government in any Member State. The Community's concern arises because it has a responsibility to ensure that its policy instruments, such as for example, its structural funds, are distributed in an effective and equitable way. But, more fundamentally, the Community has come into existence because, in the modern world, some governmental functions are best exercised at a level larger than that of the member state; as a corollary, it follows that some governmental functions may best be exercised at a level lower than that of the Member State. If power can shift away from the level of the State in one direction, so also it can shift away from the State in another. The project of European Union needs to embrace both contingencies.

The Maastricht Treaty undoubtedly centralizes power through extending the competences of the Community in areas such as energy and the environment, as well as in its proposals for economic and monetary union. But, at the same time, the Treaty signifies a first attempt to counteract the trend towards creeping centralization and to seek a new equilibrium capable of balancing power between the Community, member states, and local authorities. This is to be achieved in two ways – first through the principle of subsidiarity, and second through the establishment of a new consultative Committee of the Regions.

The principle of subsidiarity is introduced in the preamble to the Maastricht Treaty, and enacted by a newly inserted Article 3b of the Treaty. The preamble to Maastricht declares that the signatories are

> resolved to continue the process of creating an ever closer union among the peoples of Europe, in which decisions are taken as closely as possible to the citizen in accordance with the principle of subsidiarity.

Article 3b declares that:

The Community shall act within the limits of the powers conferred upon it by the Treaty and of the objectives assigned to it therein.

In areas which do not fall within its exclusive competence, the Community shall take action, in accordance with the principle of subsidiarity, only if and in so far as the objectives of the proposed action cannot be sufficiently achieved by the Member States and can therefore, by reason of the scale or effects of the proposed action, be better achieved by the Community.

Any action by the Community shall not go beyond what is necessary to achieve the objectives of this Treaty.

The principle of subsidiarity was put into the Treaty partly as a result of the concern of the German *Länder* that the development of the Community should not undermine its federal system of government, since it is the federal government rather than the *Länder* which is legally responsible for ensuring compliance with Community provisions. But the British government also pressed for its inclusion for a quite different reason – to reserve powers for the Member States as against the Community. For Britain, the principle of subsidiarity is a substitute for a states' rights clause, on the lines of the 10th Amendment to the American Constitution or Article 30 of the German Constitution, a provision conspicuously absent from the Treaty of Rome.

The principle of subsidiarity is binding upon the institutions of the Community, and imposes a three-fold test upon putative Community legislation. The first is whether there is a legal basis for a Community action. That was, of course, already part of Community law before the Maastricht Treaty, and Article 164 required the Court of Justice to ensure it. The second is whether, even if there is a legal basis, the Community should activate it, or whether instead the objective of the proposal might not be sufficiently achieved by the Member States. Moreover, even if the objective in question cannot be sufficiently achieved by the Member States, the question has to be asked whether the objective can be *better* achieved by the Community. The third test relates to the intensity rather than the scope of Community legislation, and asks whether the Community is leaving enough discretion to the Member States. Is it, for example, using a regulation that is directly applicable in a situation where a directive that would leave implementation to a Member State would suffice?

The second test applies to 'the areas which do not fall within' the 'exclusive jurisdiction' of the Community. It bears some similarity to Article 72 of the German Constitution providing for the role of the *Länder* in cases of concurrent powers. It does not apply, therefore, to areas such as the Common Agricultural Policy, the common commercial policy, and the external tariff, which fall within areas of admitted exclusive Community competence. The second test applies to areas where there is a mixed competence of both the

Community and Member States, so that there is a choice between Community action and national action.

The third test, however, in the final paragraph of Article 3b, known as the proportionality test, applies to *all* Community legislation, whether it lies within a field of exclusive competence or not. According to Douglas Hurd, the Foreign Secretary at the time, the British delegation at Maastricht insisted that the proportionality test be put into a separate third paragraph precisely to emphasize its contrast with the previous provision which applies only to areas where the Community lacks exclusive competence.[19] In fact, however, given the case-law of the European Court of Justice, this third paragraph adds little, if anything, to existing legal rules.

It is at the present time impossible to predict what use the European Court will make of the principle of subsidiarity. It could generate a burgeoning jurisprudence as the commerce clause and the equal protection clause have done in the American Constitution; or it could, alternatively, come to have very little juridical significance, as Article 72 of the German Constitution appears to have done. It may be that the European Court will take the view that it has to prove manifest error or abuse of powers to strike down Community legislation on grounds of subsidiarity. Many British lawyers would take this view since they believe that subsidiarity is otherwise too imprecise a term to be properly justiciable. Subsidiarity may well therefore prove to be a constitutional convention of the Community rather than a justiciable principle.

The German *Länder* and perhaps the Spanish autonomous regions might be able to bring a case before the European Court on subsidiarity grounds but British local authorities will be unable to do so. The principle cannot be invoked to protect local authority rights, since the Community cannot concern itself with the structure of government within any Member State. It is, indeed, part of the subsidiarity principle that if a competence belongs to the Member States, it must be for the Member States rather than the Community to determine how that competence should be distributed internally.

Nevertheless, the principle of subsidiarity may well influence, albeit indirectly, central–local relations. For the principle is likely to operate at the political as well as the legal level. It is likely to prove a political constraint upon Community institutions – upon the Commission when proposing legislation, the European Parliament when proposing amendments, and the Council of Ministers when making decisions. At the Lisbon summit in June 1992, the Member States agreed that all existing Community legislation had to be examined by the end of 1993 so that the Council could decide which items ought to be repealed in accordance with subsidiarity criteria. Proposals for new legislation are now accompanied by a justification from the Commission showing that they are in accordance with the principle of subsidiarity.

Although the principle of subsidiarity will not directly affect central–local relations, it may well give rise to a new mood in which decentralization is seen as a necessary complement to the transfer of competences to the Community. In such circumstances it is difficult to believe that Britain will or can remain unaffected. For, if the question: 'Has the Community made the case that this competence cannot be carried out at Member State level?' comes to be asked, so also might the question: 'Has the case been made that this competence cannot be carried out at local level?' If that happens, the principle of subsidiarity will have helped to create a new atmosphere in central–local relations, and one which is far more favourable to local government.

The principle is, moreover, complemented by Articles 198a–c of the Maastricht Treaty, establishing a Committee of the Regions. The establishment of this Committee may be regarded as an institutional means of ensuring that subsidiarity leads to the devolution of powers to subnational levels of government, as well as from the Community to Member States.

The Committee of the Regions comprises 189 members from regional and local government, and has advisory status. Britain, together with France, Germany, and Italy, has 24 members on it. Members of the Committee, although appointed by the Council of Ministers, acting unanimously on proposals from the respective Member States, may not be bound by any mandatory instructions. They must be completely independent in the performance of their duties. The British members are required to be elected local government representatives.[20]

The Council and the Commission are *required* to consult the Committee where so provided by the Treaty, and *may* consult it on other occasions. The Committee may also submit an opinion whenever its specific regional interests are involved in any Community action.

Although the Committee has solely advisory powers, its significance should not be underestimated. The Committee cannot force the Council of Ministers to come to a decision, but, since it is required to give its opinion, it has a delaying power. This power can, however, be limited by Article 198a which allows the Commission to set a time limit of one month for the Committee to give its opinion.

Nevertheless, the setting up of the Committee constitutes a clear institutional recognition on the part of the Community that the construction of European union requires the contribution of regional and local bodies, as well as that of national governments. Since the regions and localities are responsible for the implementation of some Community legislation, and often have to enforce it, logic requires that they should be given a voice in helping to determine what that legislation should be. The Maastricht Treaty transforms the regional problem from a merely economic one to a political and institutional one. It recognizes the role of subnational bodies, and seeks to organize their participation in the decision-making process of the Community.

The development of the European Community, then, offers the possibility of reversing the process of centralization which has been so marked a feature of British government over the past two decades. But local authorities in Britain have not found it easy to respond to the Community. In its report of December 1991, *A Rough Guide to Europe: Local Authorities and the European Community*, the Audit Commission concluded that 'All local authorities know that they ought to be doing something about "Europe". Some have made outstanding contributions already. But many do not seem to have a clear idea of what exactly that something is or how to do it' (p.1).

Part of the difficulty is that the internal management of local authorities still based largely on the committee system which has dominated local government since the 1835 Municipal Corporations Act. This tends to disperse and fragment power among committee chairmen. It is not conducive to strong local leadership of the kind routinely exercised by, for example, French mayors. This is a weakness in competing for funds in the Community, since such competition often depends upon marketing skills more likely to be found in clearly identifiable local leaders than in committees. Joseph Chamberlain would have been able to market Birmingham, in the way that Pierre Mauroy has been able to market Lille; but there do not seem to be any successors to Chamberlain in British local government, for the committee system does not generate them.

In 1991, the Department of the Environment issued a consultation paper on *The Internal Management of Local Authorities in England*, which paid considerable attention to the methods by which local government was organized in other countries, especially in the other Member States of the Community. It found that local government in Britain was almost unique in lacking a clear separation of powers between the council, with representative and legislative functions, and a leadership group with executive functions. This consultation paper led to the establishment of a working party which duly reported in July 1993. Its report, *Community, Leadership and Representation* called for the Secretary of State to allow local authorities to adopt new models of internal management. It did not advocate a strong mayoral system, but it did suggest as one possibility a cabinet-type model, which could yield stronger and more identifiable local leadership. A model of this type would make local government in Britain more effective in bidding for Community funds.

A further difficulty which local government faces in dealings with the Community is that its structure is out of line with that of the other Member States. In particular, Britain is the only large Member State without a regional layer of government. Yet many Community projects are planned on a regional basis, while the regions are often the administrative units which have to compete for or administer Community funds. Moreover, as the Community develops, direct transnational regional links such as those between the Four Motors Regions – Catalonia, Lombardy, Rhône-Alpes and Baden-Württemberg – are likely to become more important. In a briefing in London in June 1991, Bruce Millan, the Commissioner responsible for regional policies, after declaring that the administrative arrangements between central and local government were a matter for Member States to decide, went on to say that 'I find it easy to work with strong regional bodies. There is no question of that. In terms of economic development, they are more effective than dividing everything up into small authorities.' Member States such as Belgium and Germany which not only have elected regional bodies, but whose regions are represented in the national parliament, are likely to be able to exert greater influence in the Community than Britain which lacks a regional layer of government. It has been argued that as a result 'strong regions will drive out weak ones', so that the German *Länder* become role models which other Member States will eventually come to copy.[21] There can be little doubt that the Community presupposes a regional structure of government as necessary to the proper functioning of the Community's political system.

In the absence of regional government, however, British local authorities must be prepared to co-operate with local authorities in other parts of the Community in planning joint projects, and also to form regional groupings within British local government. 'Without effective regional groupings', the Audit Commission has commented, quoting a senior Community official, 'the UK will lose out'.[22] There are already some such regional groupings. For example, in the North of England, local authorities have formed a Northern Regional Association of Local and District Authorities. Yet, after surveying local authorities, the Audit Commission concluded that 'only 52% of authorities surveyed liaise locally, 45% regionally and 32% with the private sector on Euro-matters'.[23]

Most local authorities have recognized the importance of the Community by appointing a 'European officer'. But Europe is coming increasingly to permeate so many areas of local government activity that it has become quite unrealistic to hive it off to a special committee or officer. It no longer makes sense to demarcate 'Europe' from the rest of the work of a local authority. For local government is becoming, by its very nature, European.

As with Parliament, 'Europe' is often looked at by local authorities as a special interest or department of government on its own. It seems natural to look at different layers of government as being somehow located in separate boxes, one box being labelled 'central government', another 'local government', and a third 'Europe', each of these boxes containing politicians pursuing their own activities in an independent way. In Parliament, as we have seen, there are select and standing committees dealing with 'Europe', and in local government there are officers whose concern is with 'Europe'. Yet, if the Community is coming to permeate so many aspects of British life, this mental picture, this perspective, will have to disappear. 'Europe' can no longer be seen as a separate and independent layer of government. In place of a governmental structure comprising independent layers of administration, each located within, as it were, its own box, the Community process substitutes a structure within which the different layers interact. It replaces a structure of government in which the layers are independent with one in which they are interdependent.

Europe and the British Party System

As well as imposing strains upon parliamentary procedures at Westminster and upon local authorities, the European Community has also undermined the British party system. Indeed, it was in part responsible for a seismic shift in British politics, the split in the Labour Party and the formation of the breakaway Social Democratic Party (SDP) in 1981.

It was not until the 1970s that the European Community threatened to disrupt party alignments. During the 1960s, first the Conservative government under Harold Macmillan and then the Labour government under Harold Wilson sought entry into the Community, but both were rebuffed by de Gaulle. After the resignation of de Gaulle in 1969, however, British entry came back on to the political agenda and Edward Heath's Conservative government, elected in 1970, secured the agreement of the other Member States to Britain's admission. Labour in opposition now adopted a more sceptical stance and, in 1971 opposed the terms of entry negotiated by the Conservatives. However, 69 Labour MPs – around one-quarter of the Parliamentary Labour Party – defied a three-line Whip and joined the Conservatives on the vote of principle on entry. In 1972, the Labour Party decided that, when returned to office, it would put the renegotiated terms of entry to a referendum. This decision caused Roy Jenkins to resign the deputy-leadership of the Party.

In 1975, the referendum, itself a constitutional innovation, caused a second constitutional innovation, a suspension of collective Cabinet responsibility, something which had only happened once before, in 1932, but under a coalition government. Seven Cabinet ministers took advantage of this provision by which they were able to campaign against Britain remaining in the Community. In 1977, there was a further suspension of collective responsibility on the European Assembly Elections Bill providing for direct elections to the European Parliament when six Cabinet ministers voted against the government. At that time, Margaret Thatcher, as Leader of the Opposition, asked the Prime Minister, James Callaghan, whether the doctrine of collective responsibility applied to his government. Callaghan replied, 'I certainly think that the doctrine should apply, except in cases where I announce that it does not.'[24]

During the referendum campaign in 1975, Labour supporters of the European Community such as Roy Jenkins, David Owen, and Shirley Williams worked together with members of other parties, and came to believe that they might have more in common with the Liberals who were enthusiasts for the Community than with their colleagues on the Left, who were hostile to it. The division within the Labour Party on the European Community was one of the factors predisposing leading figures on Labour's right-wing to break from Labour in 1981 and form a new party, the Social Democrats, which formed an alliance with the Liberals.

By the end of the 1980s, however, Labour had come gradually to unite, under the leadership of Neil Kinnock, and to adopt a more pro-European orientation; and, from the time of Margaret Thatcher's Bruges speech in 1988, if not earlier, the European issue had come to threaten the internal cohesion of the Conservative Party rather than Labour. Indeed, many of the great crises of the premierships of Margaret Thatcher and John Major – the Westland affair in 1985/6, the resignations of Nigel Lawson in 1989 and of Sir Geoffrey Howe in 1990 (this latter resignation precipitating Margaret Thatcher's loss of the premiership), and the passage of the European Communities (Amendment) Bill of 1993 ratifying Maastricht – had Europe as their central theme.

In the European Parliament, the Conservatives belonged, until 1992, to a party group – the European Democratic Group – which comprised, in addition to themselves, only two Danish Conservatives. The Spanish Partido Popular had left this Group for the Christian Democrat Group shortly after the 1989 elections to the European Parliament. The Conservatives thus remained detached from the main grouping of the centre-right in the European Parliament, the Christian Democrats, whose programme was explicitly federalist. They remained members of what was essentially a national group in a multinational parliament. Until the early 1990s, Labour, too, was divorced from its Continental counterparts who were, with the exception of the Danish Social Democrats, firmly integrationist.

In the European Parliament there has been a convergence towards the two main political groups – the Socialists and Christian Democrats – who, between them, can command an absolute majority in the Parliament. The smaller political families have tended to become marginalized. Moreover, party allegiances are also becoming important in the European Council, the twice-yearly summits of Community heads of government. It has been said that 'if one wants to predict how a European Council is going to go, it is a wise thing to look at the summit which always takes place beforehand of the Christian Democrat members in it because they constitute at the moment half the membership of the European Council. They feel a sense of solidarity. Pre-Maastricht they had a very important meeting where a lot of the decisions that were taken were already anticipated by their discussions.'[25]

Thus there is a danger that the British parties in the European Parliament, and the British position on the Council of Ministers, will lack weight since the British political parties are not in the mainstream of the European party families. Since the 1980s, however, Labour's position on Europe has become much closer to that of its Continental colleagues, but on the Right there has been a growing divergence of view between the Conservatives and Christian Democrats on the basic issues of federalism, monetary union, and the social protocol to the Maastricht Treaty.

Conservative MEPs, however, exposed as they were to Community institutions, came increasingly to share the viewpoint of their Christian Democrat colleagues in the European Parliament rather than their Conservative colleagues at Westminster. Significantly, the Conservative MEPs were the only element in the Party to support Sir Anthony Meyer and Michael Heseltine in their leadership challenges to Margaret Thatcher in 1989 and 1990; and they sought alliance with the Christian Democrat Group so that they could play a larger part in the European Parliament's activities. In 1992, they joined the Christian Democrat parliamentary group in the European Parliament, but without becoming full members of the Christian Democrat transnational party, the European People's Party. The Conservatives did not, therefore, have to accept Christian Democrat policies with which they disagreed.

The Conservative Party as a whole remains sceptical of European integration, and it is divided between those who accepted the Maastricht Treaty as a lesser evil, and those who believed that the Treaty was a step too far. At the Conservative Party Conference of 1992, the then Foreign Secretary, Douglas Hurd, raised the spectre of previous Conservative splits on the Corn Laws and Tariff Reform, and warned the Party not to let such a split occur again. Nevertheless, the parliamentary conflict over Maastricht threatened to split the Conservatives during the long parliamentary debates on the Maastricht Treaty in the House of Commons in 1992–3, and to render John Major's leadership untenable. Future steps towards European integration, due to be considered at the next intergovernmental conference in 1996, threaten to split the Party even more deeply.

The political culture of the European Parliament, and indeed of the European Community as a whole, conflicts profoundly with the ethos of the

Conservative Party. For the European Parliament is elected by proportional representation, and operates by means of a consensus between Christian Democrats and Socialists which cuts across the Right/Left divisions of politics. Its ethos is essentially one of power-sharing – power-sharing within itself, between itself and other Community institutions, and between the Community and the member states – while the ethos of British politics is adversarial, centralist and exclusive. The Conservative Party, the party of British – or perhaps English – nationalism, the party which seeks to defend the British constitution, is likely to find itself under increasing strain if the Community continues to develop in the direction of greater integration.

Conclusions

The British party system, like local government and like Parliament itself, has not found it easy to adapt to the European Community. These difficulties, as stated at the beginning of this chapter, reflect deep-seated habits of mind, for it is these habits of mind which give ideological backing to Britain's system of government, a system that remains so different from that of the other Member States.

But, of course, these habits of mind need not necessarily prove permanent. For habits can change. Indeed, psychoanalysts tell us that the first step towards changing deep-seated patterns of behaviour is to recognize them for what they are.

At the beginning of this chapter, it was suggested that some of the most important dates in British history were 1066, the date of the last successful invasion of Britain, 1660, the date of the restoration of the monarchy, and 1689, the date of the Glorious Revolution. These landmarks ensured that the progress of Britain's system of government would be both evolutionary and stable.

But there are also other important dates in British history – 1746, for example, when the Jacobite revolt, the last major rebellion against the Crown, was defeated, and with it the threat of Continental invasion. The result was that Britain found herself isolated from Europe, and, coincidentally, the eighteenth century also saw the growth of empire. It may well be that the psychological differences between Britain and the countries of the Continent only came to be emphasized during this period, reinforced as they were by the French Revolution and the Napoleonic threat. But 1947, when India achieved independence, symbolized the voluntary relinquishing of Britain's imperial role. It could be argued that the intervening two centuries, even though they have so strongly coloured Britain's sense of national identity, were an aberrant period in her long history during most of which the fate of Britain and that of the Continent have been intertwined. If that is so, then the mind-set which this period of 200 years engendered need not necessarily prove permanent. Thus Britain's political habits, while deep-seated, may yet prove alterable. And perhaps future generations will perceive the fundamental conflict in British postwar politics as being not so much between Left and Right, as between those who believed that Britain's experience between the eighteenth and twentieth centuries was a deviation, and those who saw Britain's separation from the Continent as a fundamental axiom of her existence. This profound political divide cut across the parties, uniting as it did Harold Macmillan, Edward Heath, Roy Jenkins and Roy Hattersley against Hugh Gaitskell, Enoch Powell, Margaret Thatcher and Michael Foot.

Which of these two perceptions of British history is the more accurate? It is far too soon to answer this question with any degree of certainty. But upon the answer, much of the future shape of Britain's changing constitution will depend.

Notes and reference

I should like to thank Michael Ryle, Michael Steed, and Anthony Teasdale for their helpful comments on an earlier draft of this chapter. But they are not to be implicated in my conclusions.

1 *Making The Law*, Report of the Hansard Society Commission on the Legislative Process, 1992, para. 522. The writer was a member of this Commission.
2 Written submission by the Rt. Hon. Enoch Powell, MP, to Select Committee of the European Communities, *Relations between the United Kingdom Parliament and the European Parliament after Direct Elections*, vol. ii, HL 256, 1977–8, 186.
3 J. A. G. Griffith, Michael Ryle, and M. A. J. Wheeler-Booth (1989), *Parliament: Functions, Practice and Procedures*, Sweet & Maxwell, 270.
4 Bernard Crick (1970), *The Reform of Parliament*, 2nd edn, Weidenfeld & Nicolson, *passim*.
5 The reports by the Hansard Society and the Commonwealth Parliamentary Association's Study Group are quoted in Cliff Grantham and Caroline Moore Hodgson (1985), 'The House of Lords: Structural Changes: The Use of Committees', in Philip Norton (ed.), *Parliament in the 1980s*, Blackwell, 125–7. This chapter contains an excellent brief account of the working of the House of Lords Select Committee.
6 Report of the Study Group of the Commonwealth Parliamentary Association on 'The Role of Second Chambers' quoted above, para. 95.
7 Grantham and Hodgson, *op. cit.*, 130–1.
8 HC 622.
9 HC 622, Q. 371, 372.
10 HC 622–II, p. 1.
11 Ibid.
12 As proposed by Terence Higgins, MP, Chairman of the House of Commons Liaison Committee, HC 622–II, p. 158.
13 The quotations in the last three paragraphs are from HC 622, paras 88, 89 and fnn. 90 and 104.
14 HC 622–II, p. 96.

15   HC 622–II, p. 2.
16   See Vernon Bogdanor (1988), 'Britain and Europe: The Myth of Sovereignty', in Richard Holme and Michael Elliott (eds), *1688–1988: Time for a New Constitution*, Macmillan.
17   See *Fratelli Constanzo SpA v. Comune di Milano* [1990] 3 C.M.L.R., 1990, 239, and *R. v. London Boroughs Transport Committee, ex parte Freight Transport Association* [1990], 1 C.M.L.R. 229.
18   Paul Bongers (1990), *Local Government and 1992*, Longman, 89.
19   See the debate on subsidiarity in the European Communities (Amendment) Bill, Hansard, House of Commons, 11 Mar. 1993, col. 1157.
20   This followed a government defeat in the House of Commons. See the debate on the Committee of the Regions in the European Communities (Amendment) Bill in Hansard, House of Commons, 4 Feb. 1993, col. 505 ff.; and the vote, 8 Mar., col. 715.
21   By Peter Ludlow, in giving evidence to the House of Commons Foreign Affairs Committee, *Europe After Maastricht*, 2nd Report, 1992–3, HC 642, vol. ii, Q. 390.
22   Audit Commission (1991), *A Rough Guide to Europe: Local Authorities and the European Community*, HMSO, 40.
23   Ibid., 24.
24   Hansard, House of Commons, 16 June 1977, col. 552.
25   Peter Ludlow, *Europe after Maastricht*, HC 233, vol. ii, Q. 134.

9 Local Government and the Constitution

Does Local Government have any Place in the British Constitution?

When Tocqueville declared that England (sic) lacked a constitution, he did not mean simply that our various enactments were not gathered together and codified in a single document, a written constitution. He meant something rather more than this. He was drawing attention to the fact that there was, in Britain, no special category of laws connected with the organization of government or the defence of individual rights which could be called 'constitutional', such that they could be entrenched against change. In Britain, therefore, Parliament was both a legislative and constituent body. It could pass laws connected with the framework of government with the same ease as it could pass any other laws. That, of course, was a consequence of the doctrine of the sovereignty of Parliament. For, if Parliament is sovereign and can do what it likes, there is no point in drawing together a special group of enactments into a single unified document called a constitution. The statutes chosen for inclusion in the constitution would have no greater status than any other statutes. They could be altered with the same ease by a simple majority in Parliament.

Local government is as much subject to this rule as any other area of British life. It is at the mercy of a sovereign parliament – or, to put the matter more realistically, at the mercy of an omnicompetent government. For the government is generally able to control Parliament and to persuade Parliament to do its bidding. It would seem, therefore, as if, in Britain, local government can have no guaranteed role, no constitutional status at all.

Yet, there is more to the British Constitution than the simple assertion of the unbridled sovereigny of Parliament. For there are many things which Parliament could decide to do which we would have no hesitation in labelling 'unconstitutional'. If, for example, Parliament were to pass a law providing that all red-headed people should be executed tomorrow without trial, one suspects that a large number of people would label such a law as unconstitutional even though it would be perfectly valid from a legal point of view. Similarly, if Parliament were to pass a law abolishing elected local government, many would say that such a law was 'unconstitutional', even though, again, an enactment of this kind would be legally valid.

Therefore, the question of whether local government has any place in the British constitution is not to be resolved by the simple assertion that Britain is a unitary state in which Parliament is sovereign. The classical theorists of the sovereignty of Parliament never intended that the doctrine should be used in this way as an argument-stopper. A. V. Dicey (1835–1922), the first jurist to analyse the concept of the sovereignty of Parliament, was very far from believing that it gave a government the right to act as it pleased. Indeed, for much of Dicey's lifetime, government was very far from being omnicompetent and there was a real check upon its power in the form of the House of Lords. For, until 1911, Parliament was genuinely bicameral in that the Lords had an absolute veto on legislation when they wished to use it. Thus there was, within the very concept of the sovereignty of Parliament, a means of securing limited government. Perhaps even more important, the sovereignty of Parliament was, for Dicey, just one of three characteristics of our constitutional law. The other two were the rule of law and the existence of constitutional conventions. Both of these clearly limit the sovereignty of Parliament. For they imply that it is not enough just for laws to be duly passed in the proper manner by Parliament for them to be constitutional. They must also be in accordance both with the rule of law and with those conventions which 'make up the constitutional morality of the day', [1] a morality which is derived from both history and tradition. Of course, neither the rule of law nor the conventions of the constitutions have any legal status in that they can be invoked by the courts to invalidate an Act of Parliament. Nevertheless, these characteristics of the constitution represent important principles through which the aim of limited government can be secured.

Towards the end of his life, Dicey came to be concerned that too much power was accruing to the executive. In 1911, the Parliament Act limited the absolute veto of the House of Lords to three sessions in the case of non-money bills (it was further reduced to one session in 1949), and removed it entirely in the case of money bills. Dicey believed that some new check upon the power of government was urgently needed. From 1890, he had advocated the referendum as a means of controlling the power of an overweening executive; and after around 1910, he pressed for it with increasing insistence. Whatever one's viewpoint on the merit of the referendum as a checking instrument, it is clear that neither Dicey nor the traditions of British constitutionalism can be prayed in aid of a view of the constitution whose central principle is that central government is omnicompetent and can do what it likes. Indeed, to suggest that government should be omnicompetent, far from being a principle of constitutional government, is in effect to abandon constitutionalism whose leitmotiv must always be limited government. In 1978, Lord Hailsham counterposed two fundamentally conflicting viewpoints in his book *The Dilemma of Democracy,* when he declared that 'Our troubles derive from the fact that we are halting between two inconsistent opinions about the nature of democracy, indeed about the nature and function of government . . . .The two theories are the theory of centralised democracy, known to me as elective dictatorship, and the theory of limited government, in my language the doctrine of freedom under law.'[2]

Thus, although Parliament is sovereign and local authorities are statutory creations of Parliament, the sovereignty of Parliament is, in the words of the Widdicombe Report, 'underpinned by a corpus of custom and convention as to the manner in which that sovereignty should be exercised'.[3]

But, what are these conventions? While it is possible to discover without too much difficulty the relevant statutes affecting local government, it is much more problematic to isolate conventions, those tacit understandings which so underpin our system of government. For, while a judge can arbitrate between different interpretations of the law, there is no similar umpire to arbitrate between conventions, between alternative views of the role of local government in the constitution. Yet, while any interpretation of the conventions must always be open to debate, there are, it is suggested, clear historical pointers to the role of local government in the constitution, pointers laying down constitutional principles which ought to be binding on central government. This chapter seeks to outline these principles, and to do so as uncontroversially as possible in the interest of establishing a consensus on the proper role of local government in the constitution. These principles, it is hoped, are in accordance with the traditions and spirit of our constitution, best summed up perhaps in the words of Dickens' Mr Podsnap, 'Centralis-ation. No. Never with my consent. Not English'.

Constitutional Principles

Local government is, of course, a statutory creation of Parliament. It has, as the Widdicombe Committee confirmed, 'no independent status or right to exist'.[4] Nevertheless, Parliament has, since the Municipal Corporations Act in 1835, given a particular legislative form to local government, whose main features are three-fold: first, that local authorities should be directly elected, second, that they should be responsible for the delivery of various public services and third, that they should have the right to raise their own revenue. Local government is, in the words of the Redcliffe Maud Commission in

1969, 'the only representative institution in the country outside Parliament'.[5] Local authorities are not only, together with Parliament, the only elected bodies exercising public power in Britain; they are also the only bodies, aside from Parliament, with the right to tax, this right to tax buttressing their independent status. Thus, local authorities are, with Parliament, the only bodies exercising public power in the United Kingdom which enjoy democratic legitimacy. So it is that the commitment to local self-government has been said to be an 'inarticulate major premise' of the constitution, even though it does not have, and under the British Constitution cannot have, any special protection in law. And yet, precisely because we do not have a codified constitution or check upon the power of government, it is even more important for us to preserve a healthy system of local government. For it is largely to local authorities that we must look if we are to secure constraints on the power of government which in other democracies are secured through constitutional provisions. Indeed, local democratic institutions constitute in Britain the main institutional means by which power can be diffused.

It follows from this that the first constitutional principle which ought to guide government in its relations with local authorities is:

1   Directly-elected local authorities shall have the right to provide public services in the interests of their local populations.

This principle, however, is currently under serious threat through the transfer of services, hitherto run by local authorities, to agencies, boards and quangos dominated by the appointees of central government. This can be seen in almost all local government services, but most strikingly perhaps in education.

Education is perhaps the most important local government service, absorbing over half of the budget of county councils, metropolitan districts and London boroughs. If local authority provision in education is weakened, therefore, local government itself must come under threat. Yet, polytechnics, further education colleges and sixth form colleges have been entirely removed from local government, while the establishment of grant-maintained schools constitutes a creeping and insidious transfer of power away from local government. It also introduces an element of built-in instability into the system. For local authorities can no longer plan ahead with some reasonable assurance that a specific number of schools will remain under their aegis. Thus it becomes more difficult for them to make forward provision through planning for the management of surplus school places. The consequence is likely to be a less efficient management of public resources.

The local authority role in housing, the most important function of shire districts, has been similarly weakened as an increasing proportion of housing expenditure has been channelled through the Housing Corporation to housing associations, which are coming to be seen as the main source of publicly subsidized housing. Indeed, in 1989/90, new homes construction by housing associations exceeded for the first time the number of new homes built by local authorities. The establishment of Housing Action Trusts, agencies set up by central government, with powers to take over rundown estates from local authority ownership, also served to weaken the local authority housing role.

In the case of other public services, also, local authority participation has been weakened. In the 1970s, local authorities were recognized as the natural agencies for inner city regeneration; today by contrast, they are regarded as just one agency among several, enjoying as they do only minority representation in Urban Development Corporations, the majority being composed of local notables and business interests. The Urban Development Corporations, moreover, have taken over development control powers previously held by local authorities and they may also have vested in them the land-holdings of local authorities. City Action Teams and Inner City Task Forces have also assumed functions which used to be undertaken by local authorities.

Under the now defunct Manpower Services Commission, local authorities enjoyed one-third of the representation on area boards. The successor Training and Enterprise Councils make no provision for any guaranteed local authority representation. In the National Health Service, trust hospitals are no longer overseen by regional or district health authority boards on which local authorities were represented; while local authority representation on police authorities has been reduced from two-thirds to one-half. Even before these developments, Lord Jenkins of Hillhead had referred to there having been a 'steady attrition of councils resulting in the threat of civic degradation which it is almost impossible to imagine being imposed in any other country'.[6] The natural outcome seems to be for local authorities to become merely residual bodies and for local government to become a welfare state safety net dealing with pupils in special schools, council houses and some very local services such as refuse, street cleaning and local roads. Local government will become the repository for those services that no one else can be bothered to provide, rather like the Poor Law Guardians in the early days of the century before the welfare state came into existence.

Why has responsibility for so many public services been taken away from local government? The fundamental reason is less perhaps a belief that 'the man in Whitehall knows best' than the desire to make public services responsive to the market. In education, for example, the creation of grant-maintained schools is intended to increase parental choice through adoption of the market principle. When school budgets are determined largely by the number of pupils attending, popular schools, it is suggested, can be expected to attract more public funds than unpopular schools. In this way, schools can become responsive to consumers in the same way that, for example, the supply of motor cars or compact discs is responsive to consumers. A similar rationale lies at the basis of the transfer of other public services out of local government.

Whether or not one approves of this market approach will of course depend largely upon one's political preconceptions. But, even under a market philosophy, there ought still to remain a vital role for local government. The market is defended by its supporters as a spontaneous creation which does away with the politicization of public services. Yet, neither in Britain nor in any other democracy, has a market for services such as education, housing, inner-city development or training arisen spontaneously as it has for cars and compact discs. Any market in the public services, therefore, must be, to some extent, an artificial one, created and regulated by government. But how ought it to be regulated?

The answer given by the government is that it can be regulated by the individual institutions themselves such as schools and further education colleges, housing associations and trust hospitals. It is the 'managers' of these institutions who are to be the regulators. They are to be given specific performance targets and specific duties to Parliament and to their clients. But it is ministers, rather than local authorities, who will become responsible for their operations, although they may sometimes exercise these responsibilities through intermediary funding agencies and similar bodies.

In a lecture in 1993 to the Public Management Foundation, William Waldegrave, the Minister for Public Service, denied that such arrangements gave rise to a democratic deficit. On the contrary, he declared, they yielded a democratic gain, through making public services directly accountable to their clients, or 'customers'.

This argument, however, equates accountability with the provision of services. It does not meet the point that, in a democracy, government not only provides services, but also has to decide upon relative priorities; it decides how much ought to be spent on each service and what is the appropriate balance between them. Government is not only about providing, but also about deciding. Services run by central government cannot yield accountability in this sense for we have not been able to discover any method of making centralized public services properly accountable either to Parliament or to the public whom they are meant to serve. That has been the basic problem which has always bedevilled the management of the nationalized industries. Moreover, civil servants in Whitehall are protected from consumers by distance and time, while funding agencies, quangos and similar institutions serve to blur rather than clarify accountability. Local authorities are far more likely to be able to regulate the market for public services effectively than central government.

Much has been heard in recent years of a democratic deficit in the European Community. In Britain, despite William Waldegrave's remarks, we have our own democratic deficit. It consists in the replacement of elected representatives by appointed managers who are largely insulated from true democratic accountability. Yet, proper accountability in the public services is absolutely vital. For while, in services such as education and housing, there is indeed some possibility of 'exit', to use Albert Hirschman's terminology, the degree of choice can never be as great as in the case of consumer goods such as motor cars or compact discs. Therefore, the alternative mechanism of accountability – 'voice' – must be brought into play. That means strengthening, not weakening, the local authority role. For it is local government which at its best makes possible the process of public dialogue and debate over priorities which is part of the very essence of democratic self-government.

In fact, the alternative to local democracy is not the rule of the market, but the rule of unaccountable managers in quangos – people whom *The Times* journalist, Simon Jenkins, has labelled, 'the unelected in pursuit of the unaccountable'. Ministers, responsible for a wide range of public appointments, cannot possibly know in detail the qualifications of those whom they appoint, nor whether their appointees will be found acceptable to local communities. Therefore, nominated bodies will have an information base that is far inferior to that of local authorities. They will be too far removed from the local community to be in touch with local opinion.

Further, bodies composed of people nominated by central government do not have to meet the same rigorous standards of accountability as local authorities. Bodies such as the governors of grant maintained schools, National Health Service trusts, Training and Enterprise Councils and Urban Development Corporations are either not required to meet in public at all, or are required to meet in public only on infrequent occasions. In some cases, indeed, it is not at all easy to find out who the members of these bodies actually are.

Moreover, appointees do not have to declare their interests, so that conflict of interest is more likely to occur; nor do they have to face the fear of surcharge if they spend money which would not be authorized by elected local authorities. Thus bodies run by appointed managers are likely to be less accountable than local authorities. Civil servants also are less accountable than officers working in local government. Mr. Tim Hornsby, a former civil servant who became Chief Executive of Kingston upon Thames, has declared 'that in 14 months of service as a Borough Chief Executive, I had been rightly much more exposed to democratic scrutiny than in well over 14 years as a civil servant'.[7]

Moreover, single-issue bodies such as the governing bodies of grant-maintained schools or housing associations suffer from the characteristic defect of narrowly focused tunnel vision. They are concerned with one particular activity, and not with the proper balance between different activities. Elected councillors, by contrast, have to be generalists concerned with the total impact of public services upon the community.

None of this should be taken to mean that local authorities should necessarily be as heavily involved in the actual *provision* of public services as they have been in the past. Of course, the precise responsibilities which local authorities ought to exercise is, in large part, a matter of political preference, but there is no reason why local authorities should not, just as much as central government, take advantage of the purchaser/provider split, while remaining the representative of the community interest. It may well be that local authorities ought no longer to be the sole or even the main providers of, for example, education and housing.Their role is perhaps better understood as being one of ensuring that these services are properly provided in accordance with community priorities. That indeed is the fundamental rationale of the *enabling* authority.

This leads us indeed to the second constitutional principle. It is that:

2   Local authorities shall be the representatives of their communities.

Local government ought not to be seen merely as a provider of services. We do not, after all, compare central government to Harrods or Marks & Spencer. Why then should we treat local government as if it were B & Q? Local government should be seen as a cornerstone of what the Redcliffe-Maud Commission called 'a viable system of local democracy; that is a system under which government by the people is a reality . . . . The importance of local government', the Report continues, 'lies in the fact that it is the means by which people can provide services for themselves; can take an active and constructive part in the business of government; and can decide for themselves, within the limits of what national policies and local resources allow, what kind of services they want and what kind of environment they prefer'.[8] Thus, even beyond the weakening of democratic accountability, the transfer of functions out of local government involves a loss of democratic representation. For individuals are more than consumers, users or purchasers of public services. They are also members of communities with the right to help decide how their communities ought to be governed.

In a number of Continental countries, local authorities exercise this community responsibility by assuming a monitoring role even over services which are not local authority functions. In Sweden and Norway, for example, local authorities monitor services such as water, personal health and hospitals, although they are not directly responsible for the provision of these services. So also local government in Britain ought to be the representative of the community, a consumer watchdog and advocate, monitoring, for example, trust hospitals and grant-maintained schools, even though they are not responsible for providing them. Indeed, it may hardly be possible for local authorities to carry out their statutory functions in such areas as community care, without adopting this wider role by monitoring National Health Service institutions in their communities.

A responsive and responsible local authority, then, ought to concern itself with monitoring all of the public services which serve the community. It must work actively with other agencies and public bodies to bring this about. Thus the enabling authority is not simply an authority which contracts out its services and meets, as the late Nicholas Ridley once advocated, but once a year to allocate contracts. It is an authority which represents the whole community. That is why it ought to be, in the words of the Redcliffe-Maud Commission, 'more than the sum of the particular services provided. It is an essential part of English democratic government'.[9] Sadly, however, local government has become so attenuated since that Report was published that, reporting 17 years after Redcliffe-Maud, the Widdicombe Committee felt forced to declare, 'That, however, is a statement of the ideal. It might be argued that the reality is now that local government has become, or is in danger of becoming, *less* than the sum of its parts – i.e. that it lacks sufficient financial and political discretion to reflect local choice even in the basic statutory services which it delivers'.[10]

On the Continent, the responsibility of local authorities for their communities is recognized by giving them a right of general competence to exercise their initiative with regard to any matter not specifically excluded from their competence nor assigned to any other authority. In Britain, by contrast, local authorities are bound by the *ultra vires* rule, so that they can act only where statutorily empowered. Individuals are allowed to do anything that they are not specifically prohibited from doing, but local authorities are unable to act unless given specific authority to do so. That is a straitjacket hindering local authorities from acting as genuine representatives of their communities. Therefore, the third constitutional principle governing local authorities should be:

3 Local authorities shall be given freedom to experiment within the law.

There are two methods by which this might be achieved. The first is to follow the general Continental pattern and give local authorities a right of general competence such that they would have a discretion to undertake activities which they considered to be in the interests of their communities. That would entail overturning the *ultra vires* doctrine. The introduction of such a power of general competence was recommended in the late 1960s by the Maud Committee on the Management of Local Government, the Redcliffe-Maud Commission and the Wheatley Commission on Local Government in Scotland. The Wheatley Report was of the view that a power of general competence would generate 'an enterprising and forward looking attitude of mind'.[11] The Widdicombe Committee shared this view, provided that the power of general competence had appropriate safeguards attached, and was made subject to a financial limit.[12] The introduction of such a power would have an important symbolic and psychological significance, bringing local government in Britain into line with systems on the Continent, and buttressing the concept of local government as representative of the community. It would encourage the citizen to see in the local authority not just one agency among others for delivering services, but as the voice of the local community, the advocate and watchdog for all of the public services in the locality.

A second method by which the same end can be achieved is through the free commune experiment which has been adopted in the Scandinavian countries. This experiment allows certain local authorities to be considered, with the approval of Parliament, as free communes with the right to be free of statutory requirements, regulations and control procedures which they believe interfere with their capacity to be effective representatives of their communities. No local authority, however, can apply to be removed from the requirement to provide a fair distribution of services nor the protection of lives and health of the general public, nor basic legal safeguards.[13] These powers are granted for an experimental period of six years. If they prove successful, they can then be transformed into a national permission to all local authorities. One example is the alteration in the law of Sweden concerning school attendance. The law required all children to be educated for five days a week at school. One rural authority, discovering that children spent too long each day travelling to school, applied to be a free commune and, after its application had been approved, allowed children to spend only four days at school, but made them longer days. This caused no problems of any kind, and has now become an option for all local authorities. Thus, the free commune experiment allows the full value of local government as a mechanism of social learning, to be exploited. Where an experiment has failed, other local authorities will have been forewarned, and money will have been saved since there will have been no need to initiate a costly new innovation over the country as a whole But where experiments have been successful, the country as a whole will benefit. Indeed, it is in precisely this manner, through the mechanism of private bill legislation, that many public services in Britain were developed at local level in the nineteenth century.

A first approach to giving local authorities greater freedom to experiment was made in the report of the Working Party on the Internal Management of

Local Authorities in England, July 1993.This report recognizes that there is no single best method of organizing local government, and that different models might well suit different authorities. It 'deliberately [did] not identify an ideal internal management model and recommend its application as a blueprint to all local authorities. We recognise that different approaches will be appropriate for different authorities, and that it is for them and not central government to choose which arrangements to adopt' (Para. 2.10). Local authorities which wished to experiment would have to submit a proposal to the Secretary of State for the Environment. Legislation would allow approval of experiments subject to suitable safeguards. Experiments would be subject to annual review by an advisory panel and the Secretary of State would have powers to suspend or modify experiments where the panel reported that they were failing. But the panel would be able to recommend that successful experiments be given wider application in authorities which wished to adopt them.

A natural next step would be to allow local authorities to consider whether they might wish to adopt an alternative election system, one of a specified number of proportional systems, to the first-past-the-post system now required for all local elections. Shire districts are already able to choose whether to have elections by thirds, so that one-third of the councillors for each ward are elected each year except in the year of county council elections; or whether to have whole council elections, in which case three councillors are elected in multi-member wards in the year midway between county elections. In this latter case, each elector has three votes, the system of election being known technically as the block vote.

The electoral system in local government produces far greater distortions than in national elections. Sometimes a party which wins less than half the vote can win nearly all of the seats, and the opposition is unable to elect sufficient councillors to man committees. Consider, for example, Richmond-upon-Thames in 1990, a piquant example in that it was the Liberal Democrats who benefited from the system (see Table 9.1).

In national elections, there has only been one Parliament in the twentieth century in which the opposition was almost totally obliterated – the 1931 general election when the government won 554 out of 615 seats. Yet, in many local councils such election results are commonplace, and party control will never change whatever the outcome at national level. Moreover, it is in such one-party councils that the danger of corruption is at its greatest, as the Salmon Commission on Standards of Conduct in Public Life noticed:

> The local authorities most vulnerable to corruption have tended to be those in which one political party has unchallenged dominance. Not only are such authorities at particular risk because of the absence of an effective opposition which can

Table 9.1   Percentage of votes and number of seats won in Richmond-upon-Thames, 1990

Party	% votes	Seats
Liberal Democrat	48	48
Conservative	35	4
Labour	15	0

scrutinise their decisions, but investigations and the making of complaints in such areas may be inhibited by the feeling that there is no way round the 'party machine'.[14]

Another type of anomaly occurs where the vote is fairly equally divided, when the outcome is much more likely to be capricious than it is in national elections. Consider, for example, the following two examples, the last election for the Greater London Council, 1981, widely perceived as a runaway victory for the Left, and Lambeth in 1982, a result which belies the borough's reputation as a 'red' stronghold (see Table 9.2).

Table 9.2   Percentage of votes and number of seats won in GLC (1981) and Lambeth (1982) elections

Election	Party	% votes	Seats
GLC, 1981	Labour	42	50
	Conservative	40	41
	Liberal/SDP Alliance	17	1
Lambeth, 1982	Conservative	39	27
	Labour	33	32[a]
	Liberal/SDP Alliance	27	5

[a] Subsequently, one Alliance councillor switched to Labour giving Labour a clear majority of councillors on 33 per cent of the vote.

It is arguable that in each of these last two cases, an alternative voting system better able to reflect opinion at local level would have led to more responsible behaviour by the local authorities concerned, and local government would, as a result, have been in a healthier state. Indeed, it may be that the electoral system is one of the factors preventing effective co-operation between central government and local authorities by exaggerating the swing against the government of the day. Therefore, there is a strong case for allowing those local authorities which wish to do so to experiment with alternative electoral systems, in the same manner as the report of the Working Party on Internal Management encourages them to experiment with alternative internal management systems.

This report, just because it recommends experiment, constitutes something of a landmark in that it is the first such document not only to recognize the value of diversity in local government, but to make specific provision for it. If the report is to prove anything more than an isolated instance, it is important for local authorities to grasp what is offered and to show that they are prepared to experiment, boldly but responsibly, with their management structures. Otherwise, centralists will say that the case for local government has been undermined by the local authorities themselves.

No legislative arrangements for local government, however, can assure its constitutional position if local authorities have insufficient financial resources of their own to yield autonomy. Therefore the fourth constitutional principle is:

4   Local authorities shall be entitled, within national economic policy, to adequate financial resources of their own commensurate with their responsibilities, part at least of which shall derive from local taxes. They shall have the right, within the limits of national policy, to decide for themselves how much they are to raise and spend each year.

While financial arrangements alone cannot guarantee local democracy, they can encourage or hinder its achievement. For a system of finance can set up pressures, either to encourage central government intervention or to enhance local self-government. Currently, the financial resources of local authorities are far too limited to sustain a viable system of local democracy, while the capping of local taxation and central determination of local expenditure hardly allow even the limited financial resources available to local authorities to be used according to local wishes.

The 1980s saw an important constitutional change in the methods by which central government sought to control local expenditure. Previously, central government had sought to determine the global total of local government expenditure; it had sought to control the revenue available to local authorities through varying the rate support grant which consisted of monies derived from central taxation. During the 1980s, however, central government sought to determine both how much individual local authorities would be spending, and how much local revenue derived from local taxation local authorities would be able to raise.

The Local Government Finance Act of 1982, which first established expenditure targets, began the move away from influence and advice to local authorities, to direct control. Indicators came to be developed by means of which the government could decide how much each local authority ought to be spending. At the present time, the distribution of grant is determined largely by standard spending assessments, introduced in 1990/91. Increasingly, these assessments, which are no more than a very rough and ready yardstick, are being used as expenditure targets. In July 1992, introducing his Education White Paper, John Patten, the Education Secretary, attacked Birmingham as 'one of the worst education authorities in the country' because it had been 'kidnapping' £55m from its education budget. Birmingham was indeed spending £55m below its standard spending assessment. But the main reason for this was that items such as further education and training services were not run on or financed by the education department. In fact, Birmingham claimed to be spending £390 per annum per pupil on education, as compared with the average for metropolitan authorities of £358 per annum per pupil. But, in any case, why should not a local authority, providing that it is fulfilling its statutory duties and that it can obtain the support of its electors, not decide for itself what the pattern of its expenditure should be? Birmingham council is in a much better position than a minister in Whitehall to decide what pattern best suits its particular local needs; and if the council makes a mistake, it will be subject to retribution at the polls. The local authority is responsible to the local electorate of Birmingham in a way that a minister can never be.

Together with control over the expenditure levels of individual local authorities, central government in the 1980s sought to control how much revenue individual local authorities could raise. The Rates Act, 1984, empowered the Secretary of State for the Environment, for the first time, to 'cap' the rates, that is to impose maximum rate levels upon local authorities. This principle of capping was continued with the community charge (the poll tax) and the council tax which has now replaced it. The capping of local authority revenue breaches the principle that local authorities should be free to decide for themselves how much money they wish to raise locally. For central government to restrict the power of a local authority to raise its own revenue is a very different matter from central government deciding to restrict its *own* contribution to local authorities.

In these two ways, then, central government has drastically restricted the autonomy of local authorities. The introduction of standard spending assessments was a declaration by central government that it knows better than local authorities how much they should *spend*; the introduction of capping was a declaration by central government that it knows better than local authorities how much they should *raise*.

No sensible local authority would deny that central government must retain the power to limit local government expenditure and borrowing. Central government must also interest itself in how local expenditure is financed since excessive borrowing will inflate the Public Sector Borrowing Requirement. These aims can, however, be achieved perfectly satisfactorily through controls on the global total of local government expenditure, variations in the level of grant and controls on the total amount of local authority borrowing, and in particular on borrowing to finance current as opposed to capital spending. The only further control needed might be a ceiling on the permissible rate of change in the level of local authority taxation in any particular year. These controls would not be found onerous by local authorities and they would be in accordance with the principle that local authorities should decide for themselves, within the limits of national policy, how much they should raise and spend each year. Both the capping of local authority expenditure and the use of standard spending assessments as indicators of how much local authorities should spend should be abandoned.

Even so, the percentage of local expenditure financed from local taxation – currently varying in different authorities from between 15–30 per cent – is far too low to sustain local autonomy. Such an arrangement in effect makes central government responsible for the revenue of local authorities, so blurring accountability and drawing the centre into the local authority decision-making process. With ministers contributing the bulk of local revenue, they will insist upon supervising how the money is spent and so central government will come to be held responsible for what ought to be local decisions. Local authorities in turn will feel less of a sense of responsibility than if they had to spend money voted by their own electors.

Moreover, the high level of grant has a distorting effect on the tax rates levied by local authorities. Through the 'gearing effect', a local authority will have to raise its tax rate by a far higher percentage than the percentage increase it has decided upon for its local spending. Thus voters will not receive accurate signals from their tax bills about the spending policies of their local authorities. For a small increase in spending, the local authority will have to increase its tax rate by a much larger percentage. Moreover, because of the high level of grant, small changes in its calculation will produce disproportionate and disruptive effects at local level, so making sensible forward planning more difficult.

Thus, the high level of central grant is in the interest neither of local nor of central government. Central government is ill-equipped to take responsibility for a myriad of local decisions concerning individual schools and housing estates. Indeed, it was the very over-loading of central government in such traditionally centralized countries as France, Italy and Spain that has led, over the last two decades, to the devolution of power to local authorities and to regions. Ministers themselves, therefore, will come to see that it is in their interest not to be held responsible for the decisions of elected local authorities. The first step in returning responsibility to where it belongs would be to initiate discussions with local government as to how the share of local taxation *vis-à-vis* grant can be increased. There is no doubt that this can be done without disturbing central government's responsibility for price stability. Otherwise it would be difficult to explain how it is that federal systems of government, such as Germany, have been able to achieve greater economic stability in the postwar period than we have been able to achieve in Britain.

An improved system of local taxation can only be achieved if there is effective consultation between central and local government. Such consultation ought, moreover, to occur whenever there is any question of altering, not only local government finance, but the structure, powers or organization of local authorities. This, then, is the fifth principle:

5   Local authorities shall have the right to be consulted on changes in their structure, powers, organization and finance.

This principle indeed was hardly questioned until the 1980s. The reform of London government in 1964 and of local government in England in 1974 were preceded by Royal Commissions. The reform of local government finance was the subject of a Committee of Inquiry which reported in 1976. No government in the 1970s would have considered legislation in these areas without the benefit of a Royal Commission or Committee of Inquiry. Yet, in 1985, fundamental legislation abolishing the Greater London Council and the metropolitan councils was introduced without consultation; while in 1987, the community charge was introduced although all of the local authority associations declared that it would prove unworkable. The method by which these changes were introduced constituted a real constitutional innovation and perhaps it was because there was no serious consultation that legislation to abolish the community charge was announced within the first year of its application in England and Wales; while the local government arrangements for London following the abolition of the GLC were thought to be so unsatisfactory that, in the general election of 1992, all three of the major parties put forward proposals to amend local government in London.

It is time to restore the constitutional principle of consultation; and time also to seek some means by which this principle can be safeguarded through Parliament. So far, it has proved difficult for Parliament to play such a role

since there is no Select Committee in either House whose role it is to scrutinize and monitor local government. A Select Committee of the Commons
with such a remit would cut across the pattern of departmentally related
Select Committees established in 1979, and could prove a vehicle for
detailed intervention into local government affairs. It would be much more
appropriate to establish a permanent Select Committee in the House of Lords
to scrutinize central/local relations, parallel perhaps to the European
Communities Select Committee which has served largely to depoliticize the
European issue, and whose reports are extremely highly regarded. A Select
Committee on central/local relations ought not to duplicate the work of the
Commons, nor deal with substantive matters of, for example, education and
housing policy; but it would be consulted before the introduction of legislation affecting the powers and prerogatives of local authorities, just as the
Select Committee on the European Communities has as part of its remit the
consideration of Community legislation likely to be of particular significance
to Britain. A Select Committee would be able to act as a forum, monitoring
central/local relations and issuing regular reports on the health of local
democracy.[15] In 1995 it was announced that the House of Lords would in fact
establish an ad hoc Select Committee.

Since 1973, no account of the British Constitution can claim to be complete if it fails to take account of the European Community dimension.
Admittedly, the Treaty of Rome makes no reference to local government, and
the Community has no authority of any kind over the structure of government
in any member state. Yet it was inevitable that the Community would come to
concern itself with the distribution of power between central government and
local authorities. For Community legislation is bound to impinge upon local
government responsibilities. The Community, following ratification of the
Maastricht Treaty, now enjoys competence over such matters as economic
development, education, culture, consumer protection, town and country
planning and land use, all of which are in part the responsibility of local
authorities. Moreover, the Community is concerned to ensure that its policy
instruments such as, for example, its structural funds, are distributed in an
effective and equitable way. But, more fundamentally, the Community exists
because, in the modern world, some governmental functions are best exercised at a level larger than that of the member state; as a corollary, it follows
that some governmental functions might be better exercised at a level lower
than that of the member state. If power can shift from the level of the state in
one direction, so also it can shift away from the state in another.

The Maastricht Treaty, while it undoubtedly centralizes power through
extending the competences of the Community in areas such as energy and the
environment, as well as in its proposals for economic and monetary union,
also seeks to counteract centralization through the principle of subsidiarity

and its institutional complement, the Committee of the Regions.

The principle of subsidiarity declares that decisions ought to be taken as closely as possible to the citizen. The British government pressed for its inclusion in the Maastricht Treaty in order to reserve power to the Member States against the Community. The German government, however, pressed for its inclusion for a quite different reason – to protect the interests of the German regions – the *Länder* – against a process of creeping centralization to the federal government. The Germans were concerned more with the distribution of power *within* the state than with the distribution of power between the state and the Community. We in Britain ought similarly to employ the principle of subsidiarity to ensure that decisions are taken as closely as possible to the citizen. Therefore, the sixth constitutional principle which ought to inform central/local relations is:

6　Public services shall be undertaken as far as possible by those authorities closest to the citizen.

It should, however, be part of the principle of subsidiarity that power should be devolved, where possible, from local authorities to citizens themselves. For the purpose of local self-government is not just to yield extra power for councillors and officials, but to enable people to exercise more control over their own lives. This entails the admission of some element of direct democracy into local government. For, if there is a genuine demand for participation in local affairs without which local self-government is likely to become an empty husk, this demand is unlikely to be met fully merely by regular local elections which confer decision-making powers upon others. Indeed, it has been said that 'A democratic institution which does not engage the *demos* might ultimately crumble at the sound of a centralist trumpet'.[16] Local government can only be strong if it can mobilize public opinion behind it.

One difficulty, however, with proposals for referendums in local government is that it is difficult to delimit those issues on which approval by referendum would be necessary. If the power to call a referendum were to be left in the hands of the local authority itself, there would be no reason why the majority party, which, *ex hypothesi,* enjoys a majority on the council, should submit any issue at all to the electorate. One possibility worth investigating, therefore, is the introduction of the popular veto, as used in Switzerland, Italy and the United States. This would allow any local government measure to be put to referendum after being passed by the council, if demanded in a petition signed by a specified percentage of registered local voters – say 5 per cent. Use of such an instrument of direct democracy could do a great deal to sustain local self-government and yield greater power for the citizen, so completing the application of the principle of subsidiarity.

The European Community is not, however, the only European organization to which Britain belongs. We are members, also, of the Council of Europe whose Convention on Human Rights we have ratified, although we have not incorporated it into our domestic law. But, in addition to the Convention on Human Rights defining the proper rights and status of individual citizens, the Council of Europe has also produced a Charter of Local Self-Government (1985), defining the proper rights and status of local communities and their elected representatives.

Unlike the Convention, the Charter is in no way binding upon Member States choosing to adhere to it, but it implies a symbolic commitment to the values of local self-government. Unfortunately, Britain was, together with the Irish Republic, the only European Member State of the Council of Europe not to sign the Charter, even though its provisions had been watered down to make it more acceptable to the government.

The constitutional principles laid down in this chapter are derived not only from our own constitutional traditions, but are also laid down in the Charter, and they are taken for granted in almost every other democracy in Western Europe. Therefore, the government, as earnest of its intention to inaugurate a new era in central/local relations ought to announce its adherence to the Council of Europe's Charter of Local Self-Government.

But do we have to look to the Continent to seek a renewal of the constitutional principle of local self-government? It would be a sad reflection on our commitment to democracy if we had to rely on the Continent to rejuvenate our democratic traditions because we were unable to do it for ourselves. The year 1994 marked the centenary of the Local Government Act, 1894, which provided for the establishment of elective parish councils. Shortly after the passage of that Act, a great Continental constitutional lawyer, Josef Redlich, wrote that:

> The grand principle of representative democracy has now been fully applied to local government . . . . England has created for herself 'self government' in the true sense of the word. She has secured self government – that is to say, the right of her people to legislate, to deliberate, and to administer through councils or parliaments elected on the basis of popular suffrage . . . . And this is the root of the incomparable strength of the English Body Politic.[17]

At the end of the nineteenth century, Continental observers regarded our structure of government as a model to be admired rather than an example to be avoided. And yet, is there any reason why we ourselves cannot recreate our system of democratic self-government with the same self-confidence and determination as our Victorian forbears displayed over a hundred years ago?

Notes and references

1   A. V. Dicey (1959), *Introduction to the Study of the Law of the Constitution,* 10th edn, 418.
2   Lord Hailsham (1978), *The Dilemma of Democracy: Diagnosis and Prescription,* Collins, 9.
3   Report of the Committee of Inquiry into the Conduct of Local Authority Business, Cmnd. 9797, 1986, Para. 3.4.
4   Ibid; Para. 3.3.
5   Royal Commission on Local Government in England, Cmnd. 4040, 1969, Para. 28.
6   Cited in *Local Government Chronicle,* 10 March 1989.
7   Tim Hornsby (1993), 'In praise of local democracy', *AMA News,* May.
8   Cmnd. 4040, Para. 28.
9   Ibid; Para. 146.
10 Widdicombe Report, Para. 3.41.
11 Report of Royal Commission on Local Government in Scotland, 1969, Cmnd. 4150, para. 640.
12 Widdicombe Report, Para. 8.27.
13 Agne Gustafsson (1991),'The Changing Local Government and Politics of Sweden', in Richard Batley and Gerry Stoker (eds), *Local Government in Europe: Trends and Developments,* Macmillan, 181.
14 Cmnd. 6524, 1976, Para. 39.
15 The author proposed the introduction of such a Select Committee in the House of Lords in his evidence to the Jellicoe Committee, the Select Committee on the Committee Work of the House, HL 35-II, 1991–2, 216–20.
16 D. E. Regan (1980), *A Headless State: The Unaccountable Executive in British Local Government,* University of Nottingham Press, 24.
17 Cited in Bryan Keith-Lucas (1985), *Parish Councils: The Way Ahead,* The Fourth Mary Brockenhurst Lecture, Devon Association of Parish Councils, 1.

10 The English Constitution and Devolution

I

England, said Disraeli, is governed not by logic but by Parliament. Nowhere has the English attitude to constitutional thought been better summarized than in these words. The supremacy of Parliament, which is the one great constitutional principle the English possess, has so dominated our thinking about government that it has left no space for any other. The English philosophy of government therefore, instead of being found in a compendium of reasoned argument such as the *Federalist*, or the writings of Michel Debré, must be sought in Erskine May and in the rules of parliamentary procedure: for procedure, it has been said, is all the Constitution the poor Englishman has: and the principle of the supremacy of Parliament is discovered to be hostile to any genuinely constitutional thought at all.

Such a conception of government can, of course, only survive in a political community in which two factors are present – perceived ability by the rulers of the community in achieving agreed political objectives, and trust by the ruled in the competence and probity of their leaders. These achievements in turn rest upon a firm and relatively unchanging sense of identity, not incompatible with the assertion of Scottish or Welsh identity. For, unlike France, Britain has never required of its inhabitants an exclusive allegiance. The State is to be conceived, not as the guardian of society, but as an arena for conciliation: and the British system of centralized government has always been tempered, if not by kindness, then at least by a beneficent indifference.

Whatever the objective circumstances of Britain's economic decline over the last 100 years, therefore, the conditions for running a political community without a Constitution seem to have been met during long periods of British history. This must be an event of comparatively rare occurrence in political societies, rarer still perhaps in democratic societies. For this reason, perhaps, the success of England in managing the 'Westminster model' of parliamentary government ought to be attributed to good fortune rather than to conscious art.

We have deliberately spoken above of 'the success of *England* in managing the "Westminster model" of parliamentary government', for one could argue that the notion of parliamentary supremacy is the cornerstone of the *English* Constitution about which Bagehot and Dicey wrote in those unregenerate Anglocentric days.We shall consider in a moment the extent to which, for the purposes of constitutional thought, 'England' includes 'Wales', but first we must briefly point out the contrast between the English mode of thinking about constitutional matters, and that prevalent in Scotland and Northern Ireland.

The Scots have, of course, always faced the dilemma that if Westminster was supreme, the Acts of Union of 1707 had no meaning beyond that of a moral injunction. England was bound in honour to respect Scottish institutions, but she could not be bound in any other way. A. V. Dicey, when he wrote his book *Thoughts on the Union between England and Scotland*, with R. S. Rait, the then historiographer-royal for Scotland, argued that the Scots had simply made a logical mistake. They had failed to see that it was logically impossible to entrench rights under a system of parliamentary supremacy. His Anglocentric approach to the whole subject is indeed strikingly illuminated by his writing throughout of the *Act*, rather than the *Acts* of Union, as if the English Parliament was able to bind Scotland by legislative means.

When he came to deal with the Irish problem, Gladstone, a Whig even in his Radicalism, found himself in agreement with Dicey. Neither the Acts of 1707 nor the Irish Act of Union could, in his view, impose any limitation upon the supremacy of Parliament. In 1869, Gladstone disestablished the Irish Church, undeterred by Article Five establishing the union of the Churches of England and Ireland 'for ever'. Gladstone differed from Dicey, not on the need to preserve parliamentary supremacy, for this was an essential precondition of any acceptable scheme of Home Rule – but on the lesser question of whether any scheme of Home Rule would *in fact* preserve that supremacy. Gladstone assured sceptics that his Home Rule Bills would leave supremacy untarnished; Unionists argued that the Bills merely purported to preserve supremacy. No one – not even the Irish Nationalists – argued that supremacy ought not to be preserved; and Parnell contented himself with the strikingly ambiguous phrase that, under the British Constitution, no more could be asked for than Gladstone was prepared to offer.

Similar in many ways was the debate in the Commons in 1977 over Clause 1 of the Scotland Bill, claiming that nothing in the Bill would affect 'the supreme authority of Parliament to make laws for the United Kingdom or any part of it'. The Labour Government offered assurances, directed especially towards their English members reluctantly conceding devolution, that supremacy would be unaffected; the Conservatives again insisted that the clause was an unjustifiable act of faith. The SNP, however, unlike their Irish counterparts, were willing explicitly to argue that they favoured the abolition of supremacy, while the Liberals had long committed themselves to a specifically federal position. Nevertheless, the continuity of argument between 1886 and 1977 is striking and reveals, surely, the poverty of much of English constitutional thought.

During the period between the Home Rule Bill and the Scotland Bill, however, Britain had undertaken – or perhaps endured would be a better word – her one experiment in devolved government – the Parliament of Northern Ireland. For, by one of the paradoxes of history, Home Rule was foisted upon Northern Ireland, on the very political community which had done its best to retain the Union; and it was foisted on her under the misplaced assumption that the South, too, would be satisfied with Home Rule in 1920. Had it been more fully appreciated that the South would be satisfied with nothing less than a break with the British connection, then it is doubtful whether the experiment would ever have been tried at all.

The government of Northern Ireland from 1921 to 1972, although in strict constitutional terms a devolved administration, was in actual practice, at least until 1968, more akin to that of a province in a federal state. This was partly because Westminster was unwilling to devote much attention to its problems until the civil rights issue came to the fore; but also because the actual exercise of legislative supremacy by a superior Parliament demands something more than a mere supervision over a subordinate body. It requires a continual engagement in the politics and administration of a territory, if in the words of the 1920 Government of Ireland Act, supremacy is to 'remain unaffected and undiminished over all persons, matters, and things in Ireland and every part thereof'. Interestingly enough, this formula was subtly altered in the 1973 Northern Ireland Constitution Act and the Scotland and Wales Acts so that supremacy became merely the supreme right to make laws for the United Kingdom as a whole; although it must be doubtful whether the right to make laws is worth very much, leaving aside pathological political situations, if it does not include supremacy over all persons, matters and things.

One would have expected the experience of Northern Ireland to have provided a considerable amount of material for reflection for students of constitutional thought – reflection about such matters as the value of constitutional guarantees against discrimination, and of the appropriate way to transfer powers in any devolution settlement. Unfortunately for the student, however, Northern Ireland did not, in the words of a former Lord Chief Justice, 'escape this shortcoming' of appearing to have 'no great interest in either the institutions or the principles of law which determine the structure of their society and the means whereby it may change and develop'.[1] The courts, moreover, did not play a large role in the constitutional development of Northern Ireland, although it is nevertheless possible, in the one or two leading cases in Northern Ireland, to see judges beginning the task of framing a corpus of constitutional principles regulating the exercise of devolved powers, and finding these principles very like those adopted in federal States.

Those who have studied the constitution of Northern Ireland, however, have, like the Scots, become prone to doubts as to whether the notion of parliamentary supremacy is sufficiently subtle or flexible to do justice to the diversity of forms of government in the United Kingdom. Indeed, it is in Scotland and in Northern Ireland that the so-called 'new view' of the constitution has been pioneered. This view claims that the provisions of 1707, or of the now superseded Ireland Act of 1949 declaring that Northern Ireland would not cease to be a part of the United Kingdom without the consent of the Parliament of Northern Ireland, could, in certain circumstances, bind Westminster.

Such reservations were first expressed in remarks made *obiter* by Lord Cooper of Culross, 'probably the most outstanding Scottish judge of our time',[2] in *MacCormick v. Lord Advocate* (1953)[3]:

> The principle of the unlimited sovereignty of Parliament is a distinctively English principle which has no counterpart in Scottish constitutional law . . . .
> I have not found in the Union legislation any provision that the Parliament of Great Britain should be 'absolutely sovereign' in the sense that Parliament should be free to alter the Treaty at will.[4]

Professor T. B. Smith argued that the Scottish Union has the status of a fundamental law of the United Kingdom, one which 'cannot lawfully be abrogated by ordinary Act' of the United Kingdom Parliament, so that although 'Every schoolboy knows that the British Constitution has no fundamental written basis; . . . every schoolboy has been misinformed'.[5]

The 'new view' has also received the cautious support of Professor Calvert in what remains the best, if not the only, text on the constitutional law of devolution, *The Constitutional Law of Northern Ireland*, and of Professor J. D. B. Mitchell in his well-known work *Constitutional Law*. That the divergence between constitutional thinking in Scotland and Northern Ireland and the conventional view of the constitution has not led to much practical embarrassment must be put down to more than the innate English desire to (in the late J. L. Austin's words), let sleeping dogmas lie. For Northern Ireland, of course, sought to avoid constitutional conflict and not to encourage it; and, until recently at least, the Scottish interpretation of the Constitution was not in practice incompatible with an allegiance to English norms, since the assertion of Scottish nationality did not seem to pose any incompatibility with membership of the United Kingdom.

In Wales the situation was more complex since, lacking a recent history of independent statehood, Wales did not enjoy, until the end of the nineteenth century, indigenous institutions such as might sustain a constitutional challenge to the English Constitution. Writing in 1914, J. Vyrnwy Morgan in *The Philosophy of Welsh History*, insisted that the recognition of Welsh nationality did not require separate statehood, and the demands of Welsh nationalists before the First World War were less for a domestic legislature than for institutions which might sustain Welsh culture and religion. The Cymru Fydd movement, for example, claimed that the 'Old Idea of Welsh Independence' had 'perished with Llewellyn and Glendower'. 'The closer the connection' with England, 'the better it will be for the purpose of Cymru Fydd',[6] provided that this connection was not at the expense of Welsh national qualities. Wales sought not separation, but recognition as an equal partner in the United Kingdom.

The contrast between the different situations of Scotland and Wales is reflected in the approaches of their respective nationalist parties. The SNP is a political party of roughly the same type as the Labour, Conservative or Liberal parties, whilst Plaid Cymru has concentrated as much on a cultural critique of modern society as upon orthodox political activity. This critique, developed by such thinkers as Waldo Williams, J. R. Jones, E. F. Schumacher, Leopold Kohr and Ioan Bowen Rees, is not a peculiarly Welsh critique. It could be applied to any industrial society, and indeed many of its proponents see Wales as providing a laboratory within which the true conditions of happiness in an industrial society can be developed. In some ways, the nationalism advocated by Plaid Cymru is therefore not true nationalism at all, for much of its thought is *decentralist* rather than *nationalist*, and it has a good deal in common with ideas expressed by those who are not Welsh nationalists.

Devolution in Wales has come to be a part of the political agenda as the result of a Labour Party debate, and not primarily as a response to the challenge of nationalism. It is defended as much on the grounds of transforming Welsh psychology as in the straightforward political terms used by the SNP. For a key word in the Welsh critique of Wales is still *taeogrwydd* – servitude. Plaid Cymru and the Labour Party alike seek to remove the sense of Welsh inferiority as did Tom Ellis and Lloyd George before them. But, because this inferiority is seen as a cultural and not a constitutional one, Wales has been unable to mount any challenge to the dominant constitutional concepts of England. The only exception to this lies in the debate on the future of the Welsh language. For if England and Wales are constitutionally one, then, as Saunders Lewis argued in his famous radio broadcast on the future of the language in 1962, 'the existence of a separate Welsh language impairs the unity'. Constitutionally, therefore, the language did not exist until recently.

But even in the area of the language, Welsh nationalists have not succeeded in developing a theory of the State which might give meaning and content to the notion that linguistic groups as well as individuals have rights. They have proceeded, on the whole pragmatically and using well-understood techniques of pressure, to secure greater tolerance for diversity by appealing to hallowed liberal norms, long accepted by British governments. Constitutionally, therefore, it is still possible to say, in the notorious words of the encyclopedia, 'For Wales, see England'.

II

Thus the principle of parliamentary supremacy remains the constitutional sun around which all our notions of political power and right revolve. This has profound consequences for the way in which we are governed. The most important of these consequences is that we find ourselves unwilling to limit Parliament, and therefore unwilling to clarify the proper role of government – for Parliament is in Britain an institution whose function is in essence to sustain government. When we establish an institution such as the Ombudsman, whose purpose is to protect the citizen against government, we insist that complaints are made to him through MPs – as if it is the link with Parliament that gives him any constitutional existence at all. The notion that Parliament can itself scrutinize and regulate the activities of public authorities is, of course, one derived from the nineteenth century when the scope of government action was minimal. Its retention into the totally changed circumstances of the twentieth century has meant that the individual is frequently left naked in the face of authority, and the checks upon government sometimes appear to be little more than the maintenance of attenuated liberal norms – a sense of decency – and the limited competence of those set to rule over us. It is doubtful if these are entirely sufficient as regulators of power under the conditions of the modern administrative State.

A related aspect of our constitutional situation is our unwillingness to attach much weight to the creative use of the law in regulating political or administrative relationships. This is partly a corollary of traditional ideas about Parliament. For if Parliament is itself sufficient as a protector of civil liberties, if it is still the Grand Inquest of the Nation, then the law is bound to assume a subordinate role. But our hesitation to use the law as an instrument of constitutional regulation has, of course, other sources as well.

For the ideologies of both major Parties are hostile, for different reasons, to giving the courts an active role in the control of power. The Labour Party, of course, has a traditional suspicion of judges as class enemies, an hostility heightened by the working of the ill-fated Industrial Relations Act in the

1970s. It is perhaps ironic that Michael Foot, whose devolution legislation would, in effect, have set up a constitutional court in Britain, expressed this hostility in its most extreme form. Speaking to the Union of Post Office Workers at Bournemouth on 15 May 1977, he claimed[7]:

> If the freedom of the people of this country – and especially the rights of trade unionists – if these precious things of the past had been left to the good sense and fair mindedness of the judges we would have few freedoms in this country at all.

Mr Foot was supported by Mr Len Murray who said that judges had made nonsense of Acts of Parliament 'again and again in our history'.[8] But Lord Elwyn-Jones, the Lord Chancellor, qualified what Mr Foot had said[9] by insisting that he

> was not casting aspersions on any particular judge or any particular decision: he was talking about the past, starting, as he has told me, with the Tolpuddle Martyrs.

Although there are, no doubt, good reasons in the history of the trade union movement to explain Mr Foot's approach, nevertheless his sentiments would not be echoed by a radical in the United States, France or Germany, who might well welcome the protection which the courts would give to civil liberties in the face of an overweening executive. Indeed, in the United States, it can be argued that the Supreme Court has, since the *Brown* decision of 1954, been a major agent of social change in areas such as civil rights and personal freedoms.

Conservative thought places great weight upon the gradual evolution of government, which is shaped more by social trends and the growth of precedent, than by deliberate constitutional action. From this point of view, the Industrial Relations Act of 1971 was, of course, a sad aberration itself to be explained in terms of its departure from a hallowed British tradition of keeping the law out of industrial relations. The Conservative has a suspicion that the clarification of political relationships destroys that intimacy which is responsible for their practical success. He therefore prefers the decent obscurity of convention to the harsh light of constitutional thinking.

The unwillingness to clarify our political relationships is beautifully shown in official attitudes to the relationships between central and local government. The following quotation from the *Wheatley Report on Local Government in Scotland* (Cmnd. 4150) is particularly apt:

> The statutes lay down the broad limits within which central and local government may act in relation to each other. They do not determine what the day-to-day working relationship will be (p.244).

It is, on this view, the attitudes of individuals working the political system, and not any conception of law or constitutional principle, which govern, and ought to govern, central–local relations. A relationship which, if it was to support genuine local autonomy, might have to be a juridical one, dissolves into one of good fellowship. It is perhaps little wonder that, when considering how central control can be lessened, the Committee is reduced to calling for a 'policy of deliberate self-restraint by central government in its dealings with local authorities' (p. 243), while ignoring the political factors which have led to greater central control.

It was, perhaps, because it insisted that problems of central–local relations be clarified in accordance with an explicit philosophy of government that the Layfield Report of 1976 met with such hostility. Appointed to consider the future of local government finance, the Committee did not content itself with treating this as a purely technical issue; nor, unlike Redcliffe-Maud, Kilbrandon, *et hoc genus omne*, did it mistake shifting the institutional furniture for genuine constitutional reform. Indeed, it posed the uncomfortable question of whether we wanted a decentralized system of government, and were willing to pay the price in terms of a diversity of standards in public services; or whether we preferred an explicitly centralist model. The technical choices about the structure of local government finance would follow upon this choice, rather than, as with Redcliffe-Maud and Kilbrandon, being pre-empted by them.

Layfield posed a question. Typically, it was not answered. Instead the response was to return to the technical problems, and to shuffle off the substantive issues by using the rhetoric of 'partnership' and 'co-operation' which is, in fact, a mask for central control. Thus we drift heedless into a governmental structure which we never chose. From this point of view, the reception of the Layfield Report must well merit an extended case-study as indicative of our natural reflexes when confronted with questions about the nature of government.

Yet a further symptom of our constitutional situation has been our unwillingness, until very recently, to raise the question of what, for the purposes of political action, is to be construed as a majority. Traditionally, the party victorious in a general election has been deemed either to be, or to represent, 'the majority'. The fact that it has hardly ever represented a majority of the voters was brushed aside as inconvenient.

The rise of the nationalist parties in Scotland and Wales has also made the question of what majority is to count for the purpose of particular acts of legislation a contentious one. Under what circumstances and over what issues should a United Kingdom majority be able to overrule a Scottish or Welsh majority? How can a line be drawn between those issues on which the Scottish or Welsh should be allowed to decide policy for themselves, and those issues in which the United Kingdom government must retain an interest? A large part of the debate about devolution consists, of course, in precisely this argument about where to draw the line – or whether it can be drawn at all.

Thus our constitutional tradition inhibits us from sensibly discussing, let alone solving, many of the most vital political problems which we face. We have, indeed, little tradition of debate about constitutional matters and, since the 1960s, we have substituted for it a belief in the virtues of institutional change. We prefer to ask the questions which a practical administrator would ask, rather than enquire into the terms and conditions upon which we are governed. Perhaps that was what Bentham meant when he denied that we had a constitution at all:

> The Anglo-American United States have a constitution. They have a constitutional code; the constitution is a system of arrangements delineated in that Code. The French and Spanish nations have constitutions. The English monarchy has no constitution, for it has no all-comprehensive constitutional code, nor in general any constitutional code whatsoever generally acknowledged as such . . . . England, having no constitution at all, has no excellent, no matchless constitution; for nothing has no properties.[10]

It is now time to consider how this parlous state will be affected by devolution.

III

Devolution to Scotland and Wales will mean that, in the absence of pathological political situations, parliamentary supremacy over Scotland will, in effect, cease to exist. Parliament's assertion of the right to continue to make laws for Scotland on devolved matters will be vain; for nothing would unite Scottish opinion more than an attempt by Westminster to legislate on a devolved matter. Indeed, such will be the power exerted by the sentiment of nationality upon the institution of an elected assembly that the members of the Scottish Assembly may be able to demarcate for themselves the areas within which they desire autonomy. They may be able to build upon the devolutionary settlement until it appears to them a more satisfactory way of dividing powers so as to give Scotland genuine control over its domestic affairs. In practice, therefore, the relationships between the devolved administrations and the government will be akin to that between provinces and the federal government in a federal state, and new constitutional and political relationships will have to be worked out. These will have to include provision for an intergovernmental layer as a forum within which mutual accommodation is to be reached; and some means will have to be found to make this layer of government properly accountable – a problem which has exercised in vain many existing federal States.

The Scotland Act 1978 would have required the courts and the Judicial Committee of the Privy Council to determine the validity of Acts of the Scottish Assembly; also the scope for litigation with regard to Acts of the Scottish Assembly would have been much greater than it was in relation to Stormont. This is partly because Stormont had a political incentive not to arouse friction with London by attempting to circumvent the 1920 Act; but primarily because the Scotland Act, unlike the Government of Ireland Act, enumerated transferred rather than reserved powers, and it did so in an extremely detailed way, listing not only groups of subjects, such as education or health, but also the specific provisions of statutes and even existing provisions in these statutes. This left greater opportunity for dispute as to their precise scope.

For British law 'is not in the form of codes strictly limited to particular subject-matters and without overlap on other domains'.[11] Thus one result of devolution would be that, in one part of the country, the courts will play a major role in politics. Scotland would in effect have a constitution and, although that may complicate political life, it would also open up opportunities for the creative use of the law in the rest of the United Kingdom.

IV

In Wales, also, devolution, will lead to considerable constitutional changes. The Welsh model of executive devolution is a kind of bastard child of the German model. For the German system rests upon a rationalistic notion of law, according to which enactments are to be drafted impersonally and in declaratory form, rather than, as in this country, being drafted largely in terms of the powers of Ministers. This provides ample scope for the Land governments to use their powers in the implementation of legislation. The Constitutional Court is there to ensure that the principles of law-making are observed, and that both government and *Länder* act in a '*bundesfreundlich*' manner. In Britain, however, we do not have a very clear idea of the proper role of public law or the appropriate role of primary law as compared with subordinate enactments.

If there is to be effective devolution in Wales, therefore, principles will have to be devised to regulate the character of primary legislation for Wales. This would involve 'the review and rewriting of major slices of public law, and with the express intention of moving numerous powers from the hands of Ministers'.[12] If that is done, then clearly our thinking about the nature of law will be greatly changed, and it may be that principles of law-making will be developed that permit a clarification of central–local relations in England, to the benefit of supporters of local autonomy.

V

If the main argument of this chapter is correct, then devolution will first undermine and finally destroy parliamentary supremacy. For, in the absence of parliamentary supremacy, we shall be forced to develop a corpus of genuinely constitutional thought.

The late Richard Crossman viewed such a prospect with horror[13]:

> During our discussion on devolution, Michael Stewart made a speech about the danger that the terms of reference of the Committee [on the Constitution] might permit consideration of a written constitution. He really is admirable on these things and he spelt out how appallingly reactionary this would be.

Constitutionalism is, of course, bound to be a defensive movement, dedicated as it is to the control and restraint of power. Therefore, the instinct of radicals, whether of Right or Left, to oppose it is a sensible one. But those who hold a less sanguine view of the effectiveness of modern government may yet have cause to be grateful that devolution has opened up such fundamental constitutional issues.

Notes and references

1   Lord McDermott: Foreword to Harry Calvert (1968), *Constitutional Law in Northern Ireland*, Stevens.
2   T. B. Smith (1960), 'The Contribution of Lord Cooper of Culross to the Law of Scotland', *Juridical Review*, **72**, 249.
3   1953, S.C. 396.
4   *Ibid.*, 410–11.
5   'The Union of 1707 as Fundamental Law', in *Public Law* (1957), 109–10.
6   W. Llewellyn Williams (1894), *Young Wales Movement: Cymru Fydd: Its Aims and Objects*, Roberts Bros, 3.
7   *Daily Telegraph*, 16 June 1977.
8   Prison Officers' Association Conference, Weymouth, *The Times*, 24 May 1977.
9   *Hansard* (1977), H. L., 16 May, Col. 461.
10 'The Constitutional Code', in *The Works of Jeremy Bentham* (ed. Bowring, 1843), Vol. IX, 9.
11 Scottish Law Commission, Memorandum No. 32, Comments on White Paper: *Our Changing Democracy: Devolution to Scotland and Wales*, para. 13.
12 Nevil Johnson (1973), *Federalism and Decentralisation in The Federal Republic of Germany*, Commission on the Constitution, Research Paper 1, para. 134.
13 R. Crossman (1977), *Diaries of a Cabinet Minister*, Vol. 2, 243.

11 Devolution: The Constitutional Problems

I

Devolution in Britain is in large part the history of something that has not happened.[1] Of five devolution or Home Rule bills since 1886 – the four Irish Home Rule bills of 1886, 1893, 1914 and 1920, and the Scotland and Wales Acts of 1978 – only one, the Irish Home Rule Act of 1920, actually came into effect; but it came into effect in only one part of Ireland, the six counties of north-eastern Ulster which came to form Northern Ireland; the other 26 counties repudiated Home Rule and broke away entirely from the United Kingdom. Northern Ireland, however, had, paradoxically, been the one part of Ireland which had *not* sought devolution; she had wished simply to retain her membership of the United Kingdom on the same basis as every other part of the country. For Northern Ireland, devolution was, in the words of her first prime minister, Sir James Craig, in 1921, 'a *final settlement* and supreme sacrifice in the interests of peace, although not asked for by her representatives' (my italics).[2] So it is that the experience of Northern Ireland between 1921 and 1972 evades the crucial problem of whether it is possible to devolve power to one part of the country in a unitary state. For devolution is normally undertaken in order to contain ethnic nationalism; the pressures which it is designed to meet are centrifugal. In Northern Ireland, however, the pressures were not centrifugal but centripetal, the majority in the province seeking to remain within the United Kingdom, not to break away from it.

Why has the history of devolution in Britain been so largely one of failure? The answer lies deep in our constitutional thinking, or perhaps rather in our tacit understandings about the constitution, those understandings that are so rarely understood.[3] Perhaps the most important of these tacit understandings is the unitary nature of the British state. Unlike countries such as Germany and the United States, Britain has little understanding of the idea of a division of powers. We find it extremely difficult to think of government as a series of interdependent levels, each with its own rights and responsibilities.

Our fundamental – perhaps our only – constitutional principle is that of the supremacy of Parliament. Yet the idea of the supremacy of Parliament creates difficulties for us when we seek to come to terms with a territorial division of powers, whether with Europe or with Scotland. For it leads us to believe that in every political community there must be one supreme political authority. Thus we find it difficult to understand how, in our relationship with Europe, there could be any alternative to a Europe of states other than a Europe centralized in Brussels, a Europe that, as Hugh Gaitskell once said, would mean the end of a thousand years of history. We tend therefore to see Westminster and Brussels, not as complementary powers, but as engaged in a duel which only one side can win. Similarly, we find it difficult to conceive of a Scottish parliament as anything other than a half-way house to the separation of Scotland from the rest of the kingdom. Yet in each case, there is a third alternative, a genuine division and sharing of powers within which each layer of government is able to perform the tasks most suited to it so that it complements rather than dominates the others. That indeed is the rationale of European Union, the idea that power can be shared and sovereignty divided so as to create a political entity capable of carrying out common policies without compromising the identity of the component units. It is no coincidence, therefore, that those who are most sympathetic to European Union tend also to be sensitive to the needs of the non-English parts of the United Kingdom; while it is those hostile to European Union who tend, to put it mildly, to be rather sceptical of proposals to devolve power from Westminster. For them subsidiarity stops at Whitehall.

Yet, although our notion of the supremacy of Parliament seemingly condemns us to live in a uniform and homogeneous state, we have, fortunately, rarely taken our ideological presuppositions to their logical conclusion. The spirit in which Britain is administered helps to counteract its logic. For, until recently at least, Britain has been able, with Ireland remaining the one glaring exception, to accommodate identities, such as that of the Scots or the Welsh, within the framework of a unitary state. Thus it has been possible for those living in Scotland or in Wales to see themselves both as Scots or Welsh *and* as British without these identities conflicting. It has never been necessary to buttress the unitary state with an ideology of uniformity. Perhaps because of a deep sense of national self-confidence, the British state, unlike, for example, the French, has not needed to be the guardian of the nation. So it is that the United Kingdom has been able to accommodate a considerable diversity of relationships – devolution in Northern Ireland between 1921 and 1972, looser constitutional relationships with the Channel Islands and the Isle of Man, and a considerable degree of administrative devolution to

Scotland and Wales – relationships which have proved perfectly compatible with the unity of the state.

The traditional relationship between Westminster and Scotland, a relationship that might be described as one of centralization tempered by indifference, was, however, put under severe strain by the centralizing measures of the Conservative governments of the 1980s and 1990s. The centralization of power did not, of course, begin with the government first elected in 1979. But the reaction to it had a special colouring in Scotland whose national identity was affronted by a government representing a minority of Scottish voters which, nevertheless, sought to impose its own ideological prescriptions upon the Scottish people. It is true that on occasions when Labour wins a large majority, such as 1945 and 1966, there is the possibility of legislation affecting England being passed against the wishes of the majority of English MPs. But England could never find herself in the position that Scotland has faced since 1987 when Scottish legislation has been regularly passed with the support of no more than the 10 or 11 Conservative MPs out of 72 from Scotland. Such a situation undermines the unwritten contract according to which Scotland has been governed since the Union and which requires that a United Kingdom majority treat Scotland with respect and sensitivity to her particular needs.

It is this sense of a national identity under threat that gives rise to the demand for devolution, for a parliament in Edinburgh. Devolution, however, has a dual dynamic. For not only can it re-establish the terms of the contract with Scotland; it can also, in dispersing power from Westminster and Whitehall, offer an example to be followed by other parts of the United Kingdom, by Wales and the English regions. The crucial question, however, is whether a future government of the Left can avoid the pitfalls which have dogged Home Rule and devolution in the past by devising a policy which can serve both aims – accommodation of the Scottish desire for autonomy and the dispersal of power from Westminster and Whitehall to the regions and localities of the United Kingdom.

II

The Labour Party is committed to establishing a parliament in Edinburgh and a parliament or senedd in Cardiff, while the Liberal Democrats and their predecessors, the Liberals, have long been committed to Home Rule for Scotland and Wales as part of their programme for a federal system of government for the whole of the United Kingdom. Both parties propose, in the light of Scotland's separate legal system, legislative devolution for Scotland but executive devolution for other parts of the United Kingdom. But legislative devolution for just one part of the country would create a constitutional imbalance between Scotland and the rest of the country – or rather it would accentuate, unacceptably, an already existing imbalance.

For Scotland, like Wales and Northern Ireland, already has a Secretary of State who can argue her case in the Cabinet. Like Wales she is over-represented in the House of Commons, there being 72 MPs from Scotland as compared with the 57 to which she would be entitled if the same criteria were applied to Scotland as are applied to England.[4] With devolution, Scotland would enjoy the additional advantage of a directly elected parliament able to press her claims upon Westminster. The extra political weight which a parliament would give to Scotland would mean that she would probably be able to attract public funds which would otherwise go to the more deprived regions of England, especially perhaps the north of England. It was indeed a revolt from Labour MPs primarily from northern constituencies that was largely responsible for emasculating the devolution bills in the 1970s.[5]

The most striking anomaly to which legislative devolution in Scotland would give rise is the 'West Lothian Question', so named in honour of the then MP for West Lothian, Tam Dalyell, MP for Linlithgow since 1983, who pressed it with such pertinacity in the 1970s. Dalyell asked what justification there could be for the fact that, after devolution, English, Welsh and Northern Irish MPs would no longer be able to vote on Scottish domestic matters, but Scottish MPs would still be able to vote on English, Welsh and Northern Irish domestic matters. What justification was there for the fact that Scottish MPs would still be able to vote on health and education in West Bromwich, while English MPs would no longer be able to vote on health and education in West Lothian?

In May 1965, the 12 Northern Ireland MPs, then all Ulster Unionists who almost always supported the Conservatives, voted against the Labour government's Manchester Corporation bill and Rent bill, the provisions of which did not apply to Northern Ireland. The government then enjoyed a majority of only three, and the Prime Minister, Harold Wilson, gave the Ulster Unionists a veiled warning:

> I would hope that Northern Ireland Members who are here, and who are welcomed here, for the duties they have to perform on behalf of the United Kingdom in many matters affecting Northern Ireland, would consider their position in matters where we have no equivalent right in Northern Ireland.[6]

The 'West Lothian question' is, as a matter of pure logic, unanswerable short of establishing a full-scale federal state for which there is certainly no demand in England. It would be constitutionally impossible entirely to exclude Scottish MPs from Westminster while Scotland continued to remain part of the United Kingdom; and the so-called 'in and out' solution, championed by Gladstone at one time during the proceedings on the 1893 Home Rule Bill, offers the worst of all possible worlds.[7] According to the 'in and out' solution, Scottish MPs would only be allowed to vote at Westminster on non-devolved issues. But this could mean that there would be two different majorities at Westminster, according to whether domestic or non-domestic issues were being discussed. Thus, on education and health, it might be that there was a Conservative majority able to sustain a Conservative government, since Scottish MPs would be excluded from voting, while on foreign affairs and defence, when Scottish MPs would be readmitted, there might be a Labour majority able to sustain a Labour government. It would hardly be possible to govern a modern industrial state on such a basis.

The West Lothian question draws attention to an anomaly inherent in devolving legislative power to just one part of a country. There is no inherent reason, however, why an anomaly of this kind should disrupt devolution. In the European Parliament, there is an analogous anomaly. For British MEPs currently vote on matters connected with the Social Chapter, even though Britain, under the Maastricht Treaty, has opted out of it. There are also Continental examples showing that where the will to conciliate is present, special treatment for one part of a country, far from stimulating separatism, can actually help contain it. In Finland, the Aaland Islands, with their Swedish population, have long had their own assembly, while in Denmark, the Faeroes and Greenland enjoy such wide autonomy that they have been able to remain outside the European Union while Denmark remains a member.

Thus the question of whether recognition of Scotland's national identity is compatible with the maintenance of the United Kingdom should be decided not on the basis of administrative tidiness or logical symmetry but on the basis of practical judgement. The West Lothian question is worrying, not so much because of the anomaly to which it draws attention, for all constitutions contain anomalies; but because it draws attention to the fact that devolution would unacceptably accentuate an already existing constitutional imbalance, thereby making it intolerable. Without further adjustments, legislative devolution to Scotland would create a lop-sided structure of government in the United Kingdom in which the citizens of England, Wales and Northern Ireland would become second-class citizens, under-represented and without assemblies which could fight for their interests as the Scottish parliament would fight for the interests of Scotland. How can such a constitutional imbalance be mitigated?

If Scotland were to enjoy legislative devolution, there would seem to be no case for retaining the Secretaryship of State. The Scottish Office exists primarily to administer policies where a separate Scottish dimension is possible. After devolution, however, those policy areas will be in the hands of the Scottish parliament. Responsibility for policy areas where no such Scottish dimension is possible ought to be transferred to non-territorial Whitehall departments.

There would be no case, either, for continuing with the over-representation of Scotland after devolution. Northern Ireland, during the years between 1921 and 1972 when she enjoyed devolution, far from being over-represented in Parliament, was actually under-represented, returning only 12 MPs (13 before the abolition of the university seats in 1948) to the House of Commons rather than the 17 to which she would have been entitled on a population basis. Scotland ought at the very least to have her representation reduced from 72 MPs to 57 after devolution; and there is a case for reducing her representation even below that, using Northern Ireland as a precedent. Such a reduction in the number of Scottish MPs would, of course, not be an answer to the West Lothian question. But it would mitigate its effects, since it would become less likely, although still, of course, perfectly possible, that Scottish MPs would affect the balance between a Labour and Conservative government. The anomaly might, however, then become one that the English, the Welsh and the Northern Irish would be prepared to accept as a price worth paying to keep Scotland within the United Kingdom.

A devolution package of this type amounts essentially to a renegotiation of the terms of the Acts of Union of 1707. Unlike the 1978 Scotland Act, which provided for the retention of the Secretary of State for Scotland and of Scottish over-representation at Westminster, such a package imposes losses upon Scotland as well as gains. It may well be indeed that the Scottish people would not want devolution upon such terms; they might believe that a parliament purchased at the cost of the removal of the Secretary of State and a reduction in Scottish representation at Westminster is too high a price to pay, and that it would be better to maintain the status quo. It is, surely, for the Scottish people to decide which alternative they prefer, and there must, therefore, be a strong case for putting a devolution package of the type outlined to the Scottish people in a referendum.

III

When, in the 1970s, Labour ministers decided to offer devolution to Scotland, Wales seems almost to have been added on as an afterthought. The presumption seems to have been, 'If Scotland, then Wales', although the configuration of political forces in Wales was very different from that in Scotland. In the October 1974 general election, the SNP, with 30 per cent of the Scottish vote, had become the second largest party in Scotland in terms of votes and clearly threatened Labour's electoral hegemony there. Support for Plaid Cymru, on the other hand, was actually lower in October 1974 in terms of percentage of the vote per opposed candidate than it had been in 1970, having fallen from 11.5 per cent per opposed candidate to 10.7 per cent. This difference in the level of support for the two nationalist parties remains. In the 1992 general election, the SNP gained 21 per cent of the Scottish vote, but won just three seats, while Plaid Cymru's vote was 8.8 per cent, although it succeeded in winning four seats.

Nationalism in Scotland is a political force which unites, but in Wales it is divisive primarily because of the language issue. In Scotland, the institutions of nationhood – the church, the legal system, the universities – elicit wide feelings of sympathy among almost all Scots. In Wales, by contrast, the most obvious badge of Welsh identity – the language – incites conflict in a principality in which nearly 80 per cent of the population cannot speak Welsh. If, as the founder and first president of Plaid Cymru, Saunders Lewis, maintained, the language is 'more important than self-government',[8] then the electoral prospects of Plaid Cymru cannot be very great. In fact the party's successes in general elections have been confined to Welsh-speaking north and west Wales, while the SNP's vote is fairly evenly spread across Scotland.

The language issue was one of the reasons for the defeat of devolution in Wales by a majority of four to one in the 1979 referendum, despite the fact that three of the four political parties in Wales – excluding only the Conservatives – favoured it. The question is whether Welsh opinion has changed so massively since 1979 that a majority now favours devolution; or whether parties of the Left, claiming allegiance to democratic values, can be justified in imposing devolution on Wales against the wishes of the majority there.

Wales is not to be offered legislative devolution but rather executive devolution, as will any English regions to which devolution is offered. Executive devolution appears at first sight as merely a weaker variant of legislative devolution. Under executive devolution, an assembly would not have the power to pass primary legislation, but only secondary legislation, responsibility for the framework of primary laws remaining with Westminster. Executive devolution, however, is not so much a weaker form of devolution than legislative devolution, but a quite different form which would introduce into Britain a wholly new and as yet untried structure of governmental relationships.

For, while legislative devolution involves a *transfer* of powers, executive devolution involves a *division* of powers. It would be possible to ascertain the precise functions of a parliament with legislative powers simply by inspecting the provisions of the devolution legislation and looking at the statute book. With executive devolution, however, the functions which an assembly

would enjoy depend not only upon the provisions of the devolution legislation, but also upon the way in which legislation for the devolved areas is
drawn up by the government and the degree of discretion which the government thinks it right to confer upon the assemblies. For there is, in Britain at
least, no clear dividing line between policy-making and administration and
no general rule to determine whether a particular matter falls under primary
legislation in which case it is to be retained, or secondary legislation in which
case it is to be devolved.

Legislative devolution involves a decision as to whether or not to transfer
responsibility for a particular function, for example, education. Executive
devolution, by contrast, involves the additional decision as to *how much*
responsibility should be transferred. This requires an answer to the prior
question of how primary legislation ought to be drafted. It primary legislation
is drafted loosely, then there will be scope for the assembly; if, on the other
hand, it is drafted tightly, the scope for the assembly would be correspond-
ingly reduced.

It would thus be possible for a government to limit the autonomy of an
assembly by drafting legislation in such a way as to leave it with little scope
for independent action. Indeed, a Conservative government in London faced
with a Labour assembly in Cardiff or Liverpool might well be tempted to
limit the freedom of action of the assemblies to prevent them from frustrating
government policy on a policy such as, for example, the continuation of grant
maintained schools.

In Britain, legislative and executive powers have in the past been so closely
fused that, in the words of the Royal Commission on the Constitution in
1973, the division between them 'is not a precise one, and under the present
arrangements they are not clearly separated'.[9] Past legislation does not seem
to have been guided by any very clear principles in this regard. In the past the
dividing line has often been drawn simply for convenience, related, perhaps
to considerations of parliamentary time. This is because the distinction
between primary and secondary legislation was never intended to provide the
basis for a division of powers between different elected bodies. Therefore,
with regard to existing legislation, the Welsh and regional assemblies would
find that their powers were of uneven scope and depth since there would be
no reason why the division between primary and secondary legislation in one
policy area, for example health, should match the division in another, for
example education. Thus the initial powers of the assemblies would have no
clear rationale. This would make an integrated approach to policy-making
extremely difficult. There would be no alternative to accepting this situation
at the outset, for any attempt to adjust all relevant statutes to provide a more
logical dividing line would simply mean delaying devolution.

Even so, the assemblies would not be the final authorities on the policies for which they were responsible. For Westminster, under the model of executive devolution, would still retain control of all primary legislation. Moreover, the majority of devolved functions will involve the supervision of services delivered by local authorities. This means that policies involving, for example, education or the social services would have to proceed through three layers of government – central government, the assembly and the local authority. It may become more difficult, after devolution, for central government to draw up primary legislation effectively since it would have lost contact with the local authorities actually delivering the services, such contact being mediated by the assemblies. Deprived of this contact and the knowledge to which it gives rise, central government may become less well informed about the needs of the areas which enjoy devolution. The assemblies will be in a better position to appreciate these needs; but, because they will have no legislative powers, they will have to rely upon close co-operation with the Secretary of State for Wales or the Secretary of State for the Environment to promote legislation for the areas for which they are responsible. Since these ministers, however, may belong to a different party from that of the majority in the assemblies, co-operation cannot by any means be assured. What is clear is that executive devolution, even more than legislative devolution, relies upon co-operation between the assemblies and central government. Devolution is likely to work successfully only if there is a spirit of compromise between government and the assemblies, rather than an adversarial relationship.

Executive devolution, then, devolution of a 'horizontal' type, is not just a weaker form of legislative devolution than devolution of a 'vertical' type, but a wholly different kind of animal raising problems which have not hitherto been confronted in the British political system. If executive devolution is to prove effective, two fundamental problems will need to be resolved.

The first is that, since, by contrast with Scotland, there are few specifically Welsh bills, and hardly any bills specifically framed for particular regions, statutes will have to be framed differently for those regions of the country with executive devolution from those without it. For, if they were to be framed similarly, then either they would be drawn up too loosely for the regions without devolution, in which case ministers would enjoy too wide a discretion and wider delegated powers than Parliament would otherwise have chosen; or, alternatively, legislation would be drawn up too tightly for the areas with assemblies, in which case they will have insufficient scope for policy-making.

The second problem is to devise principles which might regulate the dividing line between primary and secondary legislation. This could not, as we have seen, be done immediately, but if executive devolution was to have any rationale at all, it would have to be achieved eventually. Such principles have been developed in the Federal Republic of Germany where the structure of public law 'displays a relatively high degree of coherence and homogeneity' so that 'it is possible . . . to achieve a consistency of principles . . . which is unattainable within the traditions of pragmatic positivism which have shaped both the common law and the statutory public law in Britain'. To develop similar principles in Britain, it would be necessary to review and re-write major slices of public law, with the purpose of removing powers from the hands of ministers. What is needed is to relate Westminster legislation to Wales 'framework' legislation as is done in Germany, by gradually amending existing statutes and suitably drawing up new ones. In Germany, however, the division of powers in the federal system is buttressed by a constitutional court which ensures that the demarcation lines are observed. In Britain, there is, of course, no such constitutional court and there is no way in which Parliament at Westminster could bind itself to observe principles which happened to be drawn up by a particular government at any one particular time.

Thus, if it is to prove successful, devolution to Wales and to the English regions would require a considerable alteration in British constitutional practice. It would require governments to accept principles which limit their power. It would require government and assemblies alike to be willing to share power, to co-operate rather than indulge in adversarial relationships. It would require, in short, a change in the political culture of Britain. It is not clear how such a change is to be brought about.

IV

Many, although by no means all, of the problems associated with devolution in Britain arise because it is being proposed on an asymmetrical basis. Devolution is being proposed for Scotland, for Wales and perhaps also for some of the English regions, rather than for the United Kingdom as a whole. A number of the problems could be avoided were 'Home Rule All Round' to be proposed, transforming Britain in one fell swoop from a unitary into a federal system. The strength of the federalist argument lies in the fact that the case for devolution in the English regions and Wales is not wholly dissimilar to the case for devolution in Scotland. That case is based on the need to disperse power from the centre in *every* part of the United Kingdom. For Britain is now by far the most centralized Member State of the European Union, and one of the most centralized states in the world. That centralization affects every part of the United Kingdom, although in Scotland and Wales it is felt with particular force to the extent that it seems a threat to their national identities. Thus, a policy of 'devolution all round', to relieve the over-concentration of power in Whitehall and diminish the span of control of central government could benefit every part of the United Kingdom, not just Scotland and Wales.

A policy of this kind, moreover, has been carried out in the postwar years by those Continental countries that had hitherto suffered from over-centralization – France, Italy and Spain. Indeed, the other Member States of the European Union of a similar size to Britain – France, Germany, Italy and Spain – all have regional layers of government. The Maastricht Treaty, by creating an advisory Committee of the Regions, explicitly recognized the constitutional role of the regions in building European Union. Since many European projects are planned on a regional basis, and since structural funds are administered on a regional basis also, Britain is likely, in the absence of a regional layer, to suffer in the competition for funds. Thus the argument for the dispersal of power from the centre and the creation of a regional layer of government is strengthened by developments in European Union, so making the case for a federal Britain a very strong one indeed.

Nevertheless, the introduction of a federal system of government, through one legislative act, while it would no doubt be logical, is hardly practical politics. It would either condemn parts of the country which did not want devolution to have it because Scotland wanted it; or, alternatively, it would compel Scotland to wait for devolution until every other part of the United Kingdom wanted it, and that could prove a very long time indeed. The proposal to implement a federal scheme in one fell swoop flies in the face of reality. When, in 1889, a correspondent pressed a federal solution upon Lord Salisbury, the Conservative leader replied, 'As to Home Rule in your sense – which is Federation – I do not see in it any elements of practicability. Nations do not change their political nature like that except through blood.'[10]

It is because the demand for regionalism in many parts of England is so insubstantial that the Labour Party faces such difficulty in drawing up a policy on devolution that can both meet the needs of Scotland and yet not arouse a backlash from England. The sensible solution would be to approach federalism in a piecemeal manner, granting devolution to those areas which want it, while not forcing it on those which are opposed to it. The Labour Party could derive considerable benefit from studying the experience of Spain which faced a similar problem after the death of Franco in 1975 when democracy was restored.

For, in Spain, there was a strong demand for autonomy in the historic provinces – the Basque country and Catalonia – but much less demand elsewhere. The solution was found through the principle of rolling devolution. Autonomy was given to the historic provinces immediately, but at the same time it was announced that any other region of the country which sought autonomy could enjoy it also. Because devolution in the Basque country and Catalonia seemed to be working successfully, it was not long before the demand for devolution made itself felt in the other provinces, so that Spain today is a state of autonomous communities, a quasi-federal state comprising 17 autonomous regions each with their own government and parliament.

So also in Britain, Labour should lay down two principles governing its devolution policy. The first is that devolution will be given only to those nations and regions of the United Kingdom which seek it; the second is that a nation or region which rejects devolution cannot prevent another nation or region from embracing it.

Is there, however, any region of England which would actually seek devolution? In many parts of England, the regions, it is true, are ghosts, with no reality in popular consciousness. There have, however, been suggestions that there is a demand for devolution in the north of England. In the 1970s, northern opinion was primarily directed towards preventing Scottish devolution which it believed would divert public funds from the north of England to Scotland. Had a Scottish parliament been established, however, it is perfectly possible that northern opinion would have come to the view that an assembly was necessary to defend its interests. But perhaps the primary demand of northern opinion is not an assembly for its own sake, but for public funds, and a northern assembly is seen as a means by which more funds might be attracted to the region. For the north, then, regionalism may be a means to achieve other aims, not an end in itself.

There is, perhaps, a stronger latent demand for devolution in London. It is, after all, absurd that London should be one of the very few, if not the only, capital of a democratic country to have no authority or forum of its own. Since the abolition of the GLC in 1986, London has been governed by the 32 London boroughs, by a host of government–appointed quangos, by joint bodies and committees and by central government departments. The creation of a Minister for London by the Conservatives, a junior minister in the Department of the Environment, offers tacit acknowledgement that London is, from the point of view of government, a single entity; and yet, if one asks the question, 'Who speaks for London?', there is no answer. There is no body that is responsible for London as a whole, for its transport system, its health service and its education system.

It would be sensible, then, for a government of the Left to begin its devolution policy by creating, together with a Scottish parliament and a Welsh parliament or senedd, a regional authority for London. This would not be a revived GLC, for the GLC enjoyed few functional responsibilities of its own and therefore sought to encroach upon the powers of the London boroughs. It came, indeed, to be squashed between the boroughs and central government, with no clear role of its own, and it acquired a reputation for political extremism. Even so, if survey evidence in the mid-1980s is to be believed, the majority of Londoners were opposed to the abolition of the GLC. It is likely that there remains a basic London patriotism which would welcome the creation of a London-wide authority with substantial functions of its own, devolved from central government, and which could speak for London. There are clear London-wide problems such as transport in London, the health service and the future of the London hospitals, which could be better resolved by a London authority than by central government and a jumble of assorted quangos.

Indeed, it could be argued that the condition of, for example, the London hospitals, the underground system or indeed transport planning as a whole in London, would be improved if London enjoyed an authority which represented the wishes of the users of these services, rather than, as at present, relying primarily upon appointed bodies and government departments to administer them. If the London authority were to be elected, like the Scottish parliament and the Welsh parliament or senedd by proportional representation, there would be little danger of extremists coming to control it, as occurred with the GLC. Moreover, if would be far easier to implement devolution in London than in the north of England, since London, like Scotland and Wales, already enjoys a unitary structure of local government, while much of the north of England does not. An elected assembly inserted upon a two-tier structure of local government would, as the Welsh Council of Labour said of a similar proposal in the 1970s, be 'like a jellyfish on a bed of nails'.[11] Devolution in other parts of England would seem to require, first, a reform of local government to create new unitary authorities, a problem which does not arise in London. If devolution worked well in the capital, however, it could be expected to give rise to a demand for devolution in other regions of England. Thus an effective regional authority in London could prove an excellent advertisement for a policy of rolling devolution which is the only way that a federal or quasi-federal Britain could ever come about in practice.

V

The prime purpose of devolution is to disperse power in an over-centralized state. Yet this is not to be achieved simply by establishing parliaments and legislatures unless there is a positive will to decentralize. Were the Scottish parliament or the regional assemblies to seek to take power from local authorities, the result of devolution would be, not decentralization, but the centralization of power, to Edinburgh, Cardiff, Liverpool and Newcastle, and away from local authorities within Scotland, Wales and the regions.

There is undoubtedly a real danger that a devolved parliament and assemblies would encroach upon the prerogatives of local government. For the Scottish parliament and the regional assemblies would, presumably, be responsible for distributing grant to local authorities. The amount of grant which local authorities received would largely determine the extent of the autonomy which they enjoyed. The parliament and the assemblies, however, will be composed of elected members with their own distinctive views as to the proper shape of local government spending; they will have their own geographical and functional concerns, and they may well seek to press these concerns upon local authorities and to use their control of grant to ensure that their views are taken into account. Were that to happen, local authorities could become little more than executants of the policy of the parliament and assemblies, and local choice would be drastically reduced if not eliminated.

When Scottish local authorities, for example, come to negotiate with a Scottish parliament for funds, the local authorities will be competing with the parliament itself which may wish to earmark a certain proportion of central government grant for its own purposes. If the Scottish parliament wishes, as is quite likely, to determine priorities for Scotland, then it will wish to have influence over how available monies are spent. It would be perfectly possible for the Scottish parliament to retain grant which central government believes is better distributed to local authorities. Or, alternatively, it could decide to spend more than it has been allocated, making up the shortfall by forcing Scottish local authorities to raise their rates of council tax in order to maintain the existing level of services. There seems, therefore, to be some possibility of a built-in conflict between the Scottish parliament and local authorities in Scotland.

But devolution need not necessarily lead to so malign a scenario. It could be avoided if central government were to earmark that portion of the funds which it pays to the Scottish parliament and the assemblies for distribution to the local authorities. Moreover, it could be argued that, after devolution, local authorities would be in a stronger position negotiating with a parliament or with an assembly than they are at present negotiating with central government. For such consultation as local authorities at present enjoy with cental government over the distribution of grant does not in practice give them any significant influence over either its size or its distribution which remain primarily matters for the Cabinet to decide. A Scottish parliament, by contrast, or a London assembly, will be more familiar with, and more sympathetic to, Scottish and London local authorities respectively; the parliament and the assembly will be closer to the ground and more attuned to local problems than central government can ever hope to be.

Thus local authorities might well find it easier to make their wishes known and to secure attention to these wishes when negotiating with a directly elected parliament and assemblies than they can achieve at present when negotiating in Whitehall. Moreover, the Scottish Parliament and regional assemblies will be able to take over the running of many bodies and quangos which are at present appointed by central government. That would lead to greater democratic control over an already existing layer of administration and perhaps better and more cost-effective control. Devolution could, therefore, lead to improvements in public administration and to services that are more responsive to those who use them.

VI

The prime requirement, if devolution is to work successfully, is a positive attitude towards the dispersal of powers. This poses a particular problem for a government of the Left which is dedicated to the principle of equality of treatment in the provision of public services. The Left indeed has often under-estimated the importance of local and national allegiances. Socialists in Europe 'inherited the tradition, deriving from Louis XIV but reinforced by the French Revolution and Napoleon, that large centralised states were progressive and small regional autonomies reactionary'.[12] In the 1880s, Joseph Chamberlain opposed Home Rule to Ireland in part because he believed that the problems of the Irish peasant were no different in kind from those of the Welsh agricultural labourer or the Scottish crofter. These problems would be remedied not by a parliament in Dublin but by a powerful radical government at Westminster. So, also, in the 1970s, left-wingers like Eric Heffer and Neil Kinnock opposed devolution because they believed that the problems of the Scottish and the Welsh working-class were no different in kind from the problems of the English working-class. The problems would be remedied not by devolved assemblies but by a powerful socialist government at Westminster. Arguments of this type proved crucial in defeating devolution both in the 1880s and in the 1970s. The Conservative argument that devolution would break up the United Kingdom would not of itself have been sufficient to defeat it without the Liberal Unionist revolt in the 1880s or the revolt of Labour backbenchers, many of them belonging to the left wing in the 1970s.

The development of the welfare state has made it more difficult to promulgate an effective devolution policy. For one fundamental principle of the welfare state is that benefits should depend upon need and not upon geography. A deprived child in Glasgow should not receive better benefits than a similarly deprived child in Liverpool, simply because Glasgow happens to enjoy an assembly while Liverpool does not. There is, therefore, an inherent tension between devolution which involves a dispersal of powers, and equality of treatment. A government of the Left, therefore, must define the proper scope of diversity very carefully. Would, for example, a government of the Left be prepared to allow every secondary school in a Conservative region to become grant-maintained? Would a government of the Left allow a regional authority to privatize the National Health Service within its region – and if not, by what principles could the regional authority be denied such a power? To create an elected parliament and assemblies is to hand a weapon to those who will run them. It would be unrealistic to assume that the weapon will be used only for the purposes which governments of the Left think desirable.

Devolution will only prove successful if there is a genuine will to disperse power and the spirit of co-operation that makes it possible. It would have to be accompanied by what the Royal Commission on the Constitution in 1973 called 'a new style of thinking, positively favourable to devolution and based on co-operation rather than the exercise of central authority'.[13] But how is this 'new style of thinking' to be achieved?

It will be essential, after devolution, to limit the danger of confrontation between the Scottish parliament, the Welsh and regional assemblies, and central government. The best way of achieving this is by minimizing the role of ministers in resolving disputes and giving that role to the courts. In the 1978 Scotland Act, in addition to the role of the courts in reviewing the *vires* of Acts of the proposed Scottish Assembly, the Secretary of State was given the power to override the Assembly if it used its powers in a manner contrary to the public interest or in such a way as to affect a non-devolved matter. Thus, if the Scottish Assembly had sought to use its planning powers to prevent the construction of military airfields, the Secretary of State would have been able to use the override, since defence would have been a reserved matter.

The experience of Northern Ireland, however, on the very rare occasions when the Northern Ireland Parliament sought to use its powers in a manner displeasing to the British government, shows how difficult it is in practice for the government to exercise its reserve powers. In 1922, for example, the Northern Ireland government proposed to abolish proportional representation in local government elections, a measure which lay within its legislative competence, but which, the British government believed, went against the spirit of devolution because it would be seen by the Catholic minority as a measure hostile to it. Winston Churchill, the Colonial Secretary, wrote that the measure was 'inopportune' but the Northern Ireland government declared that if the abolition of proportional representation was vetoed, it would resign. The British government was forced to give way.[14] It is a mistake, therefore, to believe that the continued assertion of unlimited sovereignty can mean very much when the use of reserve powers by the central government comes into opposition to the wishes of a directly elected devolved body. Thus, policy override powers would be risky to use in practice since they would put the British government in direct conflict with a majority in one part of the kingdom. The Scottish parliament or the assembly in question would claim that it, rather than the government, represented the feeling of the nation or region that it was responsible for, and there could be a damaging confrontation with the government.

Therefore disputes between the British government and the Scottish parliament and Welsh or regional assemblies should be resolved, so far as possible, not by the government but by the courts, as is normally the case in federal systems.

The Judicial Committee of the Privy Council would, no doubt, be the body whose function it was to determine the *vires* of legislation emanating from the Scottish parliament. If that were to happen, the Judicial Committee would become in effect an embryonic constitutional court. Admittedly, the Judicial Committee would be able to pronounce only on Scottish and not on Westminster legislation. Nevertheless, if it were to decide a dispute over the division of powers in Scotland's favour, it would be difficult to imagine Westminster deliberately choosing to legislate for Scotland on a matter which the Judicial Committee had ruled was devolved. In practice, therefore, the Judicial Committee might well come to assume something like the role of a constitutional court with respect to Scottish legislation. To this extent, devolution would provide a powerful impetus to a codified constitution for Britain as a whole. For it would be proposing a quasi-federal system of government with a politically sanctified division of powers and a court to act as arbiter of that division.

We have seen, moreover, that there are other areas where constitutional definition is likely to be required if devolution is to prove successful. If executive devolution, a category hitherto unknown in the United Kingdom, were to work, there would have to be a process of definition of the proper sphere of primary and secondary legislation such as occurs in the German constitutional system. Moreover, if the Scottish parliament and assemblies are not to encroach upon local authorities, principles would need to be worked out to ensure that devolution strengthens local autonomy rather than encroaching upon it. There would have to be a defence of the rights of local authorities, a Charter of Rights perhaps for local government so that it could secure its autonomy not only against central government, but also against a Scottish parliament or regional assembly.

The purpose of devolution is to destroy the omnicompetence of Parliament. If it succeeds in doing so, it will force us to develop a corpus of genuinely constitutional thought. Devolution will work best if it is implemented not in isolation but as part of a larger constitutional settlement, involving the judicial protection of rights and a juridically guaranteed division of powers between different layers of government. Thus devolution involves nothing less than a commitment to a new kind of constitutional relationship in Britain, a relationship based on power-sharing. That would be a reaction against the trends of over 300 years.

Notes and references

1 Richard Rose (1982), *Understanding the United Kingdom: The Territorial Dimension in Government*, Longman.
2 Vernon Bogdanor (1979), *Devolution*, Oxford University Press, 47. This book gives a history of earlier Home Rule and devolution measures.
3 Sidney Low (1904), *The Governance of England*, T. Fisher Union, 12.
4 See the unpublished paper by Iain McLean, 'The Representation of Scotland and Wales in the House of Commons'.
5 Roger Guthrie and Iain McLean (1978), 'Another Part of the Periphery', *Parliamentary Affairs*.
6 House of Commons Debates, 6 May 1965, col. 1561.
7 Bogdanor, *Devolution*, Chapter 2.
8 Cited in Bogdanor, *Devolution*, 125.
9 Royal Commission on the Constitution (1973), Cmnd. 5460, HMSO, para. 828.
10 Lord Salisbury to Rev. M. MacColl, 12 April 1889, in G. W. E. Russell (ed.), *Malcolm MacColl: Memoirs and Correspondence*, Smith, Elder, 1914, 137.
11 Bogdanor, *Devolution*, 143.
12 Hugh Seton-Watson (1977), *Nations and States*, Methuen, 445.
13 Cmnd. 5460, para. 282.
14 Bogdanor, *Devolution*, 52–3.

12 The Referendum in the United Kingdom

The British Constitution knows nothing of the people. Its central, indeed perhaps its only, principle – the sovereignty of Parliament – was first formulated in the seventeenth century, long before the era of mass suffrage. Britain's political conventions remain profoundly inimical to popular participation. The prime minister is still nominated by the sovereign, not chosen by the House of Commons. The Commons itself remains overwhelmingly dominated by the two major parties, and the choice of the electors is in practice largely confined to the endorsement or rejection of the ruling party every five years.

Traditionally, the referendum was seen as unconstitutional in Britain precisely because it conflicted with parliamentary sovereignty. Yet it was first advocated by the great constitutional lawyer, A. V. Dicey (1835–1922) in an article entitled 'Ought the referendum to be introduced into England?', published in the *Contemporary Review*, 1890. Dicey's political aim was to ensure that Irish Home Rule, to which he was strongly opposed, was submitted to the electorate before it became law. He saw the referendum as the one instrument which could check a party majority in the Commons. It was for him, as for most of those who have advocated it, an essentially conservative weapon whose effect would be to prevent or delay change.

In postwar Britain, the issue of the referendum first arose not on the mainland but in Northern Ireland, and under highly unusual circumstances; for Northern Ireland was the only part of the United Kingdom whose membership was constitutionally guaranteed. When, in 1948, Eire decided to become an independent republic outside the Commonwealth, the British government had responded by passing the 1949 Ireland Act, which provided, *inter alia*, that Northern Ireland would not cease to be a part of the United Kingdom without the consent of the Parliament of Northern Ireland – Stormont. In 1972, however, Edward Heath's government prorogued Stormont, and it had therefore to find some other way to affirm the status of Northern Ireland. It was for this reason that a referendum in Northern Ireland – the Northern Ireland border poll – was held in 1973.

Advocates of the border poll hoped that it would 'take the border out of politics' in Northern Ireland. For politics in the province was bedevilled by the dispute about the border, which polarized political opinion into a Protestant Unionist party and various Catholic Republican parties. If the issue of the border could be decided by referendum, then perhaps the party conflict could evolve away from sectarian conflict so that politics in Northern Ireland would come to resemble the politics of the rest of the United Kingdom.

Such reasoning was, however, rather simplistic. For Irish nationalists could argue that the outcome of the border poll was predetermined by the politicians who had established partition in 1920–21. Northern Ireland had been set up as it was precisely because it was the largest area that could comfortably be carved out of the island of Ireland and dominated by a permanent Protestant majority. Therefore, republicans argued, the referendum was nothing more than a propaganda exercise. It was not needed to discover the opinion of the majority in Northern Ireland. That had been predetermined by the way the boundary had been drawn in the 1920s. Resolution of the Northern Ireland problem depended, not upon displaying the obvious fact that there was a Protestant majority in the North, but in devising a satisfactory relationship that could accommodate the needs of both Protestant and Catholic communities. It was by no means clear how the border poll would contribute to that aim. For this reason, the parties representing the Catholic community advised their supporters to boycott the poll, advice that seems largely to have been taken.

The border poll asked the electors of Northern Ireland two questions:

'Do you want Northern Ireland to remain a part of the United Kingdom?' ('Yes', 591 820).

'Do you want Northern Ireland to be joined with the Irish Republic outside the United Kingdom?' ('Yes', 6 463).

The turnout was 58.6 per cent. Since 98.9 per cent of those voting supported the Union, it could be argued that it had the positive endorsement of 58.0 per cent of the Northern Irish electorate.

When the Northern Ireland Parliament was prorogued, Edward Heath promised that 'a system of regular plebiscites' scheduled at ten-yearly intervals would be held.[1] No further border poll was held in 1983. The Northern Ireland Constitution Act of 1976, however, provided that Northern Ireland should not cease to be part of the United Kingdom without the consent of the electorate of Northern Ireland. Thus the referendum served to entrench the position of Northern Ireland within the United Kingdom.

The poll might have proved a useful propaganda exercise in convincing opinion abroad that Northern Ireland remained a part of the United Kingdom entirely voluntarily, but it did nothing to resolve the basic problem of the province, which well illustrates Henry Maine's dictum:

> Democracies are quite paralysed by the plea of Nationality. There is no more effective way of attacking them than by admitting the right of the majority to govern, but denying that the majority so entitled is the particular majority which claims the right.[2]

In such a situation, the referendum has little to offer.

Not until Britain's entry into the European Community (EC) in the early 1970s did the question of a national referendum come to be raised in British politics. This occurred less as a result of constitutional doctrine than for quite accidental reasons.

The question of whether Britain should enter the European Community was, like Irish Home Rule, one that transcended party loyalties. The issue split both major parties. During the 1970s, most of Labour's left wing was hostile to entering what it saw as a capitalist cartel, but the majority of the right wing, including most of the leading figures in the party, favoured entry. Most Conservative MPs also favoured entry, but some who belonged to the old imperialist wing of the party opposed it. Others, led by Enoch Powell, also opposed entry, believing that the EC required an unacceptable curtailment of national sovereignty. Opinion was divided in the country also, nor did the divisions in popular opinion follow party lines.

By 1971, Edward Heath, the Conservative prime minister, had secured agreement among the other members of the European Community on the terms of British entry. In the preceding general election of 1970, however, all three parties had supported British entry. This meant that there was no way of telling whether the electorate supported what seemed to many the most important constitutional issue of the century, involving in effect a permanent transfer of legislative power away from Westminster. At a press conference on 2 June 1970, Heath claimed that a referendum would not be needed to ratify Britain's entry, arguing:

> I always said that you could not possibly take this country into the Common Market [as the European Community was then known in Britain] if the majority of the people were against it, but this is handled through the Parliamentary system.[3]

He did not explain, however, how 'the Parliamentary system' would reflect public opinion when all three major parties favoured entry.

The Labour party had also been opposed to a referendum but, in opposition after 1970, the leadership was being pressed by the left wing and by constituency activists to oppose entry. There seemed a real possibility that, acting in concert with Conservative opponents of the European Community, Labour might be able to defeat the government on the issue. Fearing a split, the leadership espoused the referendum, in James Callaghan's words 'a rubber life raft into which the party may one day have to climb',[4] as a device to avoid a split.

The Labour leaders accepted the referendum both to avoid having to commit a future Labour government to withdrawal from the European Community and to maintain the unity of the party. This decision was in accordance with feeling in the country. Survey evidence from February 1971 indicated that a large majority of the electorate favoured a referendum.[5]

In opposition, Labour was unable to secure a referendum to ratify Britain's entry into the European Community, which took place in January 1973. Having returned to power in the general election of February 1974, however, Labour renegotiated the terms of British entry. It put these renegotiated terms to the people on 5 June 1975, the date of Britain's only national referendum, with a recommendation that they be accepted. To maintain Labour's unity, however, the referendum was accompanied by another constitutional innovation, the suspension of collective cabinet responsibility. This had occurred only once before, in 1932, under the special circumstances of a coalition government. Seven cabinet ministers, including Michael Foot, a future leader of the party, and Tony Benn, the leader of the Left, took advantage of the suspension of collective responsibility to argue for withdrawal from the European Community, against the majority of their cabinet colleagues.

The referendum endorsed Britain's membership in the EC by a majority of 67 per cent to 33 per cent on a 65 per cent turnout. The Yes vote was spread fairly evenly across the country, varying in mainland Britain between 55 per cent and 76 per cent. In Northern Ireland, the Yes vote was a bare majority, 52 per cent, but the Western Isles and Shetland were the only counting areas to yield a No majority.

In the short run at least, it therefore seemed as if Harold Wilson had secured his two main aims: to make Britain's membership in the European Community legitimate and to preserve the unity of the Labour party. 'It means', claimed Wilson when the result was announced, 'that fourteen years of national argument are over.'

It would, however, be misleading to see the outcome of the referendum as evidence of Britain's commitment to the EC. In their book on the referendum, published shortly after the event, David Butler and Uwe Kitzinger warned presciently that the verdict was 'unequivocal, but it was also unenthusiastic. Support for membership was wide but it did not run deep.'[6] The referendum result owed as much to the fact that the political leaders most respected by the electorate advocated remaining in the EC as it did to enthusiasm for it. A 'leadership effect' was noticed by Humphrey Taylor, leader of a survey research organization conducting polls for the pro-marketeers. 'One strong card in our hands now is that the major public figures advocating EEC membership are relatively popular while those advocating leaving the EEC are relatively unpopular,' he declared.[7] The campaign took the character of a struggle between 'moderates', who included the leaders of all three parties and who were in favour of the European Community, and 'extremists' such as Enoch Powell, the Rev. Ian Paisley, the Northern Ireland Protestant leader, the Labour left wing and the trade union leaders. In such a struggle, there could be little doubt where the allegiance of the British electorate would lie.

Moreover, to attract the support of the electorate, the implications of EC membership had to be understated by its supporters. Voters were assured that membership involved no loss of sovereignty. The commitment of the European Community to securing, in the words of the preamble to the Treaty of Rome, 'an ever closer union' was never mentioned. The EC was presented as little more than a commercial arrangement, and one that could in a short time yield considerable economic benefits to Britain. Perhaps for this reason, disillusionment with the EC set in very rapidly.

In the parliamentary debates on the Maastricht Treaty in 1992–3, all three parties were once again in favour of the treaty, as they had been during the general election of 1992. Thus the elector opposed to the treaty had no means of expressing his or her opinion. Conservative Prime Minister John Major was opposed to a referendum, as Edward Heath had been, but so also was John Smith, the Labour leader, unlike his predecessor, Harold Wilson. The referendum, however, was advocated by Paddy Ashdown, the Liberal Democrat leader, who favoured the treaty, and by Margaret Thatcher, John Major's predecessor as prime minister, who was opposed to the treaty. But, with both front benches opposed to a referendum, amendments proposing it were comfortably defeated both in the Commons and in the Lords.[8] Nevertheless, Britain remains an awkward member of the Community.

Harold Wilson's second aim in holding the referendum of 1975 had been to preserve the unity of the Labour party. But this too was secured only in the short run. The Labour government held together until its election defeat in May 1979, and the device of suspending collective responsibility meant that ministers with incompatible beliefs could stay together within the same cabinet. It was a loveless marriage, however, since the Labour promarketeers had found themselves working together with those of other parties during the referendum campaign. They began to believe that they might have more in common with the Liberals than with their own colleagues on the Left. The referendum of 1975 was one of the factors predisposing leading figures on

Labour's Right – such as Roy Jenkins, David Owen and Shirley Williams – to lead a breakaway from the Labour party in 1981 and form a new party, the Social Democratic party, in alliance with the Liberals. In the long run, therefore, far from preserving traditional party alignments, the referendum may have helped to undermine them.

Britain's first and only national referendum was held less because of a principled commitment than for reasons of internal party politics. Dicey had perhaps foreseen that this would happen when he commented in 1909, a time when it seemed the Conservative party would come to favour a referendum:

> It is singular and not perhaps very fortunate that in accordance with English habits, a reform good in itself, should be proposed by men who probably do not believe in it, and who want to meet a party difficulty. Still, I hail it with satisfaction.[9]

Fifteen years earlier, Dicey had predicted that 'once established, the Referendum would never be got rid of by anything short of a revolution'.[10]

The 1975 referendum was an *ad hoc* response to what was thought of as a unique issue. It was not intended to create a precedent. 'It is not just that it is more important', declared a Labour junior minister, Gerald Fowler; 'it is of a different order. There is, and there can be, no issue that is on all fours with it. That is why we say that this issue is the sole exception, and there can be no other exception, to the principle that we normally operate through parliamentary democracy.'[11] The difficulty was, however, that once the principle had been conceded, it would be difficult to prevent if from being invoked again. Within just 18 months of the European Community referendum, the Labour government was forced by backbench pressure to concede referendums on devolution in Scotland and Wales.

In each referendum, the question has been drawn up by the government of the day. In the case of the Northern Ireland border poll, the Opposition complained that the two questions asked were by no means exhaustive of the possibilities. The shadow Secretary of State for Northern Ireland suggested that a third question be asked: 'Do you want eventually to live in a united Ireland brought about by free consent of the peoples of Northern Ireland and of the Republic of Ireland?'[12] Further, there was no mention in the first of the questions asked – 'Do you want Northern Ireland to remain a part of the United Kingdom?' of the *terms* upon which Northern Ireland would remain a part of the United Kingdom. Would the majority be required to offer the minority a place in the government of the province through power-sharing arrangements; or would the province continue to be governed by the majority as it had been between 1921 and 1972. Moreover, the two questions excluded other constitutional options which had been advocated such as condominium and confederation.

In the case of the 1975 Common Market referendum, there were, apparently, 'vehement arguments' in the Cabinet on the wording of the question. National Opinion Polls had shown that different formulations of the question produced widely divergent answers (see Table 12.1).

The question was eventually put in the following form:

> The Government have announced the results of the renegotiation of the United Kingdom's terms of membership of the European Community. DO YOU THINK THAT THE UNITED KINGDOM SHOULD STAY IN THE EUROPEAN COMMUNITY (THE COMMON MARKET)?

In the devolution referendums, the question was simply whether or not the voters wished the provisions of the Scotland or Wales Act to come into effect. There were some who argued that there should be a second question on independence for Scotland and Wales. Then, if devolution were accepted but independence rejected, the nationalists would 'be given notice that they should not abuse the terms' of devolution by attempting to use the elected assembly as a staging post to independence. The nationalists would thus have been isolated from the devolutionists.

The government, however, rejected this proposal on the grounds that it would give the independence option a credibility which it had previously lacked, and that it would also confuse the electorate.

In general, however, the issue of how the question should be worded has not been a matter of major public controversy in Britain.

In the Northern Ireland border poll, the votes were counted on a province-wide basis. This was resented by nationalists who urged a district or county count. Northern Ireland, so they claimed, was not a homogeneous unit, but had been carved artificially out of the island of Ireland by the 1920 Government of Ireland Act which defined the province as comprising six counties. Why, then, should the votes not be counted on a county basis, a procedure which would reveal that two counties – Fermanagh and Tyrone – had nationalist majorities.

The government, predictably, rejected the nationalists' claim. It was opposed to repartition and did not wish to have it publicly demonstrated that a majority in Fermanagh and Tyrone wished to join with the Irish Republic.

In both the EEC referendum and the devolution referendums, the votes were counted on a county basis. The government rejected a proposal for a constituency count on the ground that this could embarrass MPs whose views differed from those of their constituents. In the EEC referendum, the county basis for counting the vote could have led to some embarrassment if, as at one

Table 12.1   National Opinion Poll questionnaire on the Common Market referendum, 1975

	Majority 'Yes' over 'No' among intending voters %
Do you accept the Government's recommendation that the United Kingdom should come out of the Common Market? YES/NO	+0.2
Should the United Kingdom come out of the Common Market? YES/NO	+4.6
IN OUT	+10.8
Should the United Kingdom stay in the Common Market? YES/NO	+13.2
Do you accept the Government's recommendations that the United Kingdom should stay in the Common Market? YES/NO	+18.2
The Government recommends the acceptance of the renegotiated terms of British membership of the Common Market. Should the United Kingdom stay in the Common Market? YES/NO	+11.2
Her Majesty's Government believes that the nation's best interests would be served by accepting the favourably renegotiated terms of our continued membership of the Common Market. Should the United Kingdom stay in the Common Market? YES/NO	+16.2

Source: NOP, February 1975.[13]

time appeared likely, Scotland and Northern Ireland showed 'No' majorities while the United Kingdom as a whole voted 'Yes'. In the event, however, this danger was averted and only two island counties – Shetland and the Western Isles – voted 'No'.

There being no constitutional rules regulating the holding of referendums, it is up to the government of the day to decide whether or not to call a referendum. In the case of the Common Market and devolution referendums, the government agreed to a referendum to secure party unity. A referendum was the only method by which opponents of the Common Market could be brought to accept the continued *legitimacy* of British membership; while the devolution legislation would probably not have been passed by Parliament without the referendum commitment.

Those who urged the referendum sought in each case to resist change – to maintain the union between Northern Ireland and the rest of the United Kingdom, to prevent Britain joining the Common Market, to prevent devolution. In the first and third cases, the referendum achieved the result which its protagonists sought. In the Common Market referendum, however, it did not. For this occurred not when Britain was joining the Common Market in 1972, but in 1975 when Britain had already been a member for two and a half years, and leaving the Community could be interpreted as a change. In each case, therefore, the referendum result confirmed the *status quo*. Use of the referendum in Britain, therefore, has done nothing to cast any doubt upon the generalization that referendums are generally conservative in their implications.

The Northern Ireland poll had hardly any repercussions in British politics. The nationalist population, as has been seen, largely boycotted it, holding that it was no more than a propaganda exercise designed to avoid the necessity of rethinking relationships between Northern Ireland and the Irish Republic. The poll was not repeated ten years later in 1983, even though, in 1973, provision had been made for regular decennial plebiscites.

The other referendums had major consequences for British politics. The Common Market referendum of 1975 served to strengthen Harold Wilson's Labour Government against its left wing. The Left had opposed Britain's membership, but were shown, by the referendum, not to enjoy the confidence of the British people; and Harold Wilson took the opportunity, shortly after the result was declared, to demote the leader of the Left, Tony Benn, and reassert his control over the Party. The Common Market referendum did not show, however, that Britain was unequivocally committed to membership of the Community. Although opponents of membership accepted the referendum result at the time as decisive, the Labour Party fought the 1983 general election committed to withdrawal; many of the Labour Party's candidates in the 1984 elections to the European Parliament were also committed to withdrawal, although the Party leadership seemed to have grudgingly accepted that withdrawal was not practically possible.

The repercussions of the devolution referendums were striking. For they were held at a time when the Labour government was in a minority in the House of Commons and was forced to rely *inter alia* upon the votes of the 11

Scottish Nationalist MPs for survival. Because the government was unable or unwilling to press for the implementation of the Scotland Act after the referendum, the Scottish nationalists withdrew their support from the government, and it was defeated in a vote of confidence held on 28 March 1979. In the ensuing general election held on 3 May 1979, a Conservative government, hostile to devolution, was returned with a comfortable overall majority, and it proceeded to repeal the Scotland and Wales Acts.

Little information is available about the financing of the Northern Ireland border poll. But the other two referendums raise interesting questions about the financing of referendums. In the Common Market referendums, two *ad hoc* umbrella campaign organizations were established – Britain in Europe and the National Referendum Campaign. These were given legal status under the referendum legislation, and each was given a subsidy of £125 000, provided that it publicly accounted for all receipts and expenditures, including the names of those who donated more than £100. The government also circulated two 2 000-word pamphlets prepared by the umbrella organizations, as well as an explanatory pamphlet of its own, to every household in the country at an estimated cost of £4m. In addition, the umbrella organizations were allocated free broadcasting time on radio and television to present their case, by analogy with party political broadcasts. Publication of the accounts of the umbrella organizations showed that, whereas the Britain in Europe organization had raised nearly £2m, the National Referendum Campaign raised only around £133 000, i.e. about £8 000 more than the government grant.

No equivalent methods of finance were possible in the devolution referendums. The 'Yes' and 'No' sides were unable to form all-embracing umbrella organizations, because they did not share a single position. Supporters of the Scotland and Wales Acts were divided between protagonists of devolution and advocates of total independence, and the former did not want to compromise themselves by joining together with the latter. The 'No' side contained Labour dissidents at odds with their party who felt that their chance of securing working-class votes would be lessened if they were seen to be working with Conservatives. No government grants were made available, and there were no explanatory pamphlets. Broadcasts were initially allocated to the parties but a leading Labour campaigner for the 'No's' succeeded in obtaining an injunction which prevented them taking place on the grounds that, with three of the four parties advocating devolution, they violated the requirements of political balance. It may be that the absence of pamphlets and broadcasts played a part in lowering the turnout thus, in Scotland, possibly militating against the chances of securing a 40 per cent 'Yes' vote. In none of the referendums held in Britain have there been ceilings on expenditure or contributions. It would, indeed, be difficult to impose such ceilings.

They are imposed in general elections upon candidates in constituencies (but not nationally) by applying the law of agency through which candidates are answerable for what is spent on their behalf. Such a principle, however, is hardly applicable to an umbrella organization. Moreover, a candidate who exceeds his permitted expenditure can be punished – perhaps by the loss of his seat. It is difficult to see what sanction can be applied to an umbrella organization which breaks the rules.

The *ad hoc* arrangements which have regulated the financing of referendums in Britain mirror the pragmatic way in which governments approached this novel institution in the 1970s. There has been an unwillingness to lay down general rules or provide for new circumstances before they arise. If the referendum is now an established part of the British Constitution, this has resulted less from deliberate intent than from the vicissitudes of party politics. Introduced to meet the interests of the political parties, the referendum yet remains one of the most powerful methods of curbing their power. The role which it comes to play in Britain is dependent, therefore, upon the future of party politics. For in Britain, more than any other democracy, it is the parties which are the main arbiters of what is constitutional and what is not. It would be only a slight exaggeration to adapt the words of Chief Justice Hughes by saying that in Britain the Constitution is what the parties say it is.

Since the referendums held in Britain have all been advisory, parliamentary sovereignty has remained formally intact. In practice, however, a referendum that produces a decisive result clearly limits the power of Parliament. In practice if not in theory, then, the referendum constitutes a method of demarcating some laws from others as fundamental, such that they require ratification by the people.

Precisely because Britain lacks a codified constitution, however, and because the referendum was introduced in an unplanned way, there has been hardly any discussion of what its scope should be. For there is no clear method of demarcating those laws that *are* fundamental and require the special protection of the referendum from laws that are not fundamental. Dicey's friend, James Bryce, asked him in 1915:

1   What is to be the authority to decide when a Bill should be referred?
2   How can 'constitutional changes' be defined in a country that has no [rigid] constitution?[14]

Without a codified constitution, these questions cannot be satisfactorily answered. Since Britain has an elastic Constitution, so also use of the referendum must be elastic.

So far, the referendums that have been held in Britain have all been concerned with the legitimacy of transferring the powers of Parliament, either by excluding an area from Parliament's jurisdiction (the Northern Ireland border poll), by the transfer of powers to the European Community, or by limiting the power of Parliament to legislate for Scotland and Wales (devolution referendums). Such transfers of the powers of Parliament are likely to be in practice irreversible. It may seem, therefore, as if a persuasive constitutional convention has been built up that the powers of Parliament should not be transferred without popular endorsement.[15]

There is a clear rationale for such a convention. For proposals to transfer the powers of Parliament involve the machinery by which laws are made, the framework within which legislation is enacted. The electorate, it might be said, entrusts its MPs as agents with legislative power, but it gives them no authority to transfer that power. Such authority, it may be argued, can be obtained only through a specific mandate – that is, a referendum. The idea that power is entrusted to the nation's representatives only for specific purposes reflects one of the most enduring themes of liberal constitutionalism, whose origins lie in the political thought of John Locke. 'The Legislative', Locke claimed, 'cannot transfer the power of making laws to any other hands. For it being but a delegated power from the People, they who have it cannot pass it to others.'[16] So it is that the introduction of the referendum into British politics has served to emphasize the commitment to liberal constitutionalism that lies at the heart of the British system of government. The accidental and quite unintended way in which this has come about bears some resemblance perhaps to what Hegel would have called the Cunning of Reason.

Notes and references

1   House of Commons, 24 March 1972, *Hansard*, col. 1862.
2   Henry Maine (1897), *Popular Government*, 5th ed, London: John Murray, 28.
3   Edward Heath, quoted in Vernon Bogdanor, *The People and the Party System*, p. 38.
4   Quoted in David Butler and Uwe Kitzinger (1976), *The 1975 Referendum*, London: Macmillan, 12.
5   See Stanley Alderson (1975), *Yea or Nay? The Referendum in the United Kingdom*, London: Cassell, 2.
6   Butler and Kitzinger, *The 1975 Referendum*, 280.
7   Ibid., 259.
8   The relevant debates occurred in the House of Commons on 21 and 22 April 1993, and in the House of Lords on 14 July 1993.
9   Dicey to Leo Maxse, 12 October 1909, cited in Richard A. Cosgrove (1980), *The Rule of Law: Albert Venn Dicey, Victorian Jurist*, London: Macmillan, 108.
10   Dicey to Maxse, 2 February 1894, cited in ibid., 107.
11   *Hansard*, House of Commons, 22 November 1974, col. 1743.
12   House of Commons Debates: Vol. 846, Col. 1100, 21 November 1972.

13   Butler and Kitzinger, *The 1975 Referendum*, 60.
14   Bryce to Dicey, 6 April 1915: Bryce papers, Bodleian Library, MS 4 fo. 84.
15   In 1993, however, the Labour opposition declared that, if returned to power, it would put the issue of electoral reform to referendum. John Smith, the Labour leader, declared that, while personally opposed to any change in the electoral system, he thought that this was an issue that ought to be settled by referendum. Electoral reform, like entry into the European Community and devolution in the 1970s, was an issue on which Labour was deeply divided; and so here too the referendum was being advocated to preserve party unity.
16   John Locke, *Second Treatise of Government*, para. 141.

13 The Forty Per Cent Rule

The 40 per cent rule was a provision inserted into the Scotland Act of 1978 against the wishes of the Government. It stated that in the referendum to be held before the Act could come into force, if it appeared to the Secretary of State for Scotland that less than 40 per cent of those entitled to vote had voted 'Yes', he was to lay before Parliament an Order repealing the Act. The genesis and constitutional status of this provision are of great interest for a number of reasons. Resulting from an amendment by a back-bench MP on the Government side of the House, it has some claim to be the most significant back-bench initiative in British politics since the war for it played a crucial part in securing the repeal of the Scotland Act, depriving the Scots of an Assembly for which a majority had voted. The 40 per cent rule thus represents a constitutional innovation as the first occasion in British politics when the *status quo* has been successfully entrenched by requiring a qualified majority to overturn it. It implies that constitutional changes require more than bare majority support if they are to secure legitimacy, and it may form a precedent of considerable significance for the future

I

The precise role of the provision cannot, however, be understood without considering the political background to the Labour Government's devolution legislation. The Government had committed itself to devolution as a central part of its legislative programme. But a large number of Labour back-benchers – perhaps the majority representing English constituencies – were unenthusiastic, if not positively hostile, to devolution, with a small minority being willing to do all they could to defeat it. They did not, however, wish to defeat the legislation if that involved bringing down the Government which was, from April 1976, in a minority in the House of Commons; they needed to be careful also not to allow the SNP to win a propaganda victory with the claim that the Scotland Bill, although desired by a majority of Scottish voters and Scottish MPs, had been defeated by an unholy cross-bench alliance of English MPs.

Labour back-benchers therefore demanded that a referendum should be held before the legislation came into force; and this was conceded by the Government in order to secure the passage of the first devolution bill – the Scotland and Wales Bill. The referendum was an instrument perfectly adapted to this difficult situation. For, as S.E. Finer has noticed, it is 'the Pontius Pilate of British politics'.[1] It enabled Government back-benchers to vote for the Bill while preparing to campaign for a 'No' vote in the referendum; it therefore offered an escape route by which the defeat of devolution could be compatible with the maintenance in office of the Government. 'It is', said Mr Malcolm Rifkind, then one of the few Conservative supporters of devolution, 'a unique constitutional matter that this Parliament is likely to put on the statute book a Bill in which it does not believe.'[2]

For some Labour back-benchers, however, this concession was unsufficient; and indeed the attempt to guillotine the Scotland and Wales Bill failed, owing to opposition to the guillotine motion by 22 Labour MPs and the abstention of a further 21 back-benchers from the Government side. Consequently the Scotland and Wales Bill was abandoned, but reintroduced with minor alterations as two bills, one for Scotland and one for Wales, in the 1977–78 session. By this time, however, it had become clear that if devolution were defeated in Parliament, the Labour Government would fall. The collapse of the first bill had put the future of the Government at risk since the SNP, seeking to capitalize upon the supposed discontent in Scotland and its position in the opinion polls as the leading party in Scotland, decided to seek an immediate general election. The Government survived only through the Lib–Lab pact and it could not afford to allow the Liberal defections which would result from a second defeat of the devolution legislation. Therefore Labour opponents of devolution had to find further ways of inflicting damage upon the Scotland Bill without actually preventing its passage through Parliament.

Clause 82(2) of the Scotland Bill gave the Secretary of State for Scotland a considerable amount of discretion in determining whether or not the Scottish electorate had endorsed devolution in the proposed referendum. The clause in question read:

> If it appears to the Secretary of State, having regard to the answers given in a referendum and all other circumstances, that this Act should not be brought into effect, he may lay before Parliament the draft of an Order in Council providing for its repeal.

Of course the Secretary of State could hardly refuse to lay a repeal Order before Parliament if the referendum showed a 'No' majority – and, in any case, Parliament could still refuse to allow devolution to go ahead by refusing to vote for the commencement Order required to give birth to the Assembly. Suppose, however, that there was a very narrow 'Yes' majority on a low turnout: the Secretary of State might take the view that the Scotland Act should remain on the statute book, while Parliament would wish to repeal it. For the support which many MPs were willing to give to the Scotland Act depended upon there being a powerful demand in Scotland for devolution. For a small number of MPs, no doubt, devolution was a positive good in itself; there were others who were opposed to devolution under any conditions – even if they could be convinced that a settled majority of the Scottish electorate wanted it. But the attitude of perhaps the majority of MPs depended upon their assessment of the state of Scottish opinion. Moreover, one of the arguments put forward by the Government to persuade Parliament to pass the legislation was that the unity of the kingdom would otherwise be at risk.

An important part of the case for the Scotland Act, therefore, was that it met a powerful demand in Scotland. The referendum was a means of testing this case. But would the argument from the strength of Scottish opinion be vindicated by a bare majority on a low turnout, or should a stiffer test be necessary? That was the issue which the Cunningham Amendment, introduced into the Commons on 25 January 1978, attempted to settle. Requiring an Order for the repeal of the Act to be laid before parliament if there was not a 40 per cent 'Yes' vote, it was preceded by an amendment moved by Mr Douglas-Mann, Labour, laying down a $33^{1}/_{3}$ per cent requirement. He stated the rationale of his amendment in the following way:

> I regard this amendment as absolutely central to the support I give to the Bill. I abstained on Second reading of the Scotland and Wales Bill and I voted against the timetable motion for that Bill. By the end of the summer, I had come to the conclusion that if – it is a large 'if' – a substantial majority of the people of Scotland were determined on this measure, it was not for English members to defeat it.[3]

Mr Cunningham also needed convincing that 'a substantial majority of the people of Scotland were determined on the measure' but, for him this substantial majority would need to be 40 per cent of the electorate. To Mr Robin Cook, another Labour back-bench opponent of devolution, this figure was 'not seen to be fair in Scotland'.[4] Whereas the $33^{1}/_{3}$ per cent criterion was in his view a 'backstop', the 40 per cent rule was a 'hurdle'.[5] For, while no Government since the war had secured the support of 40 per cent of the electorate, every government except, ironically, the Labour Government returned in the two elections of 1974 had secured the support of at least a third of the electorate. But the supporters of the Cunningham Amendment could reply that, whereas the actions of any Government were for the most part reversible by a later administration, the act of setting up an assembly in Scotland was in practice irrevocable. 'It is quite clear', said Mr Willie Hamilton, 'that Parliament being sovereign could overturn it.' 'But', he added in a picturesque metaphor, 'it is a bit like falling off a cliff. One cannot change one's mind and go back.'[6]

Devolution, therefore, was an irreversible constitutional change and, just as in many countries with written constitutions some special method of validating constitutional changes is prescribed, so also in Britain the unitary state ought not to be abandoned without convincing evidence that such a change was sought by the people of Scotland.

To the surprise of the Government, the Cunningham Amendment was carried by 166 to 151 votes. Although many Conservatives voted for the Amendment, the Conservative front bench was hesitant about offering its support and Mr Pym, who led for the Opposition on devolution, abstained. Four Conservatives, including Mr Heath, voted against the Amendment. But, of course, the Amendment could not have been carried if Labour members had turned out in force to support the Government. Why did they not do so? It appears that the Government Whips were unaware of the strength of the Labour rebellion which was organized by George Cunningham. In any case, there was little that they could do in the face of the profound indifference displayed by many Labour MPs who, in the words of Ian Mikardo, 'were fed up to the back teeth with devolution and everything connected with it. It had become one bloody great bore.' Some Labour MPs therefore 'went missing' when the Cunningham Amendment was raised; others, 'who had been voting with the Government, in a bored and listless way . . . were actually convinced or converted by George's speech, which was a massive piece of advocacy'.[7]

The Government made an attempt at the report stage of the Scotland Bill to have the Amendment deleted; but the motion was moved by a Labour backbencher, Dennis Canavan, and not by a minister, signifying that the Government did not believe that it had a very strong chance of success. For the Conservatives abandoned their earlier hesitancy and turned out in force to support the Amendment, with Mr Pym now offering it his blessing. Mr Canavan's motion was defeated by 298 votes to 243, and an attempt by Mr Robin Cook to reduce the requirement was also defeated by 285 votes to 240.

II

The Cunningham Amendment, which became Section 85(2) of the Scotland Act, provided: 'If it appears to the Secretary of State that less than 40 per cent of the persons entitled to vote in the referendum have voted "yes" . . . he shall lay before Parliament the draft of an Order-in-Council for the repeal of this Act.'

The first problem raised by this provision was how the number of persons 'entitled to vote' should be determined. The electoral register could record only those who were entitled to vote at a particular moment in time and would therefore be out of date by the time it was published. The register used in the devolution referendum came into force on 16 February 1979, two weeks before the referendum was held, and was based on a qualifying date of 10 October 1978. Of course, between October and February some of those on the electoral register would have died or been convicted of a felony and so legally disqualified from voting. Others would have moved house and, although legally qualified and able to vote, would be unlikely to do so. Thus one illogicality of the 40 per cent rule was that in practice the possible turnout would depend upon the age of the register. The devolution referendum was, in fact, held on a new register; had it been held in, say, October 1978, the practicable turnout would have been considerably lower, for the electoral register becomes .75 per cent out of date each month after the qualifying date.

Moreover, the register itself is unlikely to be completely accurate. A 1967 Home Office survey made in England and Wales (P. Gray and F. A Gee, *Electoral Registration for Parliamentary Elections,* HMSO), showed that there were 4 per cent of omissions. The 1971 Census 'showed that the electoral register contained 98.8 per cent of the census names which, with allowance for aliens, is pretty close'.[8] So if 4 per cent of the electorate was missing from the electoral register, yet it was nearly accurate in terms of total numbers, there must be further errors or duplications. Presumably the bias of the officers responsible for registration would operate so as to place individuals on the register where there was some element of doubt, rather than take the risk of disfranchising anyone. Mr J. S. Gardner, the Electoral Registration Officer for the Lothian Region in the referendum, claimed that before 1979 he had never heard of formal hearings of objections to registration such as were now being requested by the SNP. He added:

> I made it my business not to lose sight of the purpose of the register. It is a *register of electors,* and my task in preparing it is to ensure, as far as I reasonably can, that all those entitled to the franchise are included in it. The exclusion of those not so entitled is not to be ignored, but this is a matter of considerably less importance, in my judgment . . . Accordingly, insofar as the register may contain names that ought not to have been included, this is the result of deliberate policy.[9]

Even if defects in the register are ignored, however, there were still many electors who were properly on the register but would, for most practical purposes, be unable to vote. The *Scotsman*[10] estimated that there would be

51 500 hospital patients on any given day in Scotland and that, of these, 39 000 would be of voting age. In Italy and Finland polling booths are provided in hospital premises, but no such provision was available in Scotland. Admittedly, a hospital patient was entitled to apply for a postal or proxy vote (although many of course would not do so), unless he had entered hospital within the fortnight preceding 1 March when he would be too late for a postal or proxy vote and effectively disfranchised. The *Scotsman* also estimated that 100 000 people of voting age were seriously disabled and that a further 150 000 would be too ill to vote, although legally qualified to do so.

However, the major cause of practically unavoidable non-voting on the part of those who were on the register resulted from home removals. The 1967 Home Office survey showed that .67 per cent of those registered moved home every month: this would mean a removal rate between October, when the register was compiled, and the 1 March referendum date of 3 per cent, which represented 114 000 voters. According to the same survey 40 per cent of those moving would still be living in the same local authority area, and therefore 68 000 would be a fairer estimate of those who would have to travel some distance in order to vote if they had not secured postal votes.

Thus, in determining who was to be 'entitled to vote' for the purposes of the Cunningham Amendment, any decision which the Government made was bound to be controversial. The electoral register was not designed for the task of determining the number of those 'entitled to vote' and could not be used for that purpose.

On 20 February 1979, Mr Millan, the Secretary of State for Scotland, announced that the terms of the Amendment bound him to discount only those not legally entitled to vote; he would be acting illegally if he also discounted for those unable to vote. Moreover, he could only make a discount for those not legally entitled to vote where there was some authoritative estimate for the size of the category in question.[11] He therefore proposed to make a discount for four categories. The first was that of young people who were on the electoral register but would not reach the age of 18 before 1 March: this category could be identified from the electoral register and was calculated as 49 802. Secondly, there were those who had died between October and March: the Registrar-General for Scotland estimated the number of deaths in Scotland during this period as 26 400. Thirdly, there were students and student nurses living away from home but in Scotland and registered both at home and at their college/hospital address: their numbers could be discovered from the results of a 'carefully constructed sample survey'[12] and amounted to 11 800. Finally, there were 2 000 convicted felons, legally disbarred from voting but registered at their home address: this figure was assessed by the Scottish Office.

One can compare Mr Millan's deductions with the maximum possible number which he could have made if he had taken account of all the main categories of unavoidable non-voting. Mr Millan's deductions of 90 002 were composed as follows:

1	Voters reaching 18 years after 1 March	49 802
2	Voters dead since registration	26 400
3	Double-registered students and student nurses	11 800
4	Prisoners	2 000

This discount amounted to 2.3 per cent of the February 1979 electoral register of 3 837 114 and reduced the target for a 40 per cent 'Yes' vote from 1 534 846 to 1 498 845. One may, however, include the following further categories:[13]

1	Errors in register (say 6 per cent)	230 226
2	Hospital patients	39 000
3	Seriously disabled	100 000
4	Ill at home	150 000
5	Removals	68 000

This adds up to a further 587 226 from which we may subtract the 52 000 valid postal ballots cast in the referendum, giving 535 226. Adding Mr Millan's deductions, we obtain a total of 625 228 which would equal 16.3 per cent of the total register. The target for a 40 per cent 'Yes' vote would then be not 1 498 845 but 1 284 754, only 53 817 more than the actual 'Yes' vote in the referendum.

It is clear, therefore, that the 40 per cent rule placed upon the electoral register a weight which it was ill-equipped to bear. A Secretary of State less scrupulous than Mr Millan could easily have made extra discounts from the register so as to assist those campaigning for a 'Yes' response. As it was, however, the pro-devolutionists could complain that they were being handicapped to the extent of over 200 000 votes, the difference between the 1 498 845 announced by Mr Millan and the figure of 1 284 754 which would result from taking into account all possible deductions. It is to be hoped, therefore, that one result of the 40 per cent rule will be to encourage a close scrutiny of the degree of efficiency of the electoral register and of how it might be improved.

III

Even more complex than the electoral arrangements, however, is the precise significance of the Cunningham Amendment. What was the nature of the hurdle which it imposed? By using the proportion of the electorate rather than the proportion of the voters as the criterion, it subtly combined two different requirements, the first being that a minimum percentage of the electorate should turn out to vote and the second that there should be a decisive majority in favour of devolution for the Scotland Act to come into force. For the lower the turnout, the higher the majority would need to be to secure implementation of the Scotland Act. On a turnout of 80 per cent, precisely 50 per cent of the voters would need to vote 'Yes'; if the turnout was 70 per cent, there would need to be a 57 per cent 'Yes' vote; and with a 60 per cent turnout, a 67 per cent 'Yes' vote would be required. Mr Cunningham drew attention to the fact that the average poll in Scotland in general elections since 1950 was 77.4 per cent: with that turnout in the devolution referendum, the 'Yeses' would have to secure only 51.7 per cent of the vote to satisfy the 40 per cent rule.[14] In the EEC referendum, when Scotland was held to have decisively endorsed the EEC, the turnout was 61.7 per cent of the electorate in Scotland and the 'Yes' vote 58.4 per cent, but the percentage of the electorate voting 'Yes' was only 35.75 per cent (in the UK as a whole it was 42.9 per cent). If the turnout in the devolution referendum was similar to that in the EEC referendum, roughly 60 per cent of the voters would have to vote 'Yes' for the 40 per cent rule to be satisfied.

However, as Mr Cunningham himself appreciated, the failure of the Scotland Act to meet his test would not necessarily mean that it would be repealed, for the referendum was still an advisory one, and not mandatory. The relevant provision only required the Secretary of State to 'lay before Parliament the draft of an Order-in-Council for the repeal of this Act'. It would certainly be possible to imagine circumstances in which Parliament could decide that the draft Order should be voted down. If the result was, as in the EEC referendum, a 'Yes' vote of roughly 36 per cent of the electorate and a 'No' vote of roughly 25 per cent, Parliament would hardly have refused to allow devolution to go ahead. So the test did not 'decide whether devolution takes place or not, but only whether the matter goes back before Parliament in the event of an inconclusive referendum result'.[15] The outcome of the referendum would determine not whether the Scotland Act came into force but whether or not the draft repeal Order needed to be laid.

Even the Conservative Opposition was anxious not to commit itself to a rigid interpretation of the 40 per cent rule. When the referendum Order was debated in the Commons, Mr Leon Brittan, a Conservative spokesman on devolution, argued only that there needed to be a 'clear majority' for the Scotland Act to come into force; and in the debate on the Welsh Order, the following revealing exchange took place:

Mr Gwynfor Evans (Plaid Cymru): What is a sufficient vote? Let us suppose that 35 per cent were in favour of the Assembly and 25 per cent were against it. Would that be a sufficient vote?

Mr Donald Anderson (Labour, anti-devolution): Yes.

Mr Evans: I wonder whether the House would interpret it in that way. I am sure that the Conservative Opposition would not so interpret it.

Mr Nicholas Edwards (Conservative, Shadow Secretary of State for Wales): We would.[16]

Thus the comment frequently made that the 40 per cent provision allowed abstainers to be treated as 'No' voters is not correct: for it would be for Parliament to decide whether to repeal the Act and this decision would be based principally upon the balance between the 'Yes' and 'No' votes. The situation would have been very different if the referendum had been mandatory. The Danish Constitution contains a provision that no constitutional change can take place unless approved by at least 40 per cent of the electorate: before 1953 the figure was 45 per cent. In 1939, a proposal to reform the Danish Upper House secured a 91.9 per cent 'Yes' vote, but because only 44.5 per cent of the electorate supported it, it failed. Such an outcome would hardly be possible with an advisory referendum which allowed Parliament an element of flexibility.

The Cunningham Amendment, therefore, gave to Parliament the discretion to decide whether a majority which did not meet the 40 per cent requirement was sufficient. The 40 per cent test also indicated to Scottish voters how Parliament intended to use its discretion. If Parliament intended not to establish the Assembly unless 40 per cent of those entitled to vote had voted 'Yes', it was surely fairer to announce this beforehand rather than proposing new tests after the referendum. In passing the Scotland Act, Parliament accepted the view that if Scotland wanted devolution, it would be granted. The issue, however, was how to ensure that devolution was not forced upon a reluctant Scotland after an inconclusive referendum result.

One cannot give a precise figure for the majority which Parliament would have required for the repeal Order to be defeated in the event of the 40 per cent criterion not being met. Probably few MPs had formulated precise figures in their own minds. What the criterion would achieve, however – and did, in fact, achieve – was to prevent the Scottish Assembly being established as the result of a small majority on a low turnout. If the majority had been a large one – say a 10 per cent majority – then a 35 per cent 'Yes' vote by the electorate might have been accepted; if the turnout had been high and the 40 per cent requirement had been met, a narrow majority would have sufficed to ensure that the Scotland Act came into force.

IV

The result of the referendum in Scotland, on a turnout of 62.9 per cent, was as follows:

Yes   1 230 937:   51.6% of those voting; 32.85% of the electorate.
No   1 153 502:   48.5% of those voting; 30.78% of the electorate.

These figures posed a dreadful dilemma for Mr Callaghan. If the 'Yes' majority had been 3 or 4 per cent higher, he could have asked Parliament to vote down the repeal Order with a fair chance of success. If, on the other hand, there had been a 'No' majority, the SNP could not have pressed him to establish the Assembly. With such an indecisive result, however, the Prime Minister was trapped between the demands of the SNP and the insistence of back-bench opponents of devolution, their numbers swelled by the unexpected success of the 'No's' to repeal the Scotland Act. Moreover, the Government was supported by only a minority in the Commons. On 1 March, the day of the referendum, the Conservatives succeeded in retaining two safe seats in the Clitheroe and Knutsford by-elections. The Parliamentary position then was as shown in Table 13.1. (These figures allow for two vacancies at Liverpool, Edge Hill, and Chipping Barnet.) The Liberals had voted against the Government on all votes of confidence since the end of the Lib–Lab pact in the summer of 1978, but the SNP had been unwilling to drive the Government from office before the referendum in Scotland since it believed that a Labour Government would be more disposed than a Conservative one to look favourably on an indecisive result.

Table 13.1   The parties in the House of Commons, 1 March 1979

Government		*Others*	
Labour	307	Conservatives	281
Scottish Labour Party	2	Liberals	13
	——	SNP	11
	309	Ulster Unionists	10
		Plaid Cymru	3
		Irish non-Unionists	2
			——
			320

Without the Cunningham Amendment, the narrow 'Yes' majority might well have been sufficient for the Scotland Act to be put into force; it is highly unlikely that, if the original version of the Bill had survived, the Government would have laid the repeal Order. But, of course, the 40 per cent rule not only changed the significance of the results, it may also have altered the terms on which the referendum campaign was fought: it may have seemed to many voters that an abstention was equivalent to a 'No' vote. In the absence of the Cunningham Amendment, therefore, a sufficient number of the abstainers would have voted 'No' to ensure a 'No' majority. Indeed, Mr Teddy Taylor, then Shadow Secretary of State for Scotland, declared that the 40 per cent rule (which he had supported) 'may have kept us from achieving an outright majority'.[17]

A further consideration was the unevenness of the vote. Only the regions in the central belt of Scotland (Strathclyde, Central, Lothian and Fife) together with the Highlands and the Western Isles showed a 'Yes' majority. The other outlying areas (Borders, Dumfries and Galloway, Grampian, Tayside, Orkney and Shetland) had all voted 'No', reflecting the fears of those in the rural parts of Scotland that they would be consistently outvoted in the Assembly by the Labour machine in the industrial areas. The 'Yes' majority in Strathclyde alone – 87 920 – was, in fact, larger than the overall 'Yes' majority of 77 435. An evenly spread 'Yes' majority across the regions would have made it easier for the Government to avoid the repeal of the Scotland Act.

It was these three factors – the narrow 'Yes' majority; the fact that the 'Yes' vote was itself too small, representing less than a third of the Scottish electorate; and the geographical distribution of the vote – which prevented the Scotland Act coming into force. The failure of the 'Yes' vote to reach the 40 per cent requirement was not by itself the crucial factor, and the effect of the Cunningham Amendment is to be seen in allowing Parliament to make the final decision rather than in any automatic rejection of devolution.

Nevertheless, the Government sought, through manoeuvre and delay, to avoid repealing the Scotland Act. Since the Amendment had been passed with the aid of Labour back-benchers, it knew that the Commons would be unwilling to vote down the repeal Order once it had been laid. According to Sir Harold Wilson: 'There had been some hope in the Cabinet that, having laid the repeal Order, their own supporters would vote the other way and keep devolution alive. But strenuous inquiries by the Government Whips revealed that some forty or so Government back-benchers would join the Conservatives in killing devolution.'[18] Mr Callaghan was reduced to proposing that inter-party talks be held on devolution, an option which he had previously rejected when it had been put to him by the Conservatives. The SNP, however, immediately tabled a motion of no-confidence and the

Conservatives, scenting victory, followed with a similar motion which was carried on 28 March by one vote. Thus, as Sir Harold Wilson indicates, the immediate cause of the collapse of the Government was not the industrial or economic troubles which had plagued it since its formation, but 'the impasse caused by the response of the Scots and Welsh in the devolution vote'.[19]

The SNP's decision to turn out the Labour Government was widely regarded as suicidal, 'the first time in recorded history', in Mr Callaghan's words, that 'turkeys have been known to vote for an early Christmas'. But the SNP sought to benefit from a polarization between Scottish and English opinion: the majority of Scottish MPs had voted against the Cunningham Amendment while a majority of English MPs had voted for it: moreover, after the referendum result, a majority of Scottish MPs remained – officially at least – committed to the establishment of an Assembly while English MPs were determined to destroy it. For Mr Gordon Wilson, an SNP member, '1 March was a threshold: we broke through a psychological barrier by getting a majority of people to vote for home rule. If the House of Commons now turns it down, we will have material for campaign after campaign.'[20]

The parliamentary manoeuvrings after the referendum revealed clearly the differences between the Labour and SNP attitudes to devolution. Labour's commitment seemed half-hearted and, by refusing to vote down the repeal Order, Labour MPs exposed themselves to the SNP jibe that they preferred Mrs Thatcher in Downing Street to a Scottish Assembly in Edinburgh. Thus a Scottish voter who sought self-government for Scotland would know that he could secure it only by voting for the SNP, the only party which 'stood for Scotland'. Support for the SNP seemed to have varied inversely with the plausibility of Labour's devolution commitment; after the failure of the first devolution bill – the Scotland and Wales Bill – opinion polls showed the SNP to be the most popular party in Scotland. No doubt the SNP hoped to capitalize upon a feeling that Scotland was being robbed through an artificial hurdle imposed by English MPs.

If that was the calculation, it proved, in the short run at least, a mistaken one. For devolution played hardly any role at all in the general election campaign. A *Glasgow Herald* poll found only 3 per cent who were prepared to regard it as a key issue, as compared with 47 per cent who felt that the cost of living was the key issue, while 28 per cent mentioned jobs and employment. The 1979 general election was fought not on self-government but on more familiar economic issues: it was perhaps not surprising that the SNP's electoral campaign was a failure, and that its representation in the Commons fell from 11 to 2 MPs. If, however, the Scottish electorate had regretted its lukewarm commitment to devolution on 1 March, it could still have atoned for it by supporting the SNP in the general election. For if the SNP had increased its parliamentary representation, the new Government would have been compelled to take the devolution issue seriously. Scots voters were thus offered a further opportunity to overcome the 40 per cent hurdle. The fact that they did not take it showed that, for the time being at least, Scots accepted that the narrow majority in the referendum offered no mandate for fundamental constitutional change: and the incoming Conservative Government repealed the Scotland Act on 20 June 1979.

In the long run, however, it is perfectly possible that the SNP could benefit from the devolution fiasco, since it has established itself so clearly as the party of Scottish self-government. The SNP no doubt exaggerated both its unhappiness at the repeal of the Scotland Act (which, if it had worked successfully, might have killed the demand for further self-government) and also the myth of English hostility to Scottish aspirations. The 40 per cent rule provides convenient material for the growth of a powerful nationalist myth to the effect that Scotland was cheated, that an extra hurdle was erected by those who knew that devolution could not be defeated on a straight vote. If the failure of devolution were to lead in the long run to a polarization of opinion in Scotland, the way would be clear for a party which claimed that there was no middle path between the *status quo* and full self-government. It would be a terrible irony if the SNP proved to be the eventual beneficiary of the Cunningham Amendment; but it would not be the first time that history played such tricks.

V

In his *Introduction to the Study of Law of the Constitution*, first published in 1885, A. V. Dicey claimed that one of the corollaries of the sovereignty of Parliament, 'the dominant characteristic of our political institutions', was that 'There is under the English (*sic!*) constitution no marked or clear distinction between laws which are not fundamental or constitutional and laws which are fundamental or constitutional'.[21] Dicey was not, however, an uncritical admirer of this state of affairs. He was passionately hostile to Irish Home Rule and he realized that sooner or later, as a result of the electoral swing of the pendulum, a Liberal Government would be returned, claiming a mandate for a measure which he believed was opposed by the majority of the electorate. Only the referendum could prevent a government backed by the power of the party machine from destroying the Union against the wishes of the electorate. Such a check against the tyranny of an elective dictatorship was to become even more urgent with the weakening of the power of the House of Lords.[22]

Where a referendum is advisory – and the four referendums held in the United Kingdom (the Northern Ireland border poll, the referendum on the

EEC and the devolution referendums) have all been advisory – then Parliamentary sovereignty remains formally intact. In practice, however, a referendum which produces a decisive result clearly limits the power of Parliament, since a government cannot easily ignore it. The referendum, therefore, in practice if not in law, constitutes an alternative method of validating laws in the United Kingdom.

The 40 per cent test goes further in drawing a distinction between constitutional laws, requiring some extra means of validation, and laws which are not fundamental and require no such extra validation. It seeks to entrench the unitary state as a part of the constitution. For the implication of the Cunningham Amendment is that the powers of Parliament ought not to be devolved unless it is clear beyond all possible doubt that this is desired by the electorate. In proposing the repeal of the Scottish Act, Mr George Younger, the Secretary of State for Scotland, suggested that 'it would be improper to promote any further version of a Scottish Assembly with legislative and executive powers without holding another referendum'.[23] Mr George Gardiner, a Conservative back-bench opponent of devolution, went further in claiming that 'it will be difficult for a future Government to refuse a referendum on any significant constitutional proposals that they bring forward . . . Moreover . . . I hope that when that happens, it will be judged relevant also to retain the 40 per cent hurdle, . . . that rule has set a precedent that cannot lightly be ignored by any future Government proposing constitutional changes.'[24]

The 40 per cent rule offers a graphic illustration of how a barrier to fundamental change can be constructed in a country lacking a written constitution. It is too early to say whether its final effect has been beneficial. If devolution disappears as an issue, it will be remembered as the instrument through which the United Kingdom was prevented from making an important constitutional change unwanted by the majority of Scots. If, on the other hand, the issue returns, possibly in a less manageable form, then the 40 per cent rule may be seen as a foolish and mischievous one which succeeded only in driving a wedge between English and Scottish opinion and prevented the adoption of an essentially moderate reform.

Did the referendum yield any short-term benefits? A number of critics have concluded that it was a fiasco because it did not settle the Scottish question. But, given the fairly even division of opinion in Scotland concerning the merits of the Scotland Act, no test of opinion could be expected to yield a definite decision. The referendum, however, if it did not settle the issue, at least defused it, and it was the only instrument which could have succeeded in doing so. If the legislation had been defeated in Parliament, the issue would have been kept alive since the SNP would have been able to say that Parliament was ignoring the will of the Scottish people. In the absence of a clear-cut result which might have settled the issue, the referendum decided it in favour of those who sought to defuse it, as against those who might have sought to keep it alive. 'The Scottish question' might well return in a different form to plague some future Parliament; but the outcome of the referendum has moved devolution away from the centre of the political stage; and in the defeat of devolution the role of the 40 per cent provision was indispensable.

Notes and references

* I should like to thank Professor A. W. Bradley, Mr George Cunningham MP and Mr P. M. Williams for comments on an earlier draft of the paper. They are not, however, responsible for my conclusions.

1   S. E. Finer (ed.) (1975), *Adversary Politics and Electoral Reform*, Anthony Wigram, 18.
2   HC Debs, 15 Feb. 1978, vol. 944, col. 595.
3   HC Debs, vol 942, col. 1462.
4   HC Debs, vol. 944, col. 566.
5   HC Debs, vol. 944, col. 567.
6   HC Debs, vol. 942, col. 1477.
7   Letter to the author, 15 September 1979.
8   *The Economist*, 19 February 1979 (discussing the research of Dr David Butler and Mr Colm O'Muircheartaigh).
9   Letter to the *Scotsman*, 26 February 1979.
10 'The Two Registers', 12 February 1979.
11 Written Answers, 20 February 1979, HC Debs, vol. 963, col. 138.
12 Ibid.
13 These figures constitute the author's view of the maximum possible number of deductions, taking account of all those in practice unable to vote. The figures are obtained from Butler and O'Muircheartaigh and the *Scotsman*, 12 February 1979.
14 'The Case for the 40 per cent Test', *Scotsman*, 1 February 1978.
15 Ibid.
16 HC Debs, vol. 958, cols. 1281/1367.
17 *Scotsman*, 3 March 1979.
18 *Final Term*, Weidenfeld & Nicolson/Michael Joseph, 1979, p. 213 fn.
19 Ibid.
20 *Financial Times*, 4 March 1979.
21 10th edn, Macmillan, 1959, 39/89.
22 See, *inter alia*, 'The referendum and its critics', *Quarterly Review*, April 1910.
23 HC Debs, vol. 968, col. 1335.
24 HC Debs, vol. 968, col. 1423.

14 The Problem of the Upper House

I

'With a perfect Lower House', says Walter Bagehot in Chapter V of *The English Constitution*, in 1867,

> it is certain that an Upper House would scarcely be of any value. If we had an ideal House of Commons, perfectly representing the nation, always moderate, never passionate, abounding in men of leisure, never omitting the slow and steady forms necessary for good consideration, it is certain that we should not need a higher chamber. The work would be done so well that we should not want any one to look over or revise it. . . . But though beside an ideal House of Commons the Lords would be unnecessary and therefore, pernicious, beside the actual House a revising and leisured legislature is extremely useful, if not quite necessary.

It is worth perhaps noticing the way in which Bagehot phrases his justification of the House of Lords. He does not say that an upper house is absolutely essential, only that it 'is extremely useful, if not quite necessary'.[1]

At the time Bagehot was writing, of course, the notion of a non-elected, aristocratic chamber was as much the norm as the exception. 'Nearly everywhere there was a mix of heredity and royal appointment.'[2] Rooted in the medieval idea of the representation of separate orders or estates, European upper houses were defended as bulwarks against the rapidly encroaching democracy, an essential limitation upon the power of the majority.

Such a defence is hardly applicable in modern times when upper houses must be justified as allies rather than opponents of liberal democratic values. Already, by 1918, the Conference chaired by Lord Bryce on the Reform of the Second Chamber in Britain, was arguing that 'The Second Chamber should aim at ascertaining the mind and views of the nation as a whole, and should recognise its full responsibility to the people, not setting itself to oppose the people's will, but only to comprehend and give effect to that will when adequately expressed'.[3] The purpose of an upper house should be to aid democracy, not to hinder it, and it can do this by correcting weaknesses inherent in democratic government, both in principle and in practice.

These weaknesses are of three kinds. There is, first, the fact that the principle of representation exemplified in the lower house might need complementing by some alternative principle of representation. This is most obvious, of course, in the case of federal states where the representation of individual electors in the lower house needs to be complemented by representation of the territorial units comprising the federation in the upper house. In a federation, the upper house does not *check* the popular will. Rather it exemplifies another mode of representing it. In a federation, therefore, each house expresses the will of the people, but in a different way.

Secondly, there is a weakness in the representative principle itself, as that principle has come to be manifested in the modern world of highly organized political parties. With a party government committed to a highly detailed political programme, it would be perfectly possible for the lower house to pass legislation involving changes, perhaps changes of a very fundamental kind, which are not supported by a majority of the electors. That a majority in the lower house represents the opinion of a majority of the electors is, after all, not a self-evident proposition but one which needs to be proved in each particular case.

Thirdly, even where the majority in the lower house *does* represent a majority in the country, it is still possible for legislation to infringe upon the rights and liberties of minorities, or to impose changes which undermine the values of liberal democracy. The erosion of liberty can occur just as easily – perhaps more easily – under a democratic parliamentary regime as under the limited suffrage regimes of the nineteenth century. Hitler, after all, came to power under a democratic regime, obtaining his dictatorial powers from a majority vote in the lower house.

Of course, it does not follow that the best way of remedying these three weaknesses – weaknesses which, first, may be inherent in the principle of representation in terms of one person, one vote; second, weaknesses in the representative principle itself, and third, the danger of a tyranny of the majority – is through an upper house. It may be that other devices would be more effective. But the argument does at least show that an unchecked single chamber could, even though democratically elected, come to threaten the foundations of liberal democratic government.

II

The classical description of the functions of an upper house was given by Lord Bryce in 1918.[4] Two of these functions – the initiation of non-controversial legislation, and 'full and free discussion of large and important questions, such as those of foreign policy' which the lower house has no time for – we may put to one side. For these functions are not perhaps so essential that they would in themselves justify the existence of an upper house. The other two functions are of considerably more importance. They are the revision of legislation, and

> the interposition of so much delay (and no more) in the passing of a Bill into law as may be needed to enable the opinion of the nation to be adequately expressed upon it. This would be specially needed as regards Bills which affect the fundamentals of the Constitution or introduce new principles of legislation, or which raise issues whereon the opinion of the country may appear to be almost equally divided.

These two functions may be called those of revision and of constitutional protection. They can be seen in their clearest form in federal states where the upper house is both revising chamber and safeguard for the states. In Australia, for example, according to one authority,

> The Senate is not merely a second chamber of revision and review . . . such as the House of Lords is supposed to be; it is that, but something more than that. It is the chamber in which the states, considered as separate entities and corporate parts of the Commonwealth, are represented. They are so represented for the purpose of enabling them to maintain and protect their constitutional rights against attempted invasions, ...[5]

It is precisely because the Senate exists to protect the rights of states in matters lying within the federal power that Art. 128 of the Australian Constitution, like Article V of the United States Constitution, prevents the proportionate representation of a state in the Senate from being altered without the consent of that state.

Each of these two functions – that of revision and of constitutional protection – provides a democratic justification for the power of delay. If it is to be an effective revising chamber, an upper house needs the power to ask the lower house to reconsider legislation. The upper house must be able to require of the lower house second thoughts. Yet it should not have the power to destroy the legislation or to defeat its fundamental aims. Thus, for the revising function to be effective, it would seem that the upper house ought to have a suspensory rather than an absolute veto, such as the House of Lords, for example, enjoys over bills other than money bills.

But, is the mere power of delay sufficient for the function of constitutional protection. Usually the power of delay is quite short – one parliamentary session in Britain, and 90 days in the Irish Republic – and so hardly sufficient to overcome a determined lower house. It may be argued that an upper house needs greater powers than this if it is to be able to act effectively as a chamber of constitutional protection. Moreover, the two functions – revision and constitutional protection – although separable, are closely related. For the power of revision may well be needed to protect some matter which is of constitutional significance. Thus, one of the purposes of a revising chamber may be precisely to secure alterations in legislation which is thought to affect the constitution.[6]

The issue of powers, however, cannot be dealt with separately from that of composition. For an upper house might have wide powers, but, because of its lack of authority, be unable to use them. The Canadian Senate, for example, has equal powers with the House of Commons on legislation, except for financial legislation. But, being a wholly nominated body, it cannot use these powers. Indeed, for this reason, the Senate normally accepts the position of the House of Commons, and there has been no need to invoke the procedure for resolving deadlocks since 1874. Similarly, the House of Lords in Britain has much wider powers than is usually thought, since the Parliament Acts, providing for the limitation of its powers, did not curtail its rights over delegated legislation which still requires its approval. Thus the Lords could, in theory, reject all such legislation, so causing grave difficulties for the government of the day. Yet, it rarely rejected delegated legislation. When it rejected the Southern Rhodesia (United Nations Sanctions) Order 1968, its action had no permanent effect since it passed an order identical in substance shortly afterwards. For the Lords, like the Canadian Senate, is unable to use its powers because its composition, based on a combination of heredity and nomination, deprives it of authority in the modern world.

One must distinguish, therefore, between the powers which an upper house enjoys in theory and the actual use that it is able to make of them. The former will be determined by the constitution, the latter by constitutional conventions and by the concatenation of political forces.

The House of Lords is an institution based upon the principle of prescription; its authority rests on historical continuity and on deference to rank. These influences, powerful until the beginning of the century, are of minimal importance today. 'An aristocratic House', declares John Stuart Mill, 'is only powerful in an aristocratic state of society.'[7] Today, so it has been said, the House of Lords 'represents nobody but itself, and therefore enjoys the full confidence of its constituents'.[8]

In the modern world, authority derives almost solely from election, and more from direct than indirect election. If one is looking for an upper house with the authority to fulfil the function of constitutional protection, therefore, the conclusion seems inescapable that it must be an elected body. Only power, as Montesquieu noticed, can check power.

If, however, it is desired to have an elected upper house, the problem arises of how it is to be elected. Some method must be found of electing it on a different basis from that of the lower house, and the method of election must be such as to ensure that, although the upper house has authority, it does not have *more* authority than the lower house. The upper house must be strong enough to challenge the lower when seeking to use its powers of revision or delay, but not so strong as to be able to prevent a government, responsible to the lower house, from governing. The Australian Senate, directly elected and with the power to withhold supply can, as the events of 1975 showed, compel a recently elected government to call a general election, a power which the House of Lords sought to exercise until the 1911 Parliament Act prevented it from doing so. The Australian Senate can give an opposition party, defeated in a general election, control over the government and the power to force a dissolution. That, surely, goes beyond any reasonable interpretation of the functions of an upper house.

III

A number of different methods have been employed in an attempt to secure a *via media* between a house exercising too little power and one enjoying excessive power. They may be divided into the following categories:

1 Indirect election
2 Direct election on the basis of territory
3 Election on a corporate basis
4 Election by members of the lower house.

1 Those European countries which select their upper house through a method of indirect election include Austria, France and the Netherlands. Austria is an example of a federal state in which the provincial assemblies elect the upper house. France has an electoral college whose composition is weighted in favour of rural areas and small towns, its method of election being intended, according to Article 24 of the Constitution, to ensure 'the representation of the territorial units of the Republic'. The upper house in the Netherlands is composed of members chosen by an electoral college composed of the provincial councils, the units of local government.

In each of these cases, representation is secured on a different basis from that of the lower house, namely territory. The upper house is supposed to represent a feeling which, claims Bagehot, 'is older than complicated politics, which is stronger a thousand times over than common political feelings – the *local* feeling. "My shirt", said the Swiss state-right patriot, "is dearer to me than my coat".'[9] This feeling is, of course, found most strongly in federal states, but it can, as the examples of France and the Netherlands show, also form the basis for an upper house in a non-federal state. The same argument could, no doubt, also be adapted to form a justification for an upper house based on some non-territorial interest – ethnicity, perhaps language, the possible basis for an upper house in Belgium; religion, or vocation, the basis of the Irish Seanad – to be considered later.

The main difficulty with such indirect methods of election is that the electoral college, the body from which the election is made, can easily become a mere plaything of party politics and lose its original purpose. An extreme example of that having occurred is the electoral college in the United States, originally intended as a deliberative body, but now a group of electors mandated to support a particular presidential candidate. If units of local government are also to become an electoral college for an upper chamber, then voters may well choose their local councillors, less on the basis of their fitness for local work, than upon their orientation in national politics. Elections for local councils will be determined by the exigencies of national party politics, and local issues will become subordinated to these exigencies. At the very least a new issue will have been introduced into local politics, and local authorities will come to have a dual function – representing their communities and acting as an electoral college.

There is, moreover, a confusion in the notion of the representation of territory. For territory itself cannot be represented, only individual electors can be. The over-representation of rural areas which occurs in Austria and France is in practice an over-representation of rural voters, whose votes come to be weighted more highly than those of urban voters, and whose political influence is thereby increased. It is difficult to see the rationale for such an arrangement in the modern world. Indeed, the US federal courts in a series of decisions in the 1960s and 1970s explicitly ruled that upper houses in the American states could no longer base representation on any factors other than population. The argument for diversity of representation thus conflicts with the norms of a modern democratic state, for it generally involves inequality of representation.

2   With direct election of an upper house, the problem is to find a method of election which avoids overlapping and duplication of function. If the cabinet system of government is to be preserved, it is essential that the supremacy of the lower house be assured. In Australia, where, as we have seen, the Senate

is able to reject supply, there is a very real conflict between federalism and the principle of cabinet government, entailing the responsibility of the government to the lower house. Wherever the two houses are equal or nearly equal in authority, the danger is that a government may find itself responsible to two mutually hostile majorities. 'A cabinet, it would seem, must be responsible to one chamber: it cannot be responsible to two.'[10] It thus seems essential that a directly elected upper house should not enjoy the power either of making and unmaking ministries or of rejecting supply which is tantamount to unmaking a ministry.

It is, therefore, not coincidental that the strongest upper houses in federal states are in Switzerland and the United States, whose systems are based not upon ministerial responsibility but upon the separation of powers. For it seems to follow that in a federal country with a cabinet system of government, the upper house cannot be a fully effective protector of states' rights. 'The conventions of cabinet government are so strong that, in the end, they will weaken if not nullify, the legal powers of the Second Chamber.'[11] Moreover, in modern democracies, party politics tends to prevent the upper house from acting as a genuine protector of states' rights. When, in 1974, the Australian Senate forced the Whitlam government to go to the country, and when, in 1975, it withheld supply from the Whitlam government, it was acting not so much as a protector of states' rights, but rather as a focus of the Liberal Party's opposition to the government. Upper houses in federal systems are as much party houses as they are state houses.

Further, in federal states, it is the courts and inter-governmental forums, such as federal/provincial conferences, linking together the states and the federal government which play at least as important a role as protectors of states' rights as the upper house. In Canada, for example, states' rights are protected in part by the convention that each Cabinet must contain 'if possible, at least one Minister from every province and from Quebec and Ontario up to ten or twelve',[12] and by conferences between provincial prime ministers and the federal government. Provincial premiers, according to one authority, 'had said they had not been interested in making representations to the Senate; they had not wanted to hand over to "understudies". One of them . . . a former Premier of Nova Scotia, had said that if he wanted to get something done and had been told to leave it to a Senator, he would have said as Premier, "I want to see the Prime Minister, nobody else will do"'.[13] Now Canada might be thought of as exceptional, precisely because its nominated upper house has so little political weight. But there seems no reason why, in federal states with directly elected upper houses, states' rights might still not be better defended by the courts and by federal/state conferences than by the upper house. The conventional argument, therefore, that in a federal state, an upper house is an essential instrument of constitutional protection for the constituent units would seem to be in need of some qualification.

3   Although the bishops in the House of Lords form a reminder of the medieval idea that political authority resides in the holding of certain offices, the Irish Republic is the only country in Europe whose upper house almost wholly reflects the principle of corporate representation. 43 of the members of the Irish Seanad are elected from five vocational panels – cultural and educational, agricultural, labour, industrial and commercial, and administrative. A further three members are selected by each of the two universities and the remaining 11 are nominated by the prime minister. In France, the Economic and Social Council, although an advisory body and not part of the legislature, also reflects the vocational principle. The idea was also exemplified in the Federal Economic Council established in the Weimar Republic.[14]

The case for such a vocational chamber came to be heard again in the 1960s and 1970s when it seemed that governments needed to be able to negotiate with the holders of economic and social power as well as with the party politicians represented in the lower house. In particular, it was widely believed that governments would not be able successfully to pursue incomes policies, thought to be essential to the fight against inflation, unless they offered the trade unions and other social and economic interests rights of participating in the making of national economic policy. In the 1960s and 1970s, when notions of economic planning played a larger role in politics than they do today, political legitimacy seemed to require not only the support of the electorate, but also the allegiance of key interests. Understandably, however, the idea of vocational representation has become less fashionable in the neo-conservative 1980s when allegiance to the market came to replace the conciliation of interests as the keystone of economic policy-making.

There are, in any case, a number of problems involved in making vocational representation the basis of an upper house of a legislature. For a vocational house, the electorate and constituency must be defined. What interests are to be represented and who determines what constitutes an interest? How long are those elected to sit in the chamber? For as long as they hold a particular office, for the duration of the legislature or for life? How is provision to be made for redefinition of interests as the balance of power in society changes? For, if there is no such provision for redefinition, the vocational chamber will rapidly become anachronistic through shifts in the number and importance of particular groups. Moreover, a vocational chamber, by its very nature, is likely to over-emphasize the importance of producer groups at the expense of the consumer and of the weakly organized, such as pensioners and the unemployed. The Economic Council in the French Fourth Republic has been accused of being 'tempted to combine against the consumer for whom, at a generous estimate, not more than a sixth of the councillors spoke'.[15] It is true that representation of the weakly organized can be secured; so can the representation of consumers – as it was in the Federal Economic Council of the Weimar period – but it might be argued that consumers do not constitute an 'interest' parallel to that of producer groups, and that their needs can best be met not through representation in a legislature, but through freedom of choice in a market economy.

However, the main objection to a vocational body being part of the legislature is that it will, in practice, be dominated by party political appointments. The Irish Seanad is, we are told, 'composed largely of party politicians not very different from their colleagues . . . and, in the case of many of them, with only tenuous connections with the interests they affect to represent'.[16] Indeed, the members of the Seanad sit, not in vocational but in party groups; and it is for this reason that one authority has argued that the Seanad 'is, in fact, not an example in practice of a vocational or functional chamber'.[17]

If a vocational body is to avoid this contamination of party politics, it seems to be necessary that it should *not* be part of the legislature. The French Economic and Social Council is able to operate as a vocational and not a party chamber precisely because it has no legislative powers.

> The answer seems inescapable that a functional or vocational chamber can work as such in association with a legislature only in an advisory capacity. If it is intended to be an integral part of the legislature its party composition becomes a matter of concern to the party politicians of the lower house and it will be converted sooner or later into another party chamber. Vocational chambers, whether as second or as third chambers in societies where politics are conducted on a free party system, cannot function effectively as an integral part of the legislature. Their proper sphere lies outside the legislature.[18]

For this reason, the idea of vocational representation, even if it is thought desirable, cannot solve the problem of the upper house.

4   In both Norway and Iceland, the upper house is composed by electing a proportion – one-quarter in Norway and one-third in Iceland – of the members of the legislature to constitute an upper house. The remainder of the legislature constitutes the lower house.

An upper house of this type is favoured by those who prefer a revising chamber which would be unable to thwart the popular will – since party strengths in the upper house will be proportional to those in the lower. An upper house so constituted could not obstruct the lower, but it might prove useful in revising legislation, in allowing for second thoughts.

Yet it is doubtful if Norway's political system can be regarded as a genuine example of bicameralism. Article 49 of the Norwegian constitution speaks of parliament, the Storting, as consisting of two 'sections' and not of two chambers. The Storting only acts as two houses in the case of 'ordinary' legislation. But even in this case, bills must be laid before the whole Storting when the two sections are unable to agree. In the case of constitutional amendments, financial legislation and motions criticizing the actions of ministers, the Storting sits as a whole. Moreover, the Storting is dissolved as a single chamber. There is no way in which one of the two 'sections' can continue its existence without the other.

The Norwegian and Icelandic upper houses lack the independent authority to fulfil the function of constitutional protection. In Norway, constitutional change, according to Article 75 of the Constitution, occurs through the Storting acting as a single chamber, and through a qualified majority of two-thirds, following a general election. Thus constitutional protection is secured not through the Lagting, the upper house, but through the Storting, acting by qualified majority and with the approval of the people.

The Norwegian Lagting may more properly be regarded perhaps as an 'upper tier standing committee of the Storting, albeit with a limited remit'[19] rather than an upper house in the strict sense of the term. It shows that the revising function does not necessarily require a separate election for an upper house, but that it can be accommodated within a single chamber. Yet, even as a revising chamber, the Lagting apparently carries little weight. Lacking independent powers, it is unable to press its objections to legislation. Only twice in the 20-year period 1962–82 has repeated opposition by the Lagting caused a joint session of the Storting to be held to resolve a deadlock; and each occasion occurred under exceptional circumstances.[20] Because the Lagting lacks weight, members of the Storting do not seem keen to belong to it, and it is generally new members who are sent to it. 'Today', according to one Norwegian commentator, 'the Lagting lives an existence completely hidden away from the glare of media publicity and except on a few occasions it is largely forgotten'.[21]

The Norwegian system, together with the Icelandic system, is more properly regarded as examples of a 'modified unicameral legislature'[22] rather than being genuinely bicameral. Therefore this method of electing an upper house cannot be regarded as resolving the problem of establishing a bicameral system within which each house fulfils complementary functions.

IV

Given the manifold problems involved in constructing an effective upper house, it is perhaps surprising that there are so few unicameral democracies. Portugal, with a population of around 10 million, is the largest unicameral state. Every democracy with a population larger than 10 million is bicameral.

This might in part be explained by the force of inertia. 'The persistence of bicameralism in nonfederal systems is a remarkable example of the tenacity of organizational forms well after their original purpose has disappeared'.[23] It might also be explained by the fact that larger states are more likely than small states to be diverse in terms of language, ethnicity or religion. However, although most of the unicameral states are homogeneous in terms of population, not all of them are. There are exceptions – Israel, for example, which has some though not all of the features associated with consociational democracy, Finland which has an important Swedish minority, and New Zealand with its Maori minority.

The unicameral democracies do not seem to have found it impossible to have the function of legislative revision performed within a single chamber, and they have developed other devices to provide the function of constitutional protection. On occasion, the prospect of abolishing the upper house has actively stimulated the search for such devices. In New Zealand, for example, the upper house was abolished in 1950 by a conservative government, but this led to 'a new and healthy interest in constitutional procedures . . .'.[24] In 1956, New Zealand adopted an Electoral Act entrenching, for the first time, those parts of its constitution dealing with the duration of parliament, the setting up and terms of reference of the Boundary Commission, the voting age, and the adjustment of constituencies following each five yearly census. A 75 per cent vote of the House is needed to alter any of these matters, or, as an alternative, a majority in a referendum.

All of the unicameral states, with perhaps the partial exception of New Zealand, have strong checks against the dangers of the dictatorship of an elected majority. Often these checks are more powerful than anything that an upper house can provide.

There seem to be three main alternatives to an upper house performing the function of constitutional protection. The first is a constitutional court with the power of judicial review of legislation. This can help to ensure the protection of minorities and also of states' rights within a federal system. The second device, which can also protect minority rights, is to make provision for a qualified majority – say two-thirds or three-quarters – so that constitutional change cannot normally be brought about by a majority government alone. Sometimes, as in Finland, Netherlands or Norway, there is a requirement for an intervening general election before constitutional changes can be made.

The third device for securing constitutional protection is the referendum. This ensures that a majority in the legislature will not undertake a change to which a majority in the country is opposed. In Denmark, when the upper house was abolished in 1953, the parties of the Right received as a quid pro quo provision for a referendum on legislation – there was already a requirement for a referendum for constitutional change. The legislative referendum can be brought into play by one-third of the members of the Folketing on any item of government legislation except the budget, taxes, salaries or pensions. For legislation to be rejected, there must be not only a majority against it, but at least 30 per cent of the registered electorate must vote against it. This is to prevent legislation being rejected through the activity of a small intense pressure group, while the sympathetic majority stays at home. The legislative referendum was used in 1963 on four land laws proposed by the Social Democratic government, all of which were defeated by the voters. Thus a government can be deterred from controversial legislation by fear of the referendum, which acts as an incentive to consensus. In such circumstances, the referendum can probably act as a more effective check upon government than an upper house would be.

Thus, for the three weaknesses of democracy mentioned at the outset, there exist remedies other than a strong upper house. For the first weakness, the fact that a single-chamber legislature represents only individuals and not, for example, constituent units in a federal state, the remedies can be found in a constitutional court with judicial review, and in federal/provincial forums. For the second weakness, the danger that a majority in the legislature may pass legislation opposed by a majority in the country, the remedy can be found in the referendum. And for the third weakness, the danger of encroaching upon minority rights, a constitutional court might provide better protection than a second chamber. Thus there is no a priori reason to believe that in unicameral democracies such as Denmark, Finland and Sweden, the citizen will have any less constitutional protection than he or she enjoys in other European democracies.

There is, however, as we have seen in Chapter 8, one area of legislative scrutiny where an anachronistic upper house – the House of Lords – has been able to show its relevance, and that is in the scrutiny of Community legislation.[25]

V

The success of the Select Committee on the European Communities offers a clue as to the proper role which the House of Lords might play within our parliamentary system. In 1918, the Bryce Committee suggested that the primary functions of the Lords included the examination and revision of bills brought from the Commons, the initiation and discussion of non-controversial bills and the interposition of sufficient delay – but no more – in the passing of a bill into law as was needed to enable the view of the nation to be adequately expressed upon it. There should also be full and free discussion of current policy issues which the Commons might not have time to consider.

The Bryce Committee, therefore, took the view that the Lords should be primarily a legislative chamber whose main function was that of revising bills. The success of the Select Committee on the European Communities, however, implies that the House of Lords should seek a different role, that of bringing expertise to bear upon issues of public policy.

The conflict between these two views – that the House of Lords should be primarily a legislative chamber and that the House of Lords, being composed on a different basis from the Commons, should be primarily a chamber seeking to exert influence based on expertise – is a fundamental one. In the period of Labour government in the 1970s, the bulk of the government's legislation reached the statute book unscathed, despite the hostility of the Conservative majority in the House of Lords to it; while in the 1980s and 1990s, it would be difficult to suggest that the Lords has substantially altered the Conservative government's legislative programme. One authority has argued that, where the House of Lords has actually been successful in pressing its amendments, this derives from its not being overtly party political.

> Paradoxically the value of the House of Lords in the legislative process appears to lie precisely in its complementarity to the Commons, based as this is on the former's non-elected (and undemocratic) character. It is the less party political character of the House which is the single most important fact differentiating its legislative role.[26]

The area in which the House of Lords has been most successful are those in which it has not sought to challenge the House of Commons, but to undertake work which complements that of the Commons. In the words of Lord Windlesham, a former Leader of the House of Lords,

> The House of Lords should not attempt to rival the Commons. Whenever it has done so in the past it has failed, and usually made itself look ridiculous in the process . . . . In any well tuned parliamentary system there is a need and a place for a third element besides efficient government and the operation of representative democracy. This third element is the bringing to bear of informed or expert public opinion . . . . It is one of the principal roles of the Lords to provide a forum in which informed public opinion can take shape and be made known.

Accordingly, 'In assessing the influence of the Lords it is worth distinguishing the influence that comes from the ability to delay legislation from the influence that comes from special knowledge or the representation of interests.'[27]

On this view, the composition of the House of Lords – a mixture of hereditary succession and appointment – is well suited to the exertion of influence deriving 'from special knowledge or the representation of interests', while, on the other hand, if it were to be able to use the power of delay, the Lords would require more democratic legitimacy than it currently enjoys.

This does not mean, however, that the House of Lords ought to have no legislative role at all. But its current procedures do not well reflect the influence which it ought to have. In so far as domestic legislation is concerned, the procedures of the Lords still reflect those of a chamber exercising nearly equal legislative power with the Commons, a position which the Lords has not held since 1911. These procedures seem more appropriate to a chamber whose main function is that of legislative revision rather than bringing expertise to bear. There is a striking contrast between the approach to domestic legislation, where bills are considered on the floor of the House at four different stages – second reading, committee stage, report and third reading – and the approach to Community legislation where the House of Lords acts as, in effect, a pre-legislative committee.

It would be natural to adapt some of the principles behind the procedures of the European Communities Committee to domestic legislation by allowing the House of Lords to establish special standing committees when it chooses to do so. These special standing committees should be able to adopt an approach paralleling, as far as possible, that of the European Communities Select Committee. They should have a pre-legislative role, with power to discuss Green and White Papers, and take evidence upon them. They should also have the power to hear oral evidence – normally in public – as well as written evidence, during the passage of a bill. This would allow the expertise of the Lords to be brought to bear through investigatory and forensic procedures, so complementing the more party-oriented approach of the Commons.

In addition to legislative scrutiny, however, the House of Lords has an important role to play in the shaping of public opinion. There is a considerable need for an institution which can bring informed expertise to bear upon major policy issues over a longer time-horizon than government or opposition are usually able to concern themselves with. The need for such an institution is particularly great in Britain because of the comparative paucity of non-partisan think tanks, the virtual abolition of the Royal Commission as an instrument of inquiry and the abolition of the Central Policy Review Staff (the 'Think Tank') in 1983. The House of Lords is well-equipped to undertake thinking about policy which falls beyond the usual time-horizon of party politicians, but which is nevertheless of importance for an advanced industrial society. It should, as Lord Fulton argued in 1977, discuss issues 'which go beyond the mandates of any one government'.[28]

The European Communities Select Committee and the Science and Technology Select Committee form prime examples of how the House of Lords can exercise this function. Each of these Committees requires considerable expertise and mastery of technical detail; and, although each deals with matters of considerable importance to the long-term future of the country, there is no immediate pay-off in electoral terms. It has indeed been claimed that the Science and Technology Committee 'may be said to support the non-party political voice of the scientific community and its procedures ensure that the Government is reminded of what that voice is saying'.[29] In addition, there have been other *ad hoc* Select Committees from time to time on matters such as Unemployment (1982) and Overseas Trade (1985).

The weakness of the Select Committee system of the House of Lords, however, is that it does not seem to be the result of any coherent plan or strategy. It would be foolish for the Lords to seek to compete with the Commons by establishing departmentally related Select Committees. Instead, it should seek to complement the Commons by establishing select committees where there are gaps in the scrutiny system of the House of Commons. These are most likely to occur where a particular subject matter cuts across departmental boundaries as is the case, of course, with the Science and Technology Select Committee. Indeed, according to one authority, 'One reason for the choice of subject matter was that with no department devoted uniquely to Science and Technology, duplication with the departmental select committees of the Commons could be avoided.'[30]

In 1995, it was announced that the House of Lords is to set up an ad hoc Select Committee on Central/Local Relations. This is a subject particularly suited to the House of Lords. There is no select committee on this subject in the House of Commons, partly because, if one were to be established in the Commons, many in local government would fear that it would prove a vehicle for detailed intervention by MPs into their affairs. Such fears do not exist *vis-à-vis* a select committee in the House of Lords. Such a select committee will be a voice neither of central nor of local government, but it ought to enable the interests of local government to be given more effective expression in Parliament.

A further possibility might be a Select Committee on Justice. This would have as its remit those areas which are, in some Commonwealth countries, the responsibility of a Minister of Justice, combining functions exercised in England by the Lord Chancellor, the Attorney-General and the Home Secretary. These functions would include keeping the statute book under review, scrutinising the administration of justice and the procedures of courts and tribunals, and ensuring the preservation of judicial independence; and, above all, monitoring the state of civil liberties, with particular emphasis on the compliance of legislation with the European Convention of Human Rights. The Select Committee would complement the work of the Law Commission by examining their reports in a critical manner. The establishment of a Select Committee on Justice is a matter of particular importance for a country such as Britain where responsibility for the state of the law and for civil liberties is divided between several government departments and where there is no codified constitution nor Bill of Rights nor constitutional court to act as a guardian of civil liberties. The weight of judicial expertise in the House of Lords also makes a Select Committee on Justice a particularly appropriate one for Britain's upper house.

Both the select Committee on Central/Local Relations and the proposed Select Committee on Justice fall within an area which might be called constitutional. It is frequently suggested that the House of Lords, being free from electoral pressures, bears a particular responsibility as a guardian of the constitution, since the Commons does not always take into account the full constitutional implications of the legislation which it passes. In this way, the House of Lords, precisely because of its peculiar composition, might be able to find a role for itself, something that it has been struggling to do ever since it was deprived of its absolute veto over legislation through the Parliament Act of 1911.

VI

The fundamental reason why it has proved so difficult to construct a satisfactory upper house is the dominance of party politics in modern democracies. As a result, the practice of bicameralism bears very little relation to the theory. The student of constitutions will note the powers of the upper house and the machinery for resolving deadlocks between them. The political scientist, however, will be more impressed by the facts of political power. Unless an upper house is directly elected, it will lack the authority to challenge a majority government. But where it is directly elected, any challenge will be as much a party battle of opposition against the government as it is a fulfilment of the functions of revision and constitutional protection.

An upper house, declared Bryce, 'should be so composed as not to incur the charge of habitually acting under the influence of party motives'.[31] Thus the task of establishing a satisfactory basis for an upper house is at the same time the task of finding some factor other than party which can yet provide an upper house with authority. The search for such a factor might appear quite hopeless, unless, in a number of the democracies of western Europe, signs of a reaction against party politics can be discerned. For it might be possible to utilize such a reaction in the construction of an upper house which, despite lacking professional politicians, yet enjoys some degree of authority.

In the absence of such a factor, however, might one not conclude with John Stuart Mill that too much attention has been given to the question of bicameralism. 'Of all topics relating to the theory of representative government', Mill wrote, none has been the subject of more discussion, especially on the Continent, than what is known as the question of the Two Chambers. It has occupied a greater amount of the attention of thinkers than many questions ten times its importance, and has been regarded as a sort of touchstone which distinguishes the partisans of limited from those of uncontrolled democracy. For my own part, I set little value on any check which a Second Chamber can apply to a democracy otherwise unchecked; and I am inclined to think that if all other constitutional questions are rightly decided, it is but of secondary importance whether the Parliament consists of two Chambers or only of one.[32]

Amidst all the changes that have occurred since Mill's time, perhaps the experience of democracy in Europe has shown that he was at least right in this – that the existence or absence of an upper house is not the crucial factor likely to determine the success of democratic government or its ability to secure constitutional protection. An upper house is a means rather than an end; and often, as we have seen, a rather cumbrous means. If the same end can be secured by a more economical means, need we necessarily bewail the absence of an upper house? 'One maxim is of all political maxims sound: never create an institution when it is not necessary. If other institutions fulfil the conditions of good government, a Second Chamber is not necessary.'[33] Perhaps one might conclude by adding – if the other institutions do not fulfil the conditions of good government, an upper house cannot remedy the deficiency.

Notes and references

1 *Collected works (1968–86)*, N. St John-Stevas ed., 15 vols; London, V, 273.
2 Arno Mayer (1981), *The Persistence of the Old Regime*, New York, 153.
3 Cd. 9038. 1918. Conference on the Reform of the Second Chamber. Letter from Viscount Bryce to the Prime Minister. Paragraph 8.
4 Ibid., paragraph 6.
5 J. Quick and R. R. Garran (1901), *The Annotated Constitution of the Australian Commonwealth*, Melbourne, 414.
6 See 'The House of Lords', Report of the Conservative Review Committee, Chairman Lord Home, March 1978, Para. 13.
7 John Stuart Mill (1861), *Considerations on Representative Government*, London, new edn, 1972, 326.
8 Carl J. Friedrich (1968), *Constitutional Government and Democracy. Theory and Practice in Europe and America*, Waltham, Mass., 4th edn, 316.
9 *The English Constitution*, 276.
10 K. C. Wheare (1963), *Legislatures*, London/Oxford, 206.
11 Ibid.
12 Senator Eugene Forsey (1982), 'The Role of Second Chambers', *The Parliamentarian*, **63**, 211.
13 Ibid., 229.
14 See Herman Finer (1923), *Representative Government and a Parliament of Industry*,

London, for a good summary of the arguments for and against such a vocational chamber. See also Vernon Bogdanor (1977), 'Postscript: A House of Industry?' in T. Raison (ed.), *The Corporate State – Reality or Myth*, Centre for Studies in Social Policy, London.

15   Philip M. Williams (1966), *Crisis and Compromise: Politics in the Fourth Republic*, Garden City, NY, 313. J. E. S. Hayward (1966), *Private Interests and Public Policy. The Experience of the French Economic and Social Council*, London, is a valuable study of the Council in the early years of the Fifth Republic.

16   Basil Chubb (1971), *The Government and Politics of Ireland*, London/Oxford, 205.

17   Wheare, *op. cit.*, 217.

18   Ibid., 218.

19   David Arter (1984), *The Nordic Parliaments: A Comparative Analysis*, London, 223.

20   Ibid., 229–30.

21   Ibid., 310.

22   Neil Elder, Alastair H. Thomas and David Arter (1982), *The Consensual Democracies? The Government and Politics of the Scandinavian States*, London, 121.

23   Gerhard Loewenberg and Samuel C. Patterson (1979), *Comparing Legislatures. An Analytic Study*, New York, 121.

24   Mr L. W. Gander, New Zealand High Commissioner to London, in 'The role of second chambers', *loc. cit.*, 227.

25   See chapter 6 'The House of Lords: Structural changes: The use of committees', in Philip Norton (ed.), *Parliament in the 1980s*, Oxford. This chapter contains an excellent brief account of the work of the House of Lords Select Committee.

26   Donald Shell (1983), *The House of Lords*, Philip Allan, 150.

27   Lord Windlesham (1975), *Politics in Practice*, Jonathan Cape, 137, 142.

28   First Report from the Select Committee of the House of Lords on Practice and Procedure, HL 41, 1977, Q. 123.

29   M. A. J. Wheeler-Booth (1989), 'The House of Lords', in J. A. G. Griffith, Michael Ryle and M. A. J. Wheeler-Booth, *Parliament: Functions, Practice and Procedure*, Sweet & Maxwell, 494.

30   Wheeler-Booth, *op. cit.*, 493, 496.

31   Para. 8.

32   *Considerations on Representative Government*, 324.

33   Herman Finer (1946), *The Theory and Practice of Modern Government*, Methuen, Vol. I, 739.

Index

Page numbers appearing in **bold** refer to tables.
Page numbers appearing in *italic* refer to figures.